This book
belongs to

_____

Southern Living

HEIRLOOM RECIPE
COOKBOOK

the food we love from the times we treasure

featuring Marian Cooper Cairns

Oxmoor
House

©2011 by Time Home Entertainment Inc.
135 West 50th Street, New York, NY 10020

Southern Living® is a registered trademark of Time Inc. Lifestyle Group. All rights reserved. No part of this book may be reproduced in any form or by any means without the prior written permission of the publisher, excepting brief quotations in connection with reviews written specifically for inclusion in magazines or newspapers, or limited excerpts strictly for personal use.

ISBN-13: 978-0-8487-3481-7
ISBN-10: 0-8487-3481-5
Library of Congress Control Number: 2011933736

Printed in the United States of America
Second Printing 2012

Oxmoor House
VP, Publishing Director: Jim Childs
Editorial Director: Susan Payne Dobbs
Senior Brand Manager: Daniel Fagan
Senior Editor: Rebecca Brennan
Managing Editor: Laurie S. Herr

Southern Living *Heirloom Recipe Cookbook*
Editor: Ashley T. Strickland
Project Editor: Emily Chappell
Senior Designer: Melissa Clark
Assistant Designer: Allison L. Sperando
Director, Test Kitchens: Elizabeth Tyler Austin
Assistant Directors, Test Kitchens:
    Julie Christopher, Julie Gunter
Test Kitchens Professionals: Wendy Ball,
    Allison E. Cox, Victoria E. Cox,
    Margaret Monroe Dickey, Alyson Moreland Haynes,
    Stefanie Maloney, Callie Nash,
    Catherine Crowell Steele, Leah Van Deren
Photography Director: Jim Bathie
Senior Photo Stylist: Kay E. Clarke
Associate Photo Stylist: Katherine Eckert Coyne
Assistant Photo Stylist: Mary Louise Menendez
Production Manager: Theresa Beste-Farley

Contributors
Editor: Katherine Cobbs
Recipe Editor: Donna Baldone
Copy Editors: Rebecca Benton, Rhonda Richards
Proofreader: Dolores Hydock
Indexer: Mary Ann Laurens
Interns: Erin Bishop, Sarah H. Doss, Laura Hoxworth,
    Alison Loughman, Lindsay A. Rozier, Caitlin Watzke
Test Kitchens Professional: Kathleen Royal Phillips
Photographers: Tanner Latham (page 309, top),
    Mary Britton Senseney
Photo Stylist: Lydia DeGaris Pursell

Southern Living
Editor: M. Lindsay Bierman
Creative Director: Felicity Keane
Managing Editor: Candace Higginbotham
Executive Editors: Rachel Hardage,
    Jessica S. Thuston
Food Director: Shannon Sliter Satterwhite
Test Kitchen Director: Rebecca Kracke Gordon
Senior Writer: Donna Florio
Senior Food Editors: Shirley Harrington,
    Mary Allen Perry
Recipe Editor: JoAnn Weatherly
Assistant Recipe Editor: Ashley Arthur
Test Kitchen Specialists/Food Styling:
    Marian Cooper Cairns, Vanessa McNeil Rocchio
Test Kitchen Professionals: Norman King,
    Pam Lolley, Angela Sellers
Senior Photographers: Ralph Anderson,
    Gary Clark, Jennifer Davick, Art Meripol
Photographer: Robbie Caponetto
Photo Research Coordinator: Ginny P. Allen
Senior Photo Stylist: Buffy Hargett
Editorial Assistant: Pat York

Time Home Entertainment Inc.
Publisher: Richard Fraiman
VP, Strategy & Business Development:
    Steven Sandonato
Executive Director, Marketing Services: Carol Pittard
Executive Director, Retail & Special Sales:
    Tom Mifsud
Director, New Product Development: Peter Harper
Director, Bookazine Development & Marketing:
    Laura Adam
Assistant Director, Brand Marketing: Joy Butts
Associate Counsel: Helen Wan

To order additional publications,
call 1-800-765-6400 or 1-800-491-0551.

For more books to enrich your life,
visit **oxmoorhouse.com**

To search, savor, and share thousands
of recipes, visit **myrecipes.com**

Cover: Fresh Corn Cakes (page 28),
    Hearty Oat-and-Walnut Bread (page 71)
Back Cover: Chocolate Mousse Cake (page 221),
    Chicken Divan (page 167),
    Hot Brown Sandwiches (page 86),
    Blackberry Jelly (page 319)

CONTENTS

INTRODUCTION

When I was in the third grade, my mother, Jane, took a job in the *Southern Living* Test Kitchen. I'd watch her get out of the car every night around 5:00 with a brown paper bag. The question always was: What's inside?

My sister and I knew it was leftovers from that day's tasting, always on a white oval Chinet plate in a zip-top plastic bag. It could be a casserole that had gone terribly wrong, poached fish, or—if we were really lucky—a dish that had gotten a high rating. The mystery of that paper bag is just one of the things I remember when I think of my mother.

I work for *Southern Living* now myself in the same job my mother held for 10 years. I've always loved food and entertaining. As a kid, I would sit on the beat-up kitchen stool, and Mom and I would talk as she cooked. She'd offer little tips along the way. I learned so much from her. We always discussed the contents of the day's brown bag during the meal. And when we went out to eat, we'd rate the food just like we were at taste testing. I just thought that was normal.

When Mom died in 2002, we were all devastated. I was a total mess. My dad had recently told me to find a career that mattered to me, so I knew I had to do that. I met my husband, Lee, six weeks before my mom died. He was the one who really encouraged me to go to culinary school. He made me believe I could do it and that it was worth doing.

When I was invited to interview for a position in the Test Kitchen, I had a real feeling of coming home. Here I was at the same dining table where my mother had taste-tested recipes for so many years, with editors who had known her. One of them said, "Marian's a legacy," just as if I were joining a sorority. I thought, "I want to be a part of that sorority." Now I am, and I absolutely love it!

The recipes on the pages that follow were born and perfected in the *Southern Living* Test Kitchen during the past four decades. Many I tasted long ago, when Mom brought them home as leftovers on those Chinet plates; others are tried-and-true classics. As you turn the pages and read the musings from notable Southerners—writers, musicians, actors, and authors—and the tasty trivia about the origins of so many of our regional favorites, I hope you will be inspired by the ingredients, people, and dishes that make Southern culture so rich and interesting. Perhaps the recipes found within will become your family heirlooms, whether served up on Chinet or bone china.

—Marian Cooper Cairns

COCKTAIL HOUR

it's always five o'clock
somewhere in the South

Both of my parents worked in the food industry, so cooking was a big part of our lives. Naturally, my folks entertained a lot while I was growing up. The silver punch bowl and ladle were always out.

a note from
Marian

In our household, it was not a gathering unless the gleaming punch bowl was front, center, and full on the marble-topped buffet table. Don't think it was sherbet and pineapples, either. At our house, there was always a well-thought-out libation mixed to rigorous standards and always fitting the occasion of the party. It might be a vat of whiskey sours in the evening or, for brunch, bubbly mimosas. Two things could be counted on: The beverage was always spirited and the punch bowl always present when a party was at hand.

Mom's days developing and testing recipes in the *Southern Living* Test Kitchen meant that she was a serial experimenter and rarely served the same thing twice. For her, joy was found in coming up with a new appetizer or a signature hors d'oeuvre for every affair. So tradition in our house meant something unexpected. What would Mom pull out of her hat this time? Tradition was not the exact same food served in the same manner, but the knowledge that a delicious surprise would be experienced each and every time. It might be a new spin on deviled eggs or aspic, and we would all love it in that moment, knowing it would probably not grace our table in the same way again.

The newly opened tearooms of the 1920s and 1930s were a perfect illustration of the connection between necessity and invention. Many a woman, finding her husband out of work, took steps to turn her kitchen skills into money, sometimes starting with only a room and two or three tables. As the proprietors were largely female, so was the clientele. Both sides benefited: Tearoom servings were small and prettily served, appealing to the presumed delicate appetite of the feminine gender and an inexpensive way to lunch "out." One such entrepreneur was Alida Harper, who started a tearoom in her historic Pink House in Savannah.

ICED TEA

Hands-on Time: 3 min.   Total Time: 6 min.

Known as the signature drink of the region, a tall glass of iced tea in the South goes with just about every event—church suppers, family meals, ladies' luncheons, and it's just perfect for porch sitting on a sizzling summer day.

3   regular-size tea bags or 1 family-size tea bag
2   cups boiling water
2   cups cold water

Warm teapot by rinsing with boiling water. Place tea bags in teapot. Pour boiling water over tea. Steep 3 to 5 minutes. Remove tea bags; stir in cold water. Cool completely; chill. Serve over ice. Makes 4 cups.

Southern Sweet Tea: After removing tea bags, add ¼ to ½ cup sugar, stirring until sugar dissolves. Then add cold water as directed.

Refreshing Lemonade

Hands-on Time: 17 min.   Total Time: 17 min.

Great for picnics and family reunions, homemade lemonade is the perfect summer beverage. Freeze it for frozen pops or slush-ies. Recipe can be halved.

1½ qt. fresh lemon juice (about 14 large
    lemons)
3¾ cups sugar
Garnishes: lemon slices, lime slices,
    lemon rind curls

1. STIR together 6 qt. water, lemon juice, and sugar in a large container. Chill thoroughly.
2. SERVE over ice, and garnish, if desired. Makes 2 gal.

MAKEOVER IN MINUTES: Make it a limeade by substituting limes for lemons. You'll need approximately 20 juicy limes to yield 1½ qt. juice.

ZESTY BLOODY MARY

Hands-on Time: 5 min.   Total Time: 5 min.

We've updated this classic cocktail to include horseradish and spicy-hot vegetable juice instead of regular tomato juice.

2¼ cups spicy-hot vegetable juice

1¼ cups vodka

2 Tbsp. fresh lime juice

1 Tbsp. refrigerated horseradish

2 tsp. Worcestershire sauce

1 tsp. hot sauce

½ tsp. garlic powder

½ tsp. pepper

¼ tsp. celery salt

Garnishes: 4 celery ribs, pickled okra, red and yellow grape tomatoes, lime wedges

Stir together first 9 ingredients in a pitcher. Serve over ice in tall glasses. Garnish, if desired. Makes 4 servings.

COFFEE PUNCH

Hands-on Time: 15 min.   Total Time: 45 min.

With long, hot summers, it's no wonder Southerners loved to cool down their favorite hot morning pick-me-up with ice cream to enjoy the rest of the day.

8 cups strong brewed coffee, chilled

2 cups milk

2 tsp. vanilla extract

½ cup superfine sugar

1 qt. vanilla ice cream, softened

1 cup whipping cream, whipped

Freshly grated nutmeg

Stir together coffee, milk, vanilla, and sugar until sugar dissolves. Scoop ice cream into punch bowl. Pour in coffee mixture; stir gently. Top with whipped cream and nutmeg. Makes 2½ qt.

Love It Lighter: Swap frozen vanilla yogurt for the ice cream, and skip the whipped cream topping for a "skinny" coffee punch.

Zesty Bloody Mary

Throughout this book, you'll find vintage photos from our magazine's history. We hope they conjure up a few food memories of your own!

MINT JULEP

Hands-on Time: 16 min.   Total Time: 31 min.

Be sure to use good bourbon in these stiff Kentucky cocktails. Serve at your next Derby party!

24 fresh mint leaves
4   tsp. powdered sugar
Crushed ice
12 oz. bourbon
Garnish: fresh mint sprigs

Place 6 mint leaves in a serving glass. Gently press leaves against glass with back of spoon to release flavors. Add 1 tsp. powdered sugar and 1 tsp. water, stirring gently until sugar is dissolved. Pack glass tightly with crushed ice, filling glass two-thirds full. Pour 2 oz. bourbon over ice; stir briskly. Add additional crushed ice to fill glass. Add 1 oz. bourbon. Place glass in freezer; chill 15 minutes. Repeat procedure with remaining ingredients. Garnish, if desired. Makes 4 servings.

TASTY TRIVIA

The New England settlers lost little time in distilling rum. The South willingly traded tobacco for the spirituous libation, and it soon became, in the opinion of many, all too popular. "Demon rum" became the impassioned denunciation from Colonial pulpits. The planter's morning draft, the julep, was made of rum long before corn whiskey made its appearance.

OLD-FASHIONEDS

Hands-on Time: 10 min.   Total Time: 1 hr., 10 min., including Sweet Citrus Syrup

This drink is believed to have been the first to be labeled as a "cocktail." It was originally served at the Waldorf Astoria bar in New York.

6   cups lemon-lime
    carbonated beverage
3   cups Canadian whiskey

Sweet Citrus Syrup
½   tsp. aromatic bitters
Crushed ice

Garnishes: orange, lemon,
    and lime slices; maraschino
    cherries; orange rind curls

Combine first 4 ingredients. Fill 12 (10-oz.) old-fashioned glasses with crushed ice; pour mixture over ice. Garnish, if desired. Makes 12 servings.

SWEET CITRUS SYRUP

Hands-on Time: 5 min.   Total Time: 1 hr., 5 min.

1   (12-oz.) can frozen
    five-fruit citrus beverage
    concentrate

½   cup grenadine syrup or
    maraschino cherry juice

1   Tbsp. sugar

Combine all ingredients in a saucepan; bring to a boil, stirring often. Remove from heat, and let cool (about 1 hour). Pour into a container; cover and refrigerate up to 2 weeks. Makes 2 cups.

For each individual serving, place ~~2 Tbsp~~ 2 Tbsp. Sweet Citrus Syrup, 5 Tbsp. lemon-lime carbonated beverage, 3 Tbsp. ~~whiskey~~ whiskey, and a dash of aromatic bitters in a (10-oz) old-fashioned glass. Stir well. Add enough finely crushed ice to fill glass; stir gently. Garnish with citrus slices and a cherry.

SANGRÍA

Hands-on Time: 10 min.   Total Time: 10 min.

French Beaujolais is a great wine to use for Sangría because it is light in body and has a fruit-forward flavor. Or substitute with a merlot or a fruity pinot noir.

1   cup sugar
4   (750-milliliter) bottles
    Beaujolais wine (or fruity
    red wine), chilled

1   (46-oz.) can pineapple
    juice, chilled
1½ cups club soda, chilled

Garnishes: maraschino
    cherries, orange slices,
    strawberries, lemon slices,
    mint sprigs

Bring sugar and ½ cup water to a boil in a small saucepan, stirring until sugar dissolves. Remove from heat; cool. Combine sugar syrup, wine, pineapple juice, and club soda; pour into a punch bowl with an ice ring, or chill until ready to serve. Garnish, if desired. Makes about 22 cups.

ORANGE-CHAMPAGNE COCKTAIL

Hands-on Time: 3 min.   Total Time: 3 min.

Somewhere between punch and a mimosa, this beverage is perfect for a brunch or wedding shower.

1   (750-milliliter) bottle
    Champagne, chilled

1   (1-liter) bottle ginger ale,
    chilled

2   cups fresh orange juice,
    chilled
    Sliced fresh strawberries

Stir together Champagne, ginger ale, and orange juice. Place a few strawberry slices in glasses, and pour in Champagne mixture just before serving. Makes 9½ cups.

CHAMPAGNE 101

Let's clarify something when it comes to sparkling wine: All Champagne is sparkling wine, but not all sparkling wine is Champagne.

In order for a sparkling wine to be called Champagne, it must be made using specific grapes—Pinot Noir, Chardonnay, Pinot Meunier—from the Champagne region of northern France. In other words, if you pick up a bottle of sparkling wine with the word "Champagne" on the label and it's not from France, put it down.

As with other wines, Champagne can range from very dry to very sweet in the following order: Extra Brut, Brut, Extra Dry, Sec, Demi-Sec, and Doux. The most popular style of Champagne, by far, is Brut, with almost all of it being designated as Nonvintage (NV). Only in exceptional years will Champagne have a vintage date.

Delicious and affordable sparkling wines are made around the world. In fact, just about every wine-producing country has a region devoted to making sparkling wine. However, the most widely available and affordable sparkling wines are from the U.S., Spain, Italy, and Australia.

Italians produce a couple of sparkling wines—most notably Prosecco (Pro-SECK-oh) from the Veneto region (home of Venice), and Spumante (the Italian word for "bubbly wine") from the region of Piedmont. It's worth noting that Prosecco—one of nature's true gifts—mixed with peach nectar or puree makes an authentic Bellini, invented at Harry's Bar in Venice.

Spain's wonderful sparkler, Cava (KAH-vuh), is made in the Penedès region near Barcelona. This may just be one of the best values around, because Cava is made in the Champagne method and can often be found for less than $10.

Chill sparkling wine for two to four hours for the proper serving temperature, and expect to get about seven or eight servings from a 750-milliliter bottle.

Best Deviled Eggs

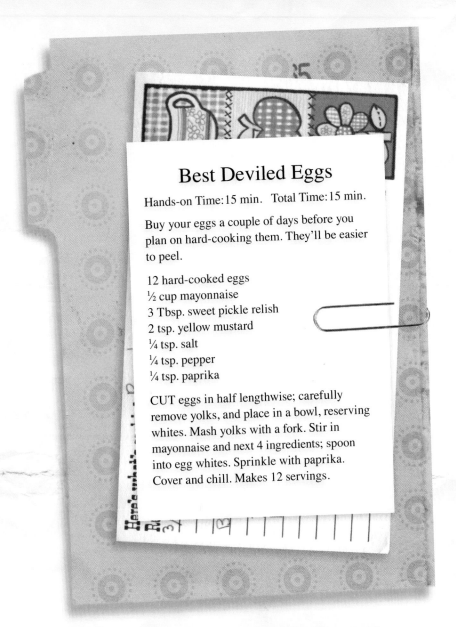

Best Deviled Eggs

Hands-on Time: 15 min. Total Time: 15 min.

Buy your eggs a couple of days before you plan on hard-cooking them. They'll be easier to peel.

12 hard-cooked eggs
½ cup mayonnaise
3 Tbsp. sweet pickle relish
2 tsp. yellow mustard
¼ tsp. salt
¼ tsp. pepper
¼ tsp. paprika

CUT eggs in half lengthwise; carefully remove yolks, and place in a bowl, reserving whites. Mash yolks with a fork. Stir in mayonnaise and next 4 ingredients; spoon into egg whites. Sprinkle with paprika. Cover and chill. Makes 12 servings.

SUGARED PECANS

Hands-on Time: 6 min.   Total Time: 36 min.

These candied nuts are perfect for nibbling with cocktails.

¼ cup butter, melted	½ cup sugar	3 cups pecan halves
2 egg whites	Dash of salt	Wax paper

1. Preheat oven to 325°. Pour butter into a 13- x 9-inch pan; tilt pan to coat.
2. Beat egg whites until soft peaks form; gradually add sugar and salt, beating until stiff peaks form. Fold in pecans. Spread pecan mixture in a single layer in prepared pan. Bake at 325° for 35 to 40 minutes or until mixture is browned and butter is absorbed, stirring every 10 minutes to coat evenly. Remove to wax paper while still warm; cool completely. Store pecans in an airtight container. Makes 4½ cups.

THE ROSES OF FAIRHOPE

by Rick Bragg

I made the trip with three old women, in a good time for roses. We had threatened to do it for years. We would pack a car with cold chicken and flip-flops and drive south like we used to, till the Alabama foothills faded into souvenir shops, shrimp shacks, and that first ragged palm. They had taken me there, when men still whistled at them and WALLACE stickers papered the bumpers of cars. How could I not take them now?

But we never got out of the driveway, somehow. My Aunt Edna's heart was failing, Aunt Juanita had to care for my homebound uncle, and my mother, Margaret, did not leave home unless blown from it by tornadoes or TNT. So I was stunned, two years ago, when my 72-year-old mother told me to come get them. I found the three oldest sisters in the yard, suitcases in their hands. Aunt Jo, the youngest sister, stayed home to watch the livestock.

Edna barbecued 250 some-odd chicken thighs and made two gallons of potato salad for the two-day trip. They packed pork and beans, raw onions, cornbread, a jar of iced tea, a hard-frozen Clorox jug of water, and not one cell phone.

As we drove they talked of childhood, dirt roads where the dark closed in like a lid on a box, and a daddy who chased the bad things away the second he walked in. By the time we hit Montgomery, they had ridden a horse named Bob, poked a dead chicken named Mrs. Rearden, and fished beside a little man named Jessie Clines. They were remembering their mama, and a groundhog who lived under the floorboards, as we drove across Mobile Bay.

I wanted them to see the sunset from the Fairhope pier, and as we rolled down the bluff, I heard them go quiet. But the sunset was just a light to see by. It was the roses. They were blooming in a circle the size of a baseball infield, more than 2,000 of them, with names like Derby horses or unrealized dreams— Mr. Lincoln, Strike It Rich, Touch of Class, Crimson Glory, Lasting Love. My mother, who never even liked roses much, said, "Oh, Lord." Juanita, tough and tiny, made of whalebone and hell, looked about to cry.

Their big sister stepped from the car as if in a trance. I had not known how sick Edna was. Her steps

were unsure, halting, as she moved into the garden. The sisters moved close, in case she fell.

Aunt Edna had sewed soldiers' clothes at the Army base, raised five girls, buried a husband, worked a red-clay garden, pieced a thousand quilts, loved on great-grandchildren, and caught more crappie than any man I have ever known. I believed she was eternal, like the red-clay bank where she built her solid, redbrick house.

"So purty," she said, again and again. She lingered in the rose garden a long time, till the sun vanished over the western shore.

She saw the Fairhope roses six times on this trip. The last time, because she was tired, we sat in the car.

A year later, I spoke at her funeral. I surprised myself, blubbered like an old fool. For the first time in a long time it mattered what came out of my head, but the words crashed together inside my skull, and I lost the fine things I wanted to say and stood stupidly in front of people who loved her.

Her daughters just hugged me, one by one, and thanked me for the roses.

BACON-HERB CUPCAKES

Hands-on Time: 25 min.   Total Time: 1 hr., 21 min.

Try these as a perfect companion to a cocktail. Marian likes to use a combination of parsley, thyme, and oregano, but sage, rosemary, basil, and chives will work just as well. Using a small cookie-dough scoop for the batter gives the baked cupcakes a pretty round top.

1½ cups sour cream	¼ cup finely chopped assorted fresh herbs	2 cups self-rising flour
½ cup cooked, finely crumbled bacon	2 green onions, chopped	6 oz. cream cheese, softened
½ cup butter, melted	½ tsp. pepper	

1. Preheat oven to 375°. Stir together first 6 ingredients. Stir in flour until blended. (Mixture will be thick.) Scoop batter into lightly greased mini muffin pans, filling completely full.
2. Bake at 375° for 26 to 28 minutes or until golden brown. Remove cupcakes from pans to a wire rack, and cool completely (about 30 minutes). Spread or pipe tops of cupcakes with cream cheese. Makes about 32.

CHEESE FONDUE

Hands-on Time: 20 min.   Total Time: 20 min.

This retro favorite is also great served with Granny Smith apple slices.

4 cups (16 oz.) shredded Swiss cheese	1 Tbsp. fresh lemon juice	2 (16-oz.) French bread loaves, cut into 1-inch cubes
3 Tbsp. all-purpose flour	⅛ tsp. freshly ground pepper	
1½ cups dry white wine	⅛ tsp. ground nutmeg	

Toss cheese with flour. Bring wine to a boil in a large heavy saucepan; reduce heat to medium-low. Add lemon juice. Gradually whisk cheese into wine, whisking constantly until melted and smooth. Stir in pepper and nutmeg. Pour into fondue pot. Serve with French bread cubes. Makes 6 to 8 servings.

Note: Add a subtle garlic flavor by rubbing the inside of the saucepan with a cut garlic clove.

SUMMER AT GRANDMOTHER'S

by Andie MacDowell

My summers were spent in Asheville in an old house that had been used as a hospital during the Civil War. It had no heat, so we would gather kindling for the wood stove to heat the water every morning.

There was a big spring-fed swimming pool just below the house that I would run down to with my sisters and cousins as soon as we had breakfast, which was usually eggs over easy, fried liver mush, bacon, tomatoes, and ripe fresh cantaloupe. Food is a big deal down here, and we would usually eat one meal while we talked about what we would have for the next one. My grandmother, who owned the house, would put a white towel on the huge box bushes as a signal that it was time for lunch, and we would run up to the house to have pimiento cheese sandwiches, fruit, and fresh-squeezed OJ, then back down the hill. At night before dinner we would sit on the porch with a bowl of boiled peanuts while my father and uncles had a beer and licked salt from their wrists. The young ones would play poker or run around catching fireflies until dinner was served, and it was always something big like shrimp and grits or my uncle's catfish stew. In my family if an uncomfortable subject came up at the dinner table, my grandmother would say, "Let's talk about brown shoes," and everyone knew it was time to change the subject. To this day I use this phrase with my children, and it always makes everyone giggle. The bedrooms in that house were large with several beds, and we would all pile into one room and talk in the dark until we drifted off.

These are the memories that drew me to live in Asheville and the ones that I wanted to instill in my children. Memories that flash back with the smell of a sun-ripened tomato, the return of fireflies each summer, and the sweet smell of boxwoods.

OLIVE-CHEESE SANDWICHES

Hands-on Time: 1 hr., 4 min.   Total Time: 1 hr., 4 min.

These sandwiches are also great served as grown-up grilled cheeses.

¾ cup mayonnaise

¼ tsp. freshly ground pepper

½ cup drained and chopped pimiento-stuffed Spanish olives

16 oz. Cheddar cheese, shredded

27 slices pumpernickel bread

Garnish: sliced pimiento-stuffed Spanish olives

1. Whisk together mayonnaise and pepper in a medium bowl. Stir in chopped olives and cheese.

2. Stack bread slices in groups of 3 or 4 slices. Cut crusts from each stack; cut each stack diagonally into quarters, creating triangles. Spread 1 heaping tsp. cheese mixture on each triangle. Garnish, if desired. Makes 36 appetizer servings.

"Cooking is a way of handing down the history of your family."

—Christy Jordan

southernplate.com

FRESH CORN CAKES

Hands-on Time: 20 min.   Total Time: 34 min.

Golden brown and hot off the griddle, these corn cakes are loaded with bits of melted mozzarella.

2½ cups fresh corn kernels (about 5 ears)
3 large eggs
¾ cup milk
3 Tbsp. butter, melted
¾ cup all-purpose flour

¾ cup plain yellow or white cornmeal
1 (8-oz.) package fresh mozzarella cheese, shredded

2 Tbsp. chopped fresh chives
1 tsp. salt
1 tsp. freshly ground pepper

1. Pulse first 4 ingredients in a food processor 3 or 4 times or just until corn is coarsely chopped.
2. Stir together flour and next 5 ingredients in a large bowl; stir in corn mixture just until dry ingredients are moistened.
3. Spoon ⅛ cup batter for each cake onto a hot, lightly greased griddle or large nonstick skillet to form 2-inch cakes (do not spread or flatten cakes). Cook cakes 3 to 4 minutes or until tops are covered with bubbles and edges look cooked. Turn and cook other sides 2 to 3 minutes. Makes about 3 dozen.

GUACAMOLE

Hands-on Time: 10 min.   Total Time: 10 min.

The Southern love affair of Tex-Mex foods heightened in the early 1980s, and parties often included this favorite dip with chips. Now our affinity for the healthy type of fat found in avocados lets us feel less guilty indulging. To easily tell if an avocado is ripe, gently press the stem end into the flesh. If it takes any effort, it's not ready.

4 large avocados
2 Tbsp. chopped fresh cilantro
2 Tbsp. fresh lime juice
1 Tbsp. fresh lemon juice

1 tsp. salt
⅛ tsp. hot sauce
2 medium tomatoes, seeded and chopped

3 jalapeño peppers, seeded and minced
1 small onion, finely chopped
Tortilla chips

Cut avocados in half. Scoop avocado pulp into bowl; mash with a fork or potato masher just until chunky. Stir in cilantro and next 7 ingredients. Serve with tortilla chips. Makes 6 cups.

CHICKEN SALAD IN
SWISS CHEESE PUFFS

Hands-on Time: 30 min.   Total Time: 52 min.

CHICKEN SALAD
- ¼ cup sliced almonds
- ½ cup mayonnaise
- 1 tsp. fresh lemon juice
- ½ tsp. salt
- Dash of freshly ground pepper
- 2 cups finely chopped cooked chicken
- ¼ cup finely chopped celery
- 2 Tbsp. finely chopped green onion

SWISS CHEESE PUFFS
- ¼ cup butter
- ½ cup all-purpose flour
- ⅛ tsp. salt
- 2 large eggs
- ½ cup (2 oz.) shredded Swiss cheese

Parchment paper
- 1 Tbsp. chopped and drained pimiento

1. Prepare Chicken Salad: Preheat oven to 350°. Bake almonds in a single layer in a shallow pan 4 to 6 minutes or until lightly toasted, stirring halfway through. Stir together mayonnaise, lemon juice, salt, and pepper in a medium bowl. Add chicken, celery, green onion, and almonds; stir well. Cover and chill thoroughly.

2. Prepare Swiss Cheese Puffs: Increase oven temperature to 400°. Combine butter and ½ cup water in a heavy saucepan; bring to a boil. Add flour and salt, all at once, stirring vigorously over medium-high heat until mixture leaves sides of pan and forms a smooth ball. Remove from heat; cool 3 minutes. Add eggs, 1 at a time, beating thoroughly with a wooden spoon after each addition; beat until dough is smooth. Stir in cheese.

3. Drop batter by heaping teaspoonfuls onto baking sheets lined with parchment paper.

4. Bake at 400° for 14 minutes or until puffed and golden brown. Pierce each puff with the tip of a knife to release steam. Cool completely on wire racks.

5. Stir pimiento into chicken salad. Cut tops off puffs, and fill with chicken salad. Replace tops, and serve immediately. Makes 16 appetizer servings.

SAUSAGE BALLS

Hands-on Time: 49 min.   Total Time: 49 min.

One bite of this traditional dish, and you'll be transported right back to the 1970s. If you don't have a chafing dish, a slow cooker set on low will work just as well.

1 lb. hot or mild bulk pork sausage	¼ tsp. ground sage	1 Tbsp. soy sauce
1 large egg, lightly beaten	¼ cup ketchup	1 Tbsp. white vinegar
⅓ cup herb-seasoned stuffing mix	¼ cup chili sauce	Cocktail picks
	2 Tbsp. light brown sugar	

Combine first 4 ingredients until blended. Shape into 30 (1-inch) balls. Brown sausage balls in a large nonstick skillet over medium-high heat; drain on paper towels, discarding drippings in skillet. Wipe skillet clean. Add ketchup, chili sauce, brown sugar, soy sauce, vinegar, and ½ cup water. Stir well; return sausage balls to skillet. Bring to a boil; reduce heat, cover, and simmer 20 minutes or until sauce thickens, stirring occasionally. Serve immediately, or chill or freeze. When ready to serve, reheat and place in a chafing dish; serve with cocktail picks. Makes 30 sausage balls (8 to 10 appetizer servings).

Note: We tested with Pepperidge Farm Herb Seasoned Stuffing.

CRAB-STUFFED MUSHROOMS

Hands-on Time: 11 min.   Total Time: 1 hr., 26 min.

Look for mushrooms similar in size so they'll cook evenly and at the same rate.

24 large fresh mushrooms (about 1 lb.)	¼ cup mayonnaise	2 large eggs, lightly beaten
1 cup zesty Italian dressing	¼ cup minced onion	1 (6-oz.) can crabmeat, drained
¾ cup soft, fresh breadcrumbs, divided	1 tsp. fresh lemon juice	

1. Rinse mushrooms, and pat dry. Remove and discard stems. Combine mushroom caps and dressing; cover and chill 1 to 2 hours. Drain well.
2. Preheat oven to 375°. Combine ½ cup breadcrumbs and next 5 ingredients; stir well. Spoon crabmeat mixture into mushroom caps; sprinkle with remaining ¼ cup breadcrumbs.
3. Place mushroom caps on a rack in a broiler pan. Bake at 375° for 12 to 15 minutes or until browned. Makes 2 dozen.

Makeover in Minutes: If you live near the ocean or a good fishmonger, splurge on jumbo lump crabmeat, or even less expensive crab claw meat, to use in place of canned.

CHESAPEAKE BAY CRAB CAKES

Hands-on Time: 21 min.   Total Time: 33 min.

These are also great served as a main dish.

1   lb. lump crabmeat, drained
1   large egg
1½ tsp. dried parsley flakes
½   tsp. Worcestershire sauce
⅛   tsp. freshly ground pepper
⅛   tsp. hot sauce
½   cup mayonnaise, divided
1¾ tsp. Old Bay seasoning, divided
4   saltine crackers, crushed
Paprika
Lemon wedges
Garnish: freshly chopped chives

1. Preheat oven to 350°. Pick crabmeat, removing any bits of shell.
2. Whisk egg in a medium bowl. Whisk in parsley flakes, next 3 ingredients, 3 Tbsp. mayonnaise, and ¾ tsp. Old Bay seasoning. Gently stir in crabmeat and cracker crumbs. Shape crab mixture into 18 (1½-inch) patties. Place on a lightly greased baking sheet.
3. Stir together remaining 5 Tbsp. mayonnaise and 1 tsp. Old Bay seasoning; spread on crab cakes, and sprinkle with paprika.
4. Bake at 350° for 12 minutes or until golden. (Do not overbake.) Serve with lemon wedges. Garnish, if desired. Makes 18 mini crab cakes.

TASTY TRIVIA

Of the many species of crab inhabiting the East Coast waters, blue crab is the most plentiful, ranking behind lobster and shrimp in commercial value. The crab most often found on the menu at beach picnics, it is available from February, when the water turns warm around Florida, until cold weather returns. The stone crab, by contrast, is rare and expensive. Concentrated around Key West and Miami, it ranges up to the Carolinas and west to Texas. Only the claw meat is eaten: trappers break off one claw, and the crab regenerates a new one.

DOWN-HOME REUNION

by Wanda McKinney

Granddaddy's voice. That would have been fine, except he's been dead for 35 years.

"This is John A. Boney," the voice said. "We are having a family reunion down in Butler. Can you come?"

When I hesitated, second cousin John A. pulled out the big guns. "I have movies of your grand-daddy from 1946." He paused for effect. "They are in color." With that, he got me. I wanted to hear John A. talk some more. I hadn't heard that South Alabama twang in a very long time.

But as the reunion drew closer, I grew more skeptical of the whole thing. "Reunions are for old people," I told my husband, Bill, remembering how my parents and grandparents enjoyed getting together with their cousins and siblings once a year. The real reason I didn't want to go—I was afraid. Afraid that it would all just make me sad. I come from a small family—just my parents and me. Now they are gone. Or so I thought.

The déjà vu moments started right away. My cousin Billie Baskin greeted me. She and her husband, Charles, had come up from Mobile. "I swan," she said, "can you believe

John A. has built an electric car?" But once again, it was her voice that caught me. The cadence and inflections, so specific to Choctaw County, Alabama, sounded so much like my mother.

We went into the First Baptist Church, where John A. had the promised movie for us to see. And by jingo, there was Granddaddy, one of the pulpwood haulers in a 1940s forestry film. I laughed to myself, seeing the rawboned young man try to leap over a small stream—Dukes of Hazzard style—in an old pickup truck.

Little by little, I became reac-quainted with my family. And I heard stories. "Your granddaddy used two boxes of matches for every pipe he smoked. He couldn't keep that thing lit." "Your mama and Aunt Emily made the cake for Grandma and Grandpa's 50th anniversary. They saved up eggs for weeks to make it."

We enjoyed a picnic lunch in Needham at the pavilion. I heard my cousin Alan explain why he came back to live in Choctaw County. "During the Civil War, my great-grandfather was captured in Charleston, South Carolina," Alan began. "Then he was in a prison

camp in Baltimore. When he got out, he walked all the way home to Alabama. When he got here, he didn't go to the house. He was so dirty and disheveled. He whistled. His wife recognized it was him, and she brought clean clothes for him to change into. Then he came on into the house. That's why it's still in the family. And when I was 8 years old, my grandfather took me here, told me the story, and deeded me this place."

Today's family pride remains strong—and hungry. The group gathered for fried catfish at Ezell's by the Tombigbee River, where cotton grows just across the road. The boisterous group—with its fondness for homegrown vegetables, family traditions, and tale-spinning—toasted the family with sweet tea and hush puppies. I watched the younger ones, entranced with the place and the stories, become hooked as I was on the lure of home.

Party Barbecued Shrimp

PARTY BARBECUED SHRIMP

Hands-on Time: 6 min.   Total Time: 2 hr., 14 min.

1   garlic clove, crushed
½   tsp. salt
½   cup vegetable oil
¼   cup soy sauce
½   cup fresh lemon juice
     (about 3 small)

3   Tbsp. finely chopped
     parsley
2   Tbsp. finely chopped
     onion
½   tsp. pepper

2   lb. unpeeled, large raw
     shrimp (21/30 count)
Cocktail picks

1. Stir together first 8 ingredients. Peel shrimp, leaving tails on; devein, if desired. Place shrimp
in a shallow dish; pour marinade over shrimp. Cover and chill 2 to 3 hours, turning often.
2. Preheat broiler or grill to 300° to 350° (medium) heat. Remove shrimp from marinade, discarding
marinade. Place shrimp on a broiler rack in a broiler pan or in a grill basket. Broil or grill shrimp,
covered with grill lid, 6 to 8 minutes, turning once, or just until shrimp turn pink. Remove shrimp from
skewers onto a serving platter. Serve immediately with cocktail picks. Makes 8 to 10 appetizer servings.

SHRIMP COCKTAIL

Hands-on Time: 20 min.   Total Time: 2 hr., 20 min.

BOILED SHRIMP
2   Tbsp. salt
2   bay leaves
1   lemon, halved
1   celery rib, cut into 3-inch
     pieces
2   lb. unpeeled, large raw
     shrimp (21/30 count)

ZIPPY COCKTAIL SAUCE
1⅓ cups chili sauce
½   cup fresh lemon juice
¼   to ⅓ cup prepared
     horseradish
1   Tbsp. Worcestershire
     sauce
½   tsp. hot sauce

2   cups shredded lettuce

1. Prepare Boiled Shrimp: Combine first 4 ingredients and 6 cups water in a Dutch oven; bring to
a boil. Add shrimp, and cook 3 to 5 minutes or just until shrimp turn pink. Drain and rinse with cold
water. Chill. Peel shrimp; devein, if desired.
2. Prepare Zippy Cocktail Sauce: Combine chili sauce and next 4 ingredients, stirring until smooth.
Cover and chill at least 2 hours.
3. Arrange lettuce on individual serving plates. Top evenly with Boiled Shrimp; drizzle with desired
amount of Zippy Cocktail Sauce before serving. Makes 8 to 10 appetizer servings.

FRIED OYSTERS

Hands-on Time: 15 min.   Total Time: 25 min.

In the South there's long been a quest for crispy fried oysters: Will it be a cornmeal breading or crumbled saltine crackers? In this version, the crackers win out...they make fried oysters extra crispy every time. These golden nuggets would make the perfect po'boy.

2 pt. fresh select oysters, drained	4 large eggs	Zippy Cocktail Sauce
3 cups cracker crumbs (about 90 crackers)	1 tsp. salt	(page 39)
	½ tsp. pepper	
	Canola oil	

1. Dredge oysters in cracker crumbs, shaking off excess. Combine eggs, salt, and pepper; beat well. Dip oysters in egg; dredge in cracker crumbs.

2. Pour oil to a depth of 2 inches into a Dutch oven; heat to 375°. Fry oysters, in batches, 3 minutes or until golden. Drain on paper towels. Sprinkle with salt while hot. Serve hot with Zippy Cocktail Sauce. Makes 12 servings.

OYSTERS ROCKEFELLER

Hands-on Time: 45 min.   Total Time: 1 hr., 3 min.

Attributed to Antoine's in New Orleans, this recipe was reportedly named after the richest man of all time, John D. Rockefeller, because of the richness of the sauce that tops the oysters.

2	dozen oysters in the shell	¼ cup finely chopped onion
¾	cup dry breadcrumbs	1 tsp. Worcestershire sauce
¼	cup butter, melted	Rock salt
3	Tbsp. dry sherry	¼ cup grated fresh
1	cup finely chopped fresh spinach	Parmesan cheese

Garnishes: lemon wedges, fresh parsley sprigs

1. Preheat oven to 400° with top oven rack 3 inches from heat. Scrub and rinse oysters. Shuck oysters, reserving deep half of shells. Drain oysters in a colander.
2. Combine breadcrumbs, butter, and sherry in a small bowl. Combine spinach and next 2 ingredients in another bowl.
3. Sprinkle a layer of rock salt in bottom of a large rimmed baking sheet. Dampen salt slightly. Place oysters in half shells; arrange shells on rock salt. Top oysters with spinach mixture; sprinkle with cheese, and top with breadcrumb mixture. Place pan on top oven rack.
4. Bake, uncovered, at 400° for 15 minutes. Increase oven temperature to broil. Broil 2 to 3 minutes or until browned and bubbly. Garnish, if desired. Makes 4 servings.

mama's way or your way

One is the tried-and-true snack to take to the ball game; the other is a Southern twist on a popular dip.

<u>MAMA'S WAY:</u>
- Simple recipe with only 2 ingredients
- Cooks low and slow
- Feeds a crowd

<u>YOUR WAY:</u>
- Option to use store-bought or home-made peanuts
- Ready to eat in 25 minutes
- Healthy snack

BOILED PEANUTS

Hands-on Time: 5 min. Total Time: 3 hr., 45 min.

2   lb. green raw peanuts
$^3/_4$ cup salt

COMBINE peanuts, salt, and 6 qt. water in a large Dutch oven; bring to a boil over high heat. Reduce heat to medium-low; cover and cook, stirring occasionally, $2^1/_2$ hours or until peanuts are tender, adding water as needed to keep peanuts covered. Remove from heat; let stand 1 hour. Drain. Makes 8 servings.

mama's way

BOILED PEANUT HUMMUS

Hands-on Time: 25 min.   Total Time: 25 min.

Chef Hugh Acheson from Athens, GA, updates a favorite Mediterranean dip with a Southern flair. He likes to season his Boiled Peanuts with Old Bay and star anise, but the simple mama's way version yields a fabulous product. You may also substitute boiled peanuts found at the grocery store or from a roadside stand.

1 cup shelled boiled peanuts
2 Tbsp. tahini
2 Tbsp. fresh lemon juice
1 Tbsp. chopped fresh
    parsley

1 tsp. minced fresh garlic
¼ tsp. ground cumin
Pinch of ground red pepper
2 Tbsp. olive oil

Garnishes: olive oil, shelled
    boiled peanuts
Pita rounds or pita chips

Process first 7 ingredients in a food processor until coarsely chopped, stopping to scrape down sides. With processor running, pour 2 Tbsp. olive oil through food chute in a slow, steady stream, processing until mixture is smooth. Stir in up to 5 Tbsp. water, 1 Tbsp. at a time, for desired spreading consistency. Garnish, if desired. Serve with pita rounds or pita chips. Makes 1 cup.

CHERISHED BREADS

baked goods that make
the heart grow fonder

In middle school I remember making home-made onion buns for hamburgers, right down to the little onions you put on top. Mom wasn't a huge baker outside of the Test Kitchen, but I remember this one occasion quite vividly—sneaking off pinches of dough to taste it, forming the rolls, and watching them bake. This was a rare occasion, of course, because typically if we were eating hamburgers for dinner, they would have come straight from Dad's Dairy Queen.

We were a big banana bread and blueberry muffin family. And those were the kinds of things that we could help ourselves to in the morning. Because Mom cooked all day for work and we always, always sat down together for a family dinner at the table, she left us to our own devices for breakfast. So grab-and-go things such as quick breads or muffins were easy. I'll even admit that since the morning meal was not her thing, it was not uncommon for us to eat store-bought breakfast strudels or sweet rolls from a refrigerated can that we baked ourselves. We loved it because it seemed like a treat to a kid who was used to eating most everything from scratch at home...or, if not, things straight from Dad's DQ.

SOUTHERN CHEDDAR SPOON BREAD

Hands-on Time: 13 min.   Total Time: 48 min.

Spoon bread is a cross between cornbread and polenta. We added cheese to this traditional Southern favorite, often served as a side dish.

1   cup plain yellow cornmeal
2   cups milk
2   Tbsp. butter, melted
1   tsp. salt
3   large eggs
1½ cups (6 oz.) shredded sharp Cheddar cheese

1. Preheat oven to 350°. Lightly grease an 11- x 7½-inch baking dish. Combine cornmeal, milk, 1 cup water, butter, and salt in a large saucepan; cook over medium heat until thickened, stirring constantly. Remove from heat.
2. Beat eggs at medium speed with an electric mixer until thick and pale. Gradually stir about one-fourth of hot mixture into eggs; add to remaining hot mixture, stirring constantly. Stir in cheese. Pour into prepared dish.
3. Bake at 350° for 35 minutes or until a knife inserted in center comes out clean. Makes 8 servings.

> Note:
> Tempering – beating a little hot milk or cream into beaten eggs, then gradually whisking the egg mixture into the hot mixture – prevents eggs from curdling.

TASTY TRIVIA

The origin of spoon bread is unclear, but one conjecture is that a seasoned cook found a heap of mush left over from breakfast. In the best Southern tradition, she simply added eggs and milk, baked it, and served it up with a spoon as a side dish for supper. Whatever the story, there are varied recipes for spoon bread throughout the South. A spoon bread containing grits is called Ovendaugh, Owendaw, or Awendaw, perhaps named after a South Carolina town and the natives that originally grew corn in that region. And one of the loveliest versions is spoon bread with egg whites folded in to make a heavenly soufflé.

ALABAMA HUSH PUPPIES

Hands-on Time: 32 min.   Total Time: 32 min.

Use a small ice-cream scoop to easily drop the batter into the hot oil.

Vegetable oil
1¾ cups plain white cornmeal
¼   cup all-purpose flour
1   tsp. baking powder
1   tsp. salt
½   tsp. ground red pepper
1   large egg, lightly beaten
1   cup milk
½   cup finely chopped onion
Tartar sauce (optional)

1. Pour oil to a depth of 3 inches into a large heavy saucepan; heat over medium-high heat to 365°.
2. Combine cornmeal and next 4 ingredients in a medium bowl; make a well in center of mixture. Stir together egg, milk, and onion; add to dry mixture, stirring just until moistened.
3. Drop batter by tablespoonfuls, 6 at a time, into hot oil. Fry 2 minutes or until browned. Drain on a wire rack over paper towels. Serve with tartar sauce, if desired. Makes 3 dozen.

TASTY TRIVIA

It would be hard to find a Southern dish that admits to as many interpretations and backgrounds as does the hush puppy. We are informed on good authority that the hush puppy came from Georgia. Or Mississippi. Certainly Marjorie Kinnan Rawlings put it in the Southern lexicon in *Cross Creek Cookery.*

The theory that the term started as a mixture of hash and batter called "hash puppy" has few adherents. Others say some fishermen were sitting by their campfire after dining on fried fish when their huntin' dawgs started to whine. The men fried some cornbread batter in the skillet they had used for frying the fish and tossed it to the dogs.

"Hush, puppies," the men said. They were nice men. Did they put chopped onion in the batter? History, even gossip, is silent on that point.

FAVORITE SOUTHERN CORNBREAD

Hands-on Time: 10 min.   Total Time: 42 min.

¼ cup bacon drippings	½ tsp. baking soda	1½ cups buttermilk
2 cups self-rising cornmeal mix	2 large eggs, lightly beaten	Butter

1. Preheat oven to 425°. Place bacon drippings in a 9-inch cast-iron skillet; heat in oven 5 minutes.
2. Combine cornmeal mix and baking soda; make a well in center of mixture. Stir together eggs and buttermilk; add to dry mixture, stirring just until moistened. Remove skillet from oven; tilt skillet in all directions to coat bottom. Pour hot drippings into batter, whisking to blend. Pour batter into hot skillet.
3. Bake at 425° for 27 minutes or until golden brown. Invert cornbread onto a serving plate; cut into wedges. Serve hot with butter. Makes 8 servings.

"The North thinks it knows how to make cornbread, but this is a gross superstition. Perhaps no bread in the world is quite as good as Southern cornbread, and perhaps no bread in the world is quite as bad as the Northern imitation of it."

—Mark Twain

REFRIGERATOR BRAN MUFFINS

Hands-on Time: 15 min.   Total Time: 32 min.

Keep this batter in your fridge for up to 1 week. The flavor improves with time, so each batch you make becomes even better.

1 (15-oz.) package wheat bran flakes cereal with raisins	3 cups firmly packed brown sugar	1 tsp. salt
5 cups all-purpose flour	1 Tbsp. plus 2 tsp. baking soda	4 large eggs, lightly beaten
	1 Tbsp. ground cinnamon	1 qt. buttermilk
		1 cup canola oil
		1 Tbsp. vanilla extract

1. Combine first 6 ingredients in a large bowl; make a well in center of mixture. Combine eggs and next 3 ingredients; add to dry ingredients, stirring just until moistened. Bake immediately, or cover batter and store in refrigerator up to 1 week.
2. Preheat oven to 400°. Spoon batter into greased muffin pans, filling two-thirds full.
3. Bake at 400° for 17 to 20 minutes. Remove from pans immediately. Makes 4 dozen.

Favorite Southern
Cornbread

BLUEBERRY STREUSEL MUFFINS

Hands-on Time: 15 min.   Total Time: 50 min.

Fresh or frozen blueberries are an excellent source of cancer-fighting antioxidants. Stock up on them when they're in season, and freeze to enjoy all year long. If using frozen blueberries, rinse and drain thawed berries; pat dry with paper towels. This will prevent discoloration of the batter.

BATTER
¼ cup butter, softened
⅓ cup sugar
1 large egg
2⅓ cups all-purpose flour
1 Tbsp. plus 1 tsp. baking powder

½ tsp. salt
1 cup milk
1 tsp. vanilla extract
1½ cups fresh blueberries

STREUSEL TOPPING
½ cup sugar
⅓ cup all-purpose flour
½ tsp. ground cinnamon
¼ cup butter, softened

1. Preheat oven to 375°. Lightly grease muffin pans.
2. Prepare Batter: Beat butter at medium speed with an electric mixer until creamy; gradually add ⅓ cup sugar, beating until light and fluffy. Add egg, beating well.
3. Combine 2⅓ cups flour, 1 Tbsp. plus 1 tsp. baking powder, and ½ tsp. salt; gradually add to butter mixture alternately with milk, beginning and ending with flour mixture and beating well after each addition. Stir in vanilla, and fold in blueberries. Spoon batter into prepared muffin pans, filling two-thirds full.
4. Prepare Streusel Topping: Combine ½ cup sugar, ⅓ cup flour, and ½ tsp. cinnamon; cut in ¼ cup butter with a pastry blender until crumbly. Sprinkle on top of muffin batter.
5. Bake at 375° for 35 minutes or until golden brown. Remove from pans immediately. Makes 1½ dozen.

Makeover in Minutes: Trade the blueberries for raspberries or blackberries for a change.

ORANGE ROLLS

Hands-on Time: 38 min.   Total Time: 2 hr., 38 min.

These sweet rolls with a bright citrus flavor are a perfect morning pick-me-up anytime, but are especially great for company.

ROLLS
- 1 (¼-oz.) envelope active dry yeast
- ¼ cup warm water (100° to 110°)
- 1 cup sugar, divided
- ½ cup butter, melted and divided

- ½ cup sour cream
- 1 tsp. salt
- 2 large eggs
- 3½ to 3¾ cups all-purpose flour
- 2 Tbsp. orange zest

GLAZE
- ¾ cup sugar
- ½ cup sour cream
- 2 Tbsp. fresh orange juice
- ½ cup butter

1. Prepare Rolls: Combine yeast and warm water (100° to 110°) in a 1-cup glass measuring cup; let stand 5 minutes.

2. Combine yeast mixture, ¼ cup sugar, 6 Tbsp. butter, and next 3 ingredients in a large mixing bowl; beat at medium speed with an electric mixer until well blended. Gradually add 2 cups flour. Beat in enough of remaining flour to make a soft dough.

3. Turn dough out onto a well-floured surface, and knead until smooth and elastic (about 5 minutes). Place in a well-greased bowl, turning to grease top.

4. Cover dough with plastic wrap, and let rise in a warm place (85°), free from drafts, 1 hour or until doubled in bulk.

5. Punch dough down. Turn dough out onto a well-floured surface. Knead 3 or 4 times. Divide dough in half. Roll each dough portion into a 12-inch circle about ¼-inch thick. Combine ¾ cup sugar and orange zest. Brush each dough circle with 1 Tbsp. remaining melted butter; sprinkle with half of orange-sugar mixture. Cut dough into 12 wedges. Roll up each wedge, beginning with wide end and rolling toward point. Repeat procedure with remaining half of dough, remaining melted butter, and remaining orange-sugar mixture.

6. Place rolls, point sides down, in 3 rows in a greased 13- x 9-inch pan. Cover and let rise in a warm place (85°), free from drafts, 30 minutes to 1 hour or until almost doubled in bulk.

7. Preheat oven to 350°. Bake at 350° for 25 minutes or until golden brown.

8. Prepare Glaze: Combine all ingredients in a saucepan. Bring to a boil over medium heat. Boil, stirring constantly, 3 minutes. Pour glaze over warm rolls. Makes 2 dozen.

Love It Lighter: Forego the glaze and opt instead for just a smear of butter or Greek yogurt.

SOUR CREAM CRESCENT ROLLS

Hands-on Time: 35 min.   Total Time: 1 hr., 50 min., plus 8 hr. for chilling

Some "old wives' tales" are true: A tiny pinch (not enough to taste) of spice, such as cinnamon, ginger, or nutmeg, does speed yeast development, according to food chemists. A pinch of sugar does the same thing, but too much actually retards the process, as does salt. With water at the precise temperature, fresh yeast, and a little patience you can proof yeast in water alone. Serve these warm rolls slathered with melted butter and your favorite preserves.

¾ cup butter, divided
1 (8-oz.) container sour cream
½ cup sugar

2 (¼-oz.) envelopes active dry yeast
½ cup warm water (100° to 110°)

4 cups all-purpose flour
1 tsp. salt
2 large eggs, beaten

1. Melt ½ cup butter in a small saucepan over medium heat. Remove from heat; stir in sour cream and sugar. Pour mixture into a large mixing bowl; cool to 100° to 110°.

2. Combine yeast and warm water (100° to 110°) in a 1-cup glass measuring cup; let stand 5 minutes.

3. Whisk together flour and salt in a bowl. Whisk eggs into sour cream mixture. Stir yeast mixture into sour cream mixture. Gradually add flour mixture, stirring well. Cover and chill at least 8 hours.

4. Punch dough down, and divide into 4 equal portions. Roll each portion into a 10-inch circle on a floured surface. Microwave remaining ¼ cup butter at HIGH 1 minute or until melted. Brush dough with melted butter. Cut each circle into 12 wedges; roll up each wedge, beginning at wide end. Place on greased baking sheets, point sides down.

5. Cover and let rise in a warm place (85°), free from drafts, 45 minutes or until almost doubled in bulk.

6. Preheat oven to 375°. Bake rolls at 375° for 10 to 12 minutes or until golden brown. Makes 4 dozen.

Note: Dough for Sour Cream Crescent Rolls may be baked in other shapes such as cloverleaf and pan rolls.

OVERNIGHT YEAST ROLLS

Hands-on Time: 22 min.   Total Time: 1 hr., 13 min., plus 8 hr. for chilling

Pour 1 cup of boiling water into a 1-cup glass measuring cup, and then place it in the oven with the dough during the rise phase.

2   (¼-oz.) envelopes active
    dry yeast
1   cup warm water (100°
    to 110°)

1   cup shortening
1   cup sugar
1   tsp. salt
1   cup boiling water

2   large eggs
6   cups all-purpose flour
Cooking spray

1. Combine yeast and warm water (100° to 110°) in a 2-cup liquid measuring cup; let stand 5 minutes.
2. Place shortening, sugar, and salt in a large mixing bowl of a heavy-duty stand mixer. Add boiling water, and beat at medium speed until smooth. Add eggs and yeast mixture, beating at low speed 1 minute or until blended; gradually beat in flour. Place dough in a bowl coated with cooking spray, turning to coat top of dough; cover with plastic wrap. Cover and chill 8 hours or overnight.
3. Lightly coat 2 (12-cup) muffin pans with cooking spray. Punch dough down. Turn dough out onto a lightly floured surface. Roll dough into 72 (1-inch) balls, and place 3 dough balls in each muffin cup.
4. Cover and let rise in a warm place (85°), free from drafts, 45 minutes or until doubled in bulk.
5. Preheat oven to 375°. Bake at 375° for 18 minutes or until golden. Makes 2 dozen.

QUICK MONKEY BREAD

Hands-on Time: 16 min.   Total Time: 1 hr., 6 min.

Make sure to butter the Bundt pan well to ensure that the bread doesn't stick to it when inverted. Soften the butter, and spread it generously over every groove of the pan.

3	Tbsp. butter	1	tsp. ground cinnamon	1	cup firmly packed light brown sugar
½	cup chopped pecans	3	(12-oz.) cans refrigerated buttermilk biscuits	½	cup butter, melted
½	cup granulated sugar				

1. Preheat oven to 350°. Grease a 10-inch Bundt pan with 3 Tbsp. butter.

2. Bake pecans in a single layer in a shallow pan at 350° for 8 to 10 minutes or until lightly toasted, stirring halfway through. Sprinkle pecans evenly in bottom of prepared Bundt pan.

3. Combine granulated sugar and cinnamon. Cut biscuits into quarters; roll each piece in sugar mixture, and layer in pan.

4. Combine brown sugar and ½ cup melted butter; pour over dough.

5. Bake at 350° for 40 minutes. Cool bread 10 minutes in pan; invert onto a serving platter. Makes 1 (10-inch) coffee cake.

"The origin of the name 'monkey bread' is anyone's guess. One reader wrote that the name is derived from the amount of 'monkeying around' needed to prepare the balls of dough. Another theory comes from the notion of pulling apart the sections of cake and playing with your food in monkey-like fashion."

—Anonymous

BISCUITS AND SAUSAGE GRAVY

Hands-on Time: 27 min.   Total Time: 46 min.

BISCUITS

3	cups self-rising soft wheat flour*
¼	tsp. baking soda
1	tsp. sugar
½	cup butter-flavored shortening
1¼	cups buttermilk
2	Tbsp. butter, melted

SAUSAGE GRAVY

½	lb. ground pork sausage
¼	cup butter
⅓	cup all-purpose flour
3¼	cups milk
½	tsp. salt
½	tsp. pepper
⅛	tsp. Italian seasoning

1. Prepare Biscuits: Preheat oven to 425°. Combine first 3 ingredients in a large bowl; cut in shortening with a pastry blender until mixture is crumbly. Add buttermilk, stirring just until dry ingredients are moistened.

2. Turn dough out onto a lightly floured surface, and knead lightly 4 or 5 times. Roll to ¾-inch thickness; cut with a 2½-inch round cutter. Place biscuits on a greased baking sheet.

3. Bake at 425° for 14 minutes or until golden. Brush tops with melted butter. Keep warm.

4. Prepare Sausage Gravy: Brown sausage in a skillet, stirring until sausage crumbles. Drain, reserving 1 Tbsp. drippings in skillet.

5. Add butter to drippings; cook over low heat until butter melts. Add flour; stir until smooth. Cook 1 minute, stirring constantly. Gradually add milk; cook, stirring constantly, over medium heat 10 minutes or until thickened and bubbly. Stir in sausage, salt, pepper, and Italian seasoning. Cook, stirring constantly, 1 minute or until thoroughly heated.

6. Split biscuits open; serve with gravy. Makes 13 servings.

*Note: We tested with White Lily self-rising flour. Staying true to the original recipe, we tested with butter-flavored shortening, but you may substitute regular shortening, if desired.

TASTY TRIVIA

One of the Southerner's prime uses for hot biscuits (right after gravy) is to sop up cane syrup, sorghum, or molasses. Cane syrup and sorghum are made from ribbon cane molasses, a by-product of sugar manufacture, much darker and stronger. Take your choice, but don't miss out on the joys of sopping. There are several ways to take part in this nourishing sport: Open several hot biscuits faceup on your plate, butter them copiously, and pour on enough syrup to drench them well. Or pour a likely amount of syrup directly on the plate and mash into it a large chunk of firm butter; use as spread for biscuits. No fork? Poke a hole in the side of the biscuit with a finger, add a lump of butter, and pour in syrup. Biscuits cold? Poke a hole and pour in syrup. This last procedure delighted children as an after-school snack for generations.

SOURDOUGH STARTER

Hands-on Time: 10 min.   Total Time: 1 hr., 15 min., plus 3 days for standing,
including Starter Food

Starters do not always "start" the first time, even though one follows the directions. Modern milk may be responsible. Starter recipes originated during the days when milk was not pasteurized, so the ferment developed more quickly. Once a starter is established, it can be kept alive and working for many years by following this method. Use this yeasty starter to make homemade bread or our Sourdough-Buttermilk Pancakes on the opposite page.

1	(¼-oz.) envelope active dry yeast	2	cups all-purpose flour	1	tsp. salt
2½	cups warm water (100° to 110°), divided	3	Tbsp. sugar		Starter Food

1. Dissolve yeast in ½ cup warm water (100° to 110°); let stand 5 minutes. Combine flour, sugar, and salt in a medium-size non-metal bowl; stir well. Gradually stir in remaining 2 cups warm water (100° to 110°). Add yeast mixture; mix well.

2. Cover starter loosely with plastic wrap or cheesecloth; let stand in a warm place (85°), free from drafts, for 72 hours, stirring 2 or 3 times daily. Place fermented mixture in refrigerator, and stir once a day. Use within 11 days.

3. To use, remove Sourdough Starter from refrigerator; let stand at room temperature at least 1 hour.

4. Stir starter well, and measure amount needed for recipe. Replenish remaining starter with Starter Food, and return to refrigerator; use starter within 2 to 14 days, stirring daily.

5. When Sourdough Starter is used again, repeat above procedure for using starter and replenishing with Starter Food. Makes 3 cups.

STARTER FOOD

Hands-on Time: 2 min.   Total Time: 2 min.

½	cup sugar	1	cup all-purpose flour	1	cup milk

Stir all ingredients into remaining Sourdough Starter. Makes about 2½ cups.

SOURDOUGH-BUTTERMILK PANCAKES

Hands-on Time: 14 min.   Total Time: 14 min.

2   cups all-purpose flour
2   Tbsp. sugar
1½ tsp. baking powder
½   tsp. baking soda

½   tsp. salt
1⅓ cups buttermilk
2   Tbsp. vegetable oil
1   large egg

1   cup Sourdough Starter
    (page 62)

1. Combine flour and next 4 ingredients in a large bowl. Whisk together buttermilk, oil, and egg. Gradually stir buttermilk mixture into flour mixture. Add Sourdough Starter, stirring just until blended.
2. Pour about ¼ cup batter for each pancake onto a hot, lightly greased griddle or large nonstick skillet. Cook pancakes 3 to 4 minutes or until tops are covered with bubbles and edges look dry and cooked. Turn and cook 1 to 2 minutes or until golden brown. Makes 12 (4-inch) pancakes.

APPLE COFFEE CAKE

Hands-on Time: 21 min.   Total Time: 56 min., including Topping

This moist coffee cake is a perfect start to any morning. Make this cake to serve for breakfast or brunch when you have company.

½ cup shortening	2 tsp. baking powder	1½ cups peeled, chopped
1 cup sugar	½ tsp. baking soda	apple
2 large eggs	¼ tsp. salt	Topping
1 tsp. vanilla extract	1 (8-oz.) container sour	
2 cups all-purpose flour	cream	

1. Preheat oven to 350°. Grease and flour a 13- x 9-inch pan. Beat shortening at medium speed with an electric mixer until creamy; gradually add sugar, beating until blended. Add eggs, 1 at a time, beating until blended. Add vanilla, beating well.

2. Combine flour, baking powder, soda, and salt; add flour mixture to shortening mixture alternately with sour cream, beginning and ending with flour mixture. Stir in apple.

3. Spoon batter into prepared pan; sprinkle with Topping. Bake at 350° for 35 minutes or until a wooden pick inserted in center comes out clean. Cut into squares, and serve warm. Makes 15 to 18 servings.

TOPPING

Hands-on Time: 5 min.   Total Time: 5 min.

½ cup chopped pecans	½ cup firmly packed light brown sugar	2 Tbsp. butter, melted
		1 tsp. ground cinnamon

Combine all ingredients until crumbly. Makes about ¾ cup.

BOSTON BROWN BREAD

Hands-on Time: 30 min.   Total Time: 1 hr., 55 min.

This dark, slightly sweet bread made from wheat flour and cornmeal is traditionally cooked in a cylinder-shaped pan or coffee can. Spread cream cheese on a slice for a special snack.

1½ cups whole wheat flour
1   cup all-purpose flour
3   Tbsp. sugar
½   cup plain white or yellow cornmeal

1½ tsp. baking powder
½   tsp. baking soda
½   tsp. salt
2   large eggs, lightly beaten

2   egg yolks
⅔   cup molasses
2   Tbsp. canola oil
1½ cups buttermilk

1. Preheat oven to 350°. Lightly grease and flour 2 (1-lb.) clean coffee cans. Stir together first 7 ingredients in a medium bowl; set aside.

2. Whisk together eggs, egg yolks, molasses, and oil in a large bowl. Add flour mixture to molasses mixture alternately with buttermilk, beginning and ending with flour mixture, beating at medium speed with a handheld mixer until blended.

3. Spoon mixture into prepared cans. Bake at 350° on middle rack in oven for 45 minutes or until a wooden pick inserted in center comes out clean. Cool in cans on a wire rack 10 minutes; remove from cans, and cool completely on wire rack (about 1 hour). Makes 2 loaves.

Note:
you can add raisins to this bread. Just toss 2/3 cup raisins with 1 Tbsp. flour, and stir into batter just before baking.

"It was a common saying among the Puritans, 'Brown bread and the Gospel is good fare.'"

—Matthew Henry

RAISIN BREAD

Hands-on Time: 30 min.   Total Time: 3 hr., 10 min.

In 1734, the Salzburgers of Bavaria, escaping religious persecution, settled about 25 miles outside Savannah, Georgia, at the invitation of General Oglethorpe. Few reminders of their brave presence remain, but this special-occasion bread or kugelhof *is a wonderful example of the diversity of our Southern foodways.*

LOAVES
3½ to 3¾ cups all-purpose
  flour, divided
¼ cup granulated sugar
2 (¼-oz.) envelopes active
  dry yeast

½ cup milk
¼ cup butter, softened
2 large eggs
1½ tsp. salt
1 tsp. vanilla extract
3 cups raisins

2 Tbsp. butter, melted

GLAZE
1 cup powdered sugar
1½ Tbsp. milk
¼ tsp. almond extract

1. Prepare Loaves: Combine 1¼ cups flour, ¼ cup granulated sugar, and 2 envelopes yeast in a large bowl. Heat milk, ½ cup water, and ¼ cup butter in a saucepan to 120° to 130°. Add to flour mixture; beat at medium speed with an electric mixer 2 minutes, scraping bowl often. Add eggs, 1 at a time, beating well after each addition. Add ¾ cup flour, 1½ tsp. salt, and 1 tsp. vanilla; beat 2 minutes at high speed. Toss together raisins and ¼ cup flour; stir into dough. Add enough remaining flour to make a soft dough.

2. Turn dough out onto a lightly floured surface; knead 5 minutes or until smooth and elastic. Place in a lightly greased bowl, turning to grease top. Cover and let rise in a warm place (85°), free from drafts, 1½ hours or until doubled in bulk. Punch dough down; let stand 15 minutes.

3. Divide dough in half; shape each half into an 8-inch loaf. Place in 2 greased 8½- x 4½-inch loaf pans. Cover; let rise in a warm place (85°), free from drafts, 30 minutes or until doubled in bulk.

4. Preheat oven to 375°. Bake at 375° for 25 minutes or until loaves sound hollow when tapped. Cool in pans 10 minutes; transfer bread to wire racks. Brush loaves with 2 Tbsp. melted butter, and cool completely.

5. Prepare Glaze: Stir together all ingredients in a small bowl until smooth. Drizzle glaze over tops of loaves. Makes 2 loaves.

BANANA BREAD

Hands-on Time: 15 min.   Total Time: 2 hr., 10 min.

This simple traditional banana bread will wow your family and friends with its moist texture and wonderful banana flavor.

½ cup butter, softened	2 cups all-purpose flour	3 ripe bananas, mashed
1½ cups sugar	1 tsp. baking soda	(about 1⅓ cups)
2 large eggs	¼ tsp. salt	Butter

1. Preheat oven to 325°. Grease and flour a 9- x 5-inch loaf pan. Beat butter and sugar at medium speed with an electric mixer until light and fluffy. Add eggs, 1 at a time, beating just until blended after each addition. Combine flour, soda, and salt; add to batter and mix just to combine. Add bananas, mixing well.

2. Spoon batter into prepared pan. Bake at 325° for 1 hour and 15 minutes or until a wooden pick inserted in center comes out clean and sides pull away from pan, shielding with aluminum foil during last 15 minutes to prevent excessive browning, if necessary. Cool in pan on a wire rack 10 minutes. Remove from pan, and cool 30 minutes on wire rack before slicing. Serve with butter. Makes 1 loaf.

LEMON TEA BREAD

Hands-on Time: 20 min.   Total Time: 2 hr., 30 min.

½ cup butter, softened
1   cup granulated sugar
2   large eggs
1½ cups all-purpose flour
1   tsp. baking powder

½ tsp. salt
½ cup milk
2   Tbsp. lemon zest, divided
1   cup powdered sugar

2   Tbsp. fresh lemon juice
1   Tbsp. granulated sugar

1. Preheat oven to 350°. Grease and flour an 8- x 4-inch loaf pan; set aside. Beat softened butter at medium speed with an electric mixer until creamy. Gradually add 1 cup granulated sugar, beating until light and fluffy. Add eggs, 1 at a time, beating just until blended after each addition.

2. Stir together flour, baking powder, and salt; add to butter mixture alternately with milk, beating at low speed just until blended, beginning and ending with flour mixture. Stir in 1 Tbsp. lemon zest. Spoon batter into prepared pan.

3. Bake at 350° for 1 hour or until a wooden pick inserted in center of bread comes out clean. Let cool in pan 10 minutes. Remove bread from pan, and cool completely on a wire rack (about 1 hour).

4. Stir together powdered sugar and lemon juice until smooth; spoon evenly over top of bread, letting excess drip down sides. Stir together remaining 1 Tbsp. lemon zest and 1 Tbsp. granulated sugar; sprinkle on top of bread. Makes 1 loaf.

Lemon-Almond Tea Bread: Stir ½ tsp. almond extract into batter. Proceed as directed.

HEARTY OAT-AND-WALNUT BREAD

Hands-on Time: 30 min.   Total Time: 4 hr., 5 min.

There was a time when homemade bread loaves were baked every day. Thanks to bread machines that knead the dough and allow it to rise without requiring attention, homemade yeast bread now fits into the lifestyle of hurried Southern cooks (see our Makeover in Minutes). Oats, walnuts, and brown sugar make this loaf a perfect partner for orange marmalade.

¼ cup firmly packed light brown sugar	3 cups bread flour	1½ tsp. active dry yeast
1 Tbsp. butter	¾ cup chopped walnuts	1½ tsp. salt
	½ cup quick-cooking oats	

1. Combine sugar, butter, and 1¼ cups water in a small saucepan; bring to a boil. Remove from heat, and let stand until mixture reaches a temperature between 100° and 110°.

2. Meanwhile, combine 2½ cups flour and next 4 ingredients in a large mixing bowl; add sugar mixture, and stir until well blended. Turn dough out onto a heavily floured surface, and knead in enough of remaining flour to make a soft dough. Knead until smooth and elastic (about 10 minutes). Place in a well-greased bowl, turning to grease top.

3. Cover dough with plastic wrap, and let rise in a warm place (85°), free from drafts, 45 minutes or until doubled in bulk.

4. Punch dough down. Turn dough out onto a floured surface, and knead lightly 4 or 5 times. Roll dough into a 14- x 7-inch rectangle. Roll up dough, starting at narrow end, pressing firmly to eliminate air pockets; pinch ends to seal. Place dough, seam side down, in a well-greased 8- x 4-inch loaf pan. Cover and let rise in a warm place, free from drafts, 1 hour or until doubled in bulk.

5. Preheat oven to 375°.

6. Bake at 375° for 40 minutes or until loaf sounds hollow when tapped. Remove bread from pan immediately; cool completely on a wire rack (about 1 hour). Makes 1 loaf.

Makeover in Minutes: This bread bakes beautifully in a bread machine. To do so, combine all ingredients in the bread machine according to the manufacturer's instructions. Select bake cycle, and start machine. When done, remove bread from pan and cool on a wire rack.

LAFAYETTE GINGERBREAD

Hands-on Time: 20 min.   Total Time: 1 hr., 56 min.

Orange juice and brandy make this gingerbread unique and give it extra flavors not found in traditional gingerbread.

¾ cup butter, softened
¾ cup firmly packed light brown sugar
¾ cup molasses
3 large eggs
3 cups all-purpose flour
1 tsp. cream of tartar
2 Tbsp. ground ginger
1 tsp. ground cinnamon
1 tsp. ground mace
1 tsp. ground nutmeg
1 tsp. baking soda
½ cup milk
½ cup brandy
2 Tbsp. orange zest
⅓ cup fresh orange juice
1 cup raisins
Garnish: powdered sugar

1. Preheat oven to 350°. Grease and flour a 13- x 9-inch baking pan; set aside.
2. Beat butter at medium speed with an electric mixer until creamy; gradually add sugar, beating well. Add molasses and eggs; beat well.
3. Combine flour and next 6 ingredients.
4. Add milk to butter mixture alternately with flour mixture, beginning and ending with flour mixture, beating well after each addition. Stir in brandy and next 3 ingredients.
5. Pour batter into prepared pan. Bake at 350° for 36 minutes or until a wooden pick inserted in center comes out clean. Cool completely on a wire rack (about 1 hour). Cut into squares to serve. Garnish, if desired. Makes 15 to 18 servings.

TASTY TRIVIA

George Washington and the Marquis de Lafayette began an enduring friendship during the Revolutionary War. In 1784, Lafayette visited his friend at Mount Vernon. Then "...he went to Fredericksburg to pay respects to the general's mother. They found her in her garden in short gown, petticoat and cap, raking leaves. Unaffectedly she greeted him, and together they went into the house where she made him a mint julep, which she served with spice gingerbread...." Lafayette praised her son; she replied, "George was always a good boy."

mama's way or your way

One is a classic baked in a cast-iron skillet; the other, a miniature twist on pecan sticky buns.

MAMA'S WAY:
- Feather-light yeast dough
- Buttery, brown sugar-pecan filling
- Rich and creamy vanilla glaze

YOUR WAY:
- Refrigerated crescent roll dough
- Decadent caramel-pecan topping
- Ready to bake in 15 minutes

mama's way

CINNAMON-PECAN ROLLS

Hands-on Time: 20 min. Total Time: 1 hr., 20 min.

1 cup chopped pecans
1 (16-oz.) package hot roll mix
½ cup butter, softened
1 cup firmly packed light
   brown sugar

2 tsp. ground cinnamon
1 cup powdered sugar
2 Tbsp. milk
1 tsp. vanilla extract

1. PREHEAT oven to 350°. Bake pecans in a single layer in a shallow pan 5 to 7 minutes or until toasted and fragrant, stirring halfway through.
2. PREPARE hot roll dough as directed on back of package; let dough stand 5 minutes. Roll dough into a 15- x 10-inch rectangle; spread with softened butter. Stir together brown sugar and cinnamon; sprinkle over butter. Sprinkle pecans over brown sugar mixture. Roll up tightly, starting at 1 long side; cut into 12 slices. Place rolls, cut sides down, in a lightly greased 12-inch cast-iron skillet or 13- x 9-inch baking pan. Cover loosely with plastic wrap and a cloth towel; let rise in a warm place (85°), free from drafts, 30 minutes or until doubled in bulk.
3. INCREASE oven temperature to 375°. Uncover rolls, and bake for 20 to 25 minutes or until center rolls are golden brown and done. Let cool in pan on a wire rack 10 minutes. Stir together powdered sugar, milk, and vanilla; drizzle over rolls. Makes 12 rolls.

Note: We tested with Pillsbury Specialty Mix Hot Roll Mix.

BITE-SIZE CINNAMON-PECAN TWIRLS

your way

Hands-on Time: 15 min.   Total Time: 33 min.

½ cup chopped pecans
¼ cup butter
¼ cup firmly packed light brown sugar

2 Tbsp. light corn syrup
1 tsp. ground cinnamon, divided

1 (8-oz.) can refrigerated crescent rolls
1½ tsp. granulated sugar

1. Preheat oven to 375°. Bake pecans and butter in a lightly greased 8-inch round cake pan 2 minutes. Swirl pan to combine, and bake 2 more minutes. Remove from oven, and stir in brown sugar, corn syrup, and ½ tsp. cinnamon; spread mixture over bottom of pan.

2. Unroll crescent roll dough, and separate into 4 rectangles, pressing perforations to seal. Stir together granulated sugar and remaining ½ tsp. cinnamon; sprinkle over rectangles. Roll up each rectangle tightly, starting at 1 long side; press edges to seal. Cut each log into 5 slices; place slices, cut sides down, in prepared pan. (Space slices equally in pan; slices will not touch.)

3. Bake at 375° for 14 to 16 minutes or until center rolls are golden brown and done. Remove from oven, and immediately invert pan onto a serving plate. Spoon any topping in pan over rolls. Makes 20 rolls.

MEMORABLE MAINS

pass-down recipes
loved by generations
of Southerners

Shrimp Destin was one of the first recipes that Mom was so impressed with that she made it over and over again—for company, for beach trips, and on my returns from college because it became my favorite too. It was a recipe that ran in the very first *Southern Living* cookbook that she worked on.

a note from
Marian

She and I both made it so many times that we could do it by heart. We served it over rice, in bread, or even on potatoes or pasta. I'm not really sure of the origins of the dish. I think it was a mainstay of the Test Kitchen staff long before the book came out. Since Birmingham folks make a beeline for the beaches of the Gulf (Destin, in particular), perhaps it has a tie to beach trips. Or maybe it's just named for the area from which the Gulf shrimp came. I'd call from college to make sure Shrimp Destin or barbecued shrimp would be on that night's menu. The latter was the last dish my mom ever made for me. It was another recipe from the *Southern Living* cookbook.

My friend Nicole from Philadelphia was coming home with me that weekend and Mom said, "Marian, we need to show her how we eat in the South...what do you want me to make?" I suggested barbecued shrimp, so we spread newsprint out on the dining table and gathered 'round and had a feast. It was so good and such a different thing for Nicole. It's a meal I'll never forget.

DIXIE FRIED CHICKEN

Hands-on Time: 43 min.   Total Time: 43 min.

This Southern staple can also be made using a "pick of the chick" package of a cut-up whole chicken to save time. Just be sure to buy one that's 3 to 4 pounds.

1 (3- to 4-lb.) whole chicken, cut up	½ tsp. ground black pepper	1 large egg
¾ tsp. salt	2 cups all-purpose flour	½ cup milk
	1 tsp. ground red pepper	Vegetable oil

1. Sprinkle chicken with salt and black pepper. Combine flour and red pepper in a shallow bowl. Whisk together egg and milk in a separate bowl.

2. Pour oil to a depth of 1 inch into a large deep skillet; heat over medium-high heat to 350°.

3. Dip chicken in egg mixture; dredge in flour mixture, shaking off excess. Add chicken to hot oil; cover, reduce heat to medium, and fry 30 minutes or until golden brown, turning occasionally. Drain chicken on a wire rack over paper towels. Makes 4 servings.

BARBECUED CHICKEN

Hands-on Time: 25 min.   Total Time: 1 hr.

2	(4½-lb.) whole chickens, quartered	1	small onion, diced	1	Tbsp. Worcestershire sauce
1	tsp. salt, divided	¾	cup ketchup	1½	tsp. hot sauce
1	tsp. pepper, divided	6	Tbsp. butter	1½	tsp. dry mustard
		3	Tbsp. light brown sugar		

1. Preheat grill to 350° to 400° (medium-high) heat. Cut off tips of wings and break joints to make chickens lie flat on grill. Sprinkle chicken with ½ tsp. salt and ½ tsp. pepper.

2. Meanwhile, combine onion, next 6 ingredients, and remaining ½ tsp. salt and ½ tsp. pepper in a small saucepan; cook over medium heat, stirring occasionally, until butter is melted and mixture comes to a boil. Remove from heat; reserve 1 cup sauce. Place chicken, skin side down, on grill. Grill, covered with grill lid, 15 minutes; turn and grill 15 to 20 minutes or until done. Baste with remaining sauce during last 5 minutes of cook time. Serve with reserved sauce. Makes 8 servings.

CHICKEN KIEV

Hands-on Time: 1 hr., 26 min.   Total Time: 2 hr., 26 min.

This retro favorite is always a hit at dinner parties. Once you cut into the crispy chicken, the herbed butter oozes out and creates a superb sauce.

6	Tbsp. butter, softened
1	Tbsp. chopped fresh parsley
½	tsp. chopped fresh rosemary

	Wax paper
6	skinned and boned chicken breasts
½	tsp. salt
¼	tsp. freshly ground pepper

	Wooden picks
½	cup all-purpose flour
2	large eggs, lightly beaten
1	cup fine, dry breadcrumbs
	Canola oil

1. Stir together butter, parsley, and rosemary in a small bowl. Shape butter mixture into 1 (5-inch) log; wrap in wax paper, and freeze about 45 minutes or until firm.

2. Place chicken breasts, 1 at a time, in a large zip-top plastic freezer bag; flatten to ¼-inch thickness, using a meat mallet or rolling pin. Sprinkle top sides of chicken breasts with salt and pepper.

3. Cut butter mixture into 6 pats; place a pat in center of each chicken breast. Fold long sides of chicken over butter; folds ends over, and secure with wooden picks. Dredge each piece of chicken in flour. Dip chicken in egg, and coat with breadcrumbs. Cover and refrigerate about 1 hour.

4. Pour oil to a depth of 1½ to 2 inches into a Dutch oven; heat to 350°. Fry chicken 15 minutes or until browned, turning with tongs. Makes 6 servings.

FYI —
Look for small chicken breast halves, about 6 ounces each. The larger breast halves take too long to cook and the breadcrumbs will get too brown. Make sure the butter is completely enclosed in the chicken and tightly secured with picks so the herbed butter pours from the center when sliced open.

Yum!

—Mom

CHICKEN À LA KING

Hands-on Time: 27 min.   Total Time: 27 min.

This is a great recipe to prepare if you have leftover cooked chicken or turkey—just substitute it for the deli-roasted chicken.

1 (10-oz.) package frozen puff pastry shells, baked
3 Tbsp. butter
⅓ cup chopped green bell pepper
½ tsp. salt
¼ tsp. freshly ground black pepper

1 (8-oz.) package sliced fresh mushrooms
¼ cup all-purpose flour
1 cup chicken broth
1 cup half-and-half
2 cups coarsely chopped deli-roasted chicken

⅓ cup chopped jarred roasted red bell peppers
Garnish: chopped fresh parsley

1. Remove centers of pastry shells to create a cavity. Set shell tops aside.
2. Melt butter in a large skillet over medium heat; add bell pepper and next 3 ingredients, and sauté until bell pepper is tender. Stir in flour. Remove from heat. Gradually stir in chicken broth and half-and-half; cook over medium heat, stirring constantly, until thickened and bubbly.
3. Stir in chicken and roasted red bell pepper; cook 1 minute or until thoroughly heated.
4. Spoon filling into pastry shells. Garnish and replace tops, if desired. Makes 6 servings.

HOT BROWN SANDWICHES

Hands-on Time: 1 hr.   Total Time: 1 hr., 20 min.

Get out your fork and knife for this saucy, open-faced sandwich from Kentucky.

6   Tbsp. butter
¾   cup all-purpose flour
½   tsp. salt
⅛   tsp. ground white pepper
1½ cups chicken broth
1½ cups milk

¾   cup grated Parmesan cheese
6   bread slices, toasted
Thinly sliced cooked turkey or chicken (about 1 lb.)
¾   tsp. paprika

2   small tomatoes, each cut into 6 slices
12   bacon slices, cooked
Garnish: fresh arugula

1. Preheat oven to 400°. Melt butter over low heat in a medium saucepan; add flour, and cook over low heat, whisking constantly, 1 minute or until smooth. Whisk in salt and pepper. Gradually add broth and milk; cook over medium-low heat, whisking constantly, until thickened and smooth. Add cheese; cook, whisking constantly, 3 minutes or until cheese is melted. (Sauce will be thick.)

2. Place 1 toast slice on each of 6 ovenproof plates. Place turkey or chicken on each toast slice; cover each with about ½ cup sauce, and sprinkle with paprika. Top each with 2 tomato slices and 2 bacon slices. Bake at 400° for 10 minutes or until sauce is bubbly. Garnish, if desired. Makes 6 servings.

Makeover in Minutes: For a hot brown breakfast, substitute English muffins for the bread and a poached egg for the sliced turkey or chicken.

CORNISH HENS WITH ORANGE RICE

Hands-on Time: 20 min.   Total Time: 1 hr., 26 min.

The sweetness of the green grapes and white wine is the perfect accompaniment to these hens and orange rice.

CORNISH HENS
2 cups seedless green grapes
6 (1½-lb.) Cornish hens
¼ cup butter, melted
1 Tbsp. all-purpose flour
1⅓ cups sweet white wine
½ cup fresh orange juice
1 cup apple jelly

1½ tsp. salt, divided
½ tsp. pepper

ORANGE RICE
¼ cup butter
1½ cups finely chopped celery and leaves
½ cup chopped onion

¾ cup fresh orange juice
1½ cups uncooked long-grain rice
½ tsp. salt
1 Tbsp. orange zest

1. Prepare Cornish Hens: Preheat oven to 450°. Place grapes in a lightly greased large roasting pan. Rinse hens; pat dry. Brown 3 hens in 2 Tbsp. melted butter in a large skillet over medium heat 4 minutes on each side. Place hens on top of grapes in roasting pan. Repeat procedure with remaining 3 hens and 2 Tbsp. butter, reserving 1 Tbsp. drippings in skillet. Whisk flour into drippings until smooth. Gradually whisk in wine, ½ cup orange juice, apple jelly, and 1 tsp. salt. Cook over medium-high heat, whisking constantly, 3 minutes or until jelly melts and sauce is reduced to 2 cups. Remove from heat, and reserve 1½ cups sauce to serve with hens.

2. Sprinkle hens with pepper and remaining ½ tsp. salt; brush with ¼ cup remaining sauce. Bake at 450° on bottom oven rack for 40 minutes or until hens are done, basting twice with ¼ cup sauce each time. Cover and let stand 10 minutes before serving.

3. Meanwhile, prepare Orange Rice: Melt butter in a large saucepan over medium-high heat; add celery and onion, and sauté 3 minutes or until tender. Stir in 2¼ cups water and ¾ cup orange juice. Bring to a boil; stir in rice and ½ tsp. salt. Return to a boil; cover, reduce heat to low, and simmer 20 minutes or until liquid is absorbed and rice is tender. Remove from heat, and stir in orange zest; fluff with a fork.

4. Arrange rice, grapes, and hens on a serving platter. Serve with reserved 1½ cups sauce. Makes 6 servings.

FRIED CHICKEN LIVERS

Hands-on Time: 32 min.   Total Time: 32 min.

Serve fried chicken livers as a main dish or snack. The crispy, crunchy crust is the best part! Cut the larger livers in half where connected, if you like.

1 (1-lb.) container chicken livers	2 tsp. seasoned salt	1 cup buttermilk
2 cups all-purpose flour	1 tsp. pepper	Vegetable oil

1. Drain chicken livers.

2. Combine flour, salt, and pepper in a large zip-top plastic bag; dredge livers in flour mixture. Dip livers in buttermilk in a shallow dish, and dredge in flour mixture again.

3. Pour oil to a depth of 2 inches into a large Dutch oven or electric fryer; heat to 365°. Fry livers, 6 at a time, 5 minutes or until browned and no pink remains. Drain on paper towels. Serve immediately. Makes 5 servings.

SMOTHERED QUAIL

Hands-on Time: 15 min.   Total Time: 1 hr., 2 min.

This preparation is an easy and delicious way to serve quail.

8 quail, dressed	1 Tbsp. olive oil	2 green onions, finely chopped
½ tsp. salt	3 Tbsp. all-purpose flour	½ tsp. salt
½ tsp. pepper	2 cups beef broth	Hot cooked rice
¼ cup butter, melted	½ cup dry sherry	

1. Preheat oven to 350°. Rinse quail; pat dry with paper towels. Sprinkle quail with salt and pepper. Brown quail in melted butter and oil in a large, heavy, deep skillet over medium-high heat 3 to 4 minutes on each side. Remove quail to a lightly greased 13-x 9-inch baking dish, reserving drippings in skillet. Remove skillet from heat; whisk flour into drippings in skillet, whisking well.

2. Place skillet back on heat, and gradually whisk in broth and sherry. Cook over medium heat, stirring constantly, until mixture is thickened. Add green onions and salt. Pour broth mixture over quail. Bake, covered, at 350° for 45 minutes or until quail is tender. Serve over hot cooked rice. Makes 8 servings.

Southern Living®

**They Leased
a Southern Plantation
for Hunting, Fishing**

BEEF WELLINGTON

Hands-on Time: 45 min.   Total Time: 2 hr., 20 min.

Duxelles (pronounced dook-SEHL) is a mixture of sautéed mushrooms, shallots, and herbs slowly cooked in butter until it forms a thick paste. It, along with pâté, is spread on beef tenderloin for Beef Wellington. The time invested in preparing duxelles delivers delicious dividends.

1 (4- to 5-lb.) beef tenderloin, trimmed and tied	1 (8-oz.) package fresh mushrooms, chopped	¼ cup Madeira
1½ tsp. salt	2 Tbsp. chopped shallots	1 (3.6-oz.) can liver pâté
½ tsp. freshly ground pepper	½ cup finely chopped cooked ham	1 (17.3-oz) package frozen puff pastry sheets, thawed
2 Tbsp. olive oil	2 Tbsp. butter	1 large egg, lightly beaten

1. Preheat oven to 450°. Sprinkle roast with salt and pepper. Brown tenderloin in hot oil in a large skillet over medium-high heat 3 to 4 minutes on each side. Remove from skillet; place in a lightly greased 15- x 10-inch jelly-roll pan, tucking narrow end under to make roast more uniformly thick. Bake, uncovered, at 450° for 35 minutes. Remove from oven. Cool to room temperature. Remove string.

2. Meanwhile, combine mushrooms, shallots, ham, and butter in a medium-size nonstick skillet; cook over medium-high heat, stirring frequently, until liquid is absorbed. Add Madeira; cook, stirring occasionally, 2 minutes or until liquid is absorbed. Let cool to room temperature (about 1 hour).

3. Spread pâté over cooled tenderloin; spread mushroom mixture over pâté.

4. Reduce oven temperature to 425°. Place 1 sheet of pastry over the other, and roll pastry on a lightly floured surface into a rectangle 1½ inches larger in width and length than roast. Place roast, top side down, in center of pastry. Bring sides of pastry up to overlap on underside of roast, forming a seam; trim ends, reserving excess pastry. Fold over ends of pastry to seal. Invert tenderloin onto an ungreased 15- x 10-inch jelly-roll pan.

5. Brush pastry with beaten egg. Roll pastry trimmings to ⅛- to ¼-inch thickness on a lightly floured surface; cut into decorative shapes, and arrange on surface of pastry, as desired. Brush shapes with beaten egg. Bake at 425° for 35 minutes or until pastry is lightly browned and a meat thermometer inserted into thickest portion registers 145° (medium rare) or to desired degree of doneness. Let stand 10 minutes. Place on a warm serving platter, and carve into ¾- to 1-inch slices. Makes 8 to 10 servings.

Makeover in Minutes: Substitute chopped prosciutto for the ham.

NOBLE ORIGINS

Historians agree that this dish was named after Arthur Wellesley, First Duke of Wellington, credited with crushing Napoleon at Waterloo, because the recipe was one of his favorites. Where exactly the dish originated is debatable. The French have their *filet de boeuf en croûte*, the British have Wellington steak and the Irish have *steig* Wellington all prepared in the same manner—each country staking claim to the recipe.

Beef Wellington became popular in America in the 1960s as a dramatic dinner party dish made to impress with its pastry crust and luxurious ingredients—foie gras or pâté, truffles or mushrooms, and cognac. The recipe fell out of fashion as recipes and entertaining became more casual.

BEEF FILLETS AU VIN

Hands-on Time: 22 min.   Total Time: 22 min.

The tenderloin is the most succulent selection of beef. It's pricey but the great flavor and tenderness make it worth it. Watch the cooking time—you don't want to dry out this prized cut.

4 (1¼- to 1½-inch-thick) beef tenderloin fillets (about 2 lb.)	½ tsp. freshly ground pepper	½ cup dry red wine
	3 Tbsp. butter, divided	1 tsp. all-purpose flour
	1 lb. sliced fresh mushrooms	1 tsp. butter, softened
½ tsp. salt	⅓ cup minced shallots	2 Tbsp. dry red wine

1. Sprinkle fillets with salt and pepper. Melt 1 Tbsp. butter in a 10-inch skillet over medium-high heat. Add fillets, and cook 4 minutes on each side; remove from skillet, reserving drippings in skillet, and keep fillets warm. Reduce heat to low.

2. Melt 1 Tbsp. butter with hot drippings in skillet; add mushrooms and shallots, and sauté 4 minutes. Stir in ½ cup wine; cook over high heat 5 minutes.

3. Combine flour and 1 tsp. softened butter; stir to form a smooth paste. Add to mushroom mixture; cook, stirring constantly, 30 seconds. Add remaining 1 Tbsp. butter and 2 Tbsp. wine; stir until butter melts. Spoon sauce over fillets. Serve immediately. Makes 4 servings.

CHUCK WAGON POT ROAST

Hands-on Time: 28 min.   Total Time: 7 hr., 38 min.

Using a slow cooker for this pot roast makes your weeknight dinner a breeze. Simply brown the roast in the morning, and toss everything into the slow cooker; it does the rest.

6   bacon slices
1   (3-lb.) boneless chuck roast
¼   tsp. pepper
½   cup all-purpose flour, divided

1   large onion, sliced and separated into rings
5   carrots, cut into 2-inch pieces
2   large potatoes, peeled and cut into 3-inch wedges

1½   tsp. salt, divided
1½   cups beef broth
½   cup brewed coffee

1. Cook bacon in a large skillet over medium-high heat 5 to 6 minutes or until crisp. Remove bacon, reserving drippings in skillet. Reserve bacon for another use.
2. Sprinkle roast with pepper; dredge in ¼ cup flour. Brown roast on all sides in hot bacon drippings in skillet. Place roast in a 6-qt. slow cooker. Place onion, carrots, potatoes, and 1 tsp. salt over roast; pour broth and coffee over roast and vegetables.
3. Cover and cook on HIGH 1 hour. Reduce heat to LOW, and cook 6 hours or until meat is tender. Remove vegetables and roast from slow cooker; keep warm.
4. Pour cooking liquid into a medium saucepan. Combine ½ cup cooking liquid, remaining ¼ cup flour, and remaining ½ tsp. salt in a small bowl. Whisk flour mixture into cooking liquid. Cook over medium heat, whisking constantly, 5 minutes or until thickened and smooth. Serve gravy with roast and vegetables. Makes 6 servings.

PEPPER STEAK

Hands-on Time: 39 min.   Total Time: 1 hr., 39 min.

Freezing the beef roast for 30 minutes makes it easier to cut into thin strips.

1 (2-lb.) boneless chuck
    roast, trimmed
5 Tbsp. olive oil, divided
¼ cup soy sauce
2 Tbsp. dry sherry
1 tsp. ground ginger
½ tsp. sugar
1 medium-size green bell
    pepper, cut into strips

1 medium-size red bell
    pepper, cut into strips
1 medium onion, cut into
    2-inch pieces
2 celery ribs, thinly sliced
¼ tsp. freshly ground pepper
1 Tbsp. cornstarch
¾ cup beef broth

2 tomatoes, each cut into
    8 wedges
Hot cooked rice, soft polenta,
    or gnocchi
Garnish: chopped fresh
    parsley

1. Cut roast across grain into 1/16-inch strips. Combine 2 Tbsp. olive oil, soy sauce, and next 3 ingredients in a large zip-top plastic freezer bag. Seal bag; shake to blend. Add beef to bag; seal and turn to coat. Chill 1 hour.

2. Remove beef from marinade, reserving marinade. Heat 2 Tbsp. olive oil in a large skillet over medium-high heat. Increase heat to high. Add beef to skillet; cook 2 to 3 minutes or until browned, stirring often. Stir reserved marinade into beef; cover, reduce heat to low, and simmer 17 to 20 minutes or until tender, stirring occasionally.

3. Meanwhile, heat remaining 1 Tbsp. olive oil in a large nonstick skillet over medium-high heat. Add green bell pepper and next 4 ingredients. Cook, stirring often, 3 to 4 minutes or until vegetables are crisp-tender. Remove from heat.

4. Combine cornstarch and broth, stirring until smooth. Stir cornstarch mixture into beef mixture. Stir in vegetable mixture and tomatoes. Serve immediately over rice, soft polenta, or gnocchi. Garnish, if desired. Makes 6 servings.

BARBECUED BRISKET OF BEEF

Hands-on Time: 19 min.   Total Time: 3 hr., 51 min.

While the brisket simmers, prepare your side dishes, such as Orange-Glazed Carrots, page 138, and Fresh Green Beans Amandine, page 137.

1	(3-lb.) beef brisket, trimmed		Hot sauce to taste (optional)	½	cup canned condensed tomato soup, undiluted
1	tsp. salt	2	Tbsp. butter	1	Tbsp. fresh lemon juice
½	tsp. pepper	3	medium onions, chopped	1	Tbsp. light brown sugar
		½	cup ketchup		

1. Brown brisket on both sides in a large Dutch oven over medium-high heat, browning fat side first. Add salt; pepper; 2 cups water; and hot sauce, if desired. Reduce heat to low. Cover and simmer 1 hour. Do not drain.

2. Melt butter in a large skillet over medium-high heat. Add onion; sauté 8 minutes or until tender. Stir in ketchup, tomato soup, lemon juice, and brown sugar, mixing well.

3. Pour onion mixture over brisket in Dutch oven. Cover and simmer 2½ hours or until meat is very tender, stirring occasionally.

4. Transfer brisket to a warm platter, and let stand 10 minutes; cut diagonally across grain into thin slices. Serve with remaining sauce. Makes 8 to 10 servings.

VEAL MARSALA

Hands-on Time: 20 min.   Total Time: 20 min.

When cooking the mushrooms, stir only twice to ensure browning.

¼   cup butter, divided
1   (8-oz.) package sliced fresh mushrooms
2   garlic cloves, minced
¼   cup all-purpose flour
1   tsp. salt, divided
½   tsp. freshly ground pepper, divided
1   lb. veal scaloppine (4 large)
⅔   cup Marsala
⅔   cup beef stock
2   Tbsp. chopped fresh parsley

1. Melt 2 Tbsp. butter in a large nonstick skillet over medium-high heat. Add mushrooms; cook 8 minutes or until browned and tender, stirring twice. Add garlic; cook 1 minute, stirring to incorporate. Transfer to a bowl.
2. Combine flour, ½ tsp. salt, and ¼ tsp. pepper in a shallow dish; dredge veal in flour mixture, and set aside.
3. Melt 1 Tbsp. butter in skillet over medium-high heat. Add half of veal, and cook 1½ minutes on each side. Transfer to a platter; keep warm. Repeat procedure with remaining 1 Tbsp. butter and veal, reserving drippings in skillet.
4. Add Marsala to skillet, stirring to loosen particles from bottom of skillet. Add beef stock, and boil 1 minute, stirring until thickened. Stir in parsley, remaining ½ tsp. salt and ¼ tsp. pepper, mushroom mixture, and any accumulated veal juices from platter; cook, stirring constantly, 1 minute. Spoon sauce over veal. Makes 4 servings.

TASTY TRIVIA

Many cultures are represented in the South's numerous veal recipes. Not surprisingly, immigrants from many countries were familiar with veal and even preferred it to beef, because they knew from experience that if a beef animal survived a harsh winter, the meat would be tough.

GERMAN-STYLE MEATBALLS

Hands-on Time: 50 min.   Total Time: 1 hr., 5 min.

This recipe calls for a panade and a slurry. The milk and bread combination forms a panade. It's used to bind the meatballs. The slurry is a thin paste of water and flour that's stirred into a hot preparation such as the sauce accompanying the meatballs. It's used as a thickener. Be sure to stir the gravy for several minutes after adding the slurry so the flour loses its raw taste.

2 (1-oz.) white bread slices, torn into small pieces	1 large egg, lightly beaten	1 tsp. Worcestershire sauce
¾ cup milk	1 tsp. salt	3 Tbsp. vegetable oil
1 Tbsp. butter	¹⁄₁₆ tsp. ground nutmeg	5 cups beef broth, divided
½ cup finely chopped onion	2 Tbsp. chopped fresh parsley	½ cup all-purpose flour
1½ lb. ground chuck	½ tsp. lemon zest	½ cup sour cream
½ lb. ground pork	1 tsp. fresh lemon juice	Hot cooked noodles

1. Place bread in a small shallow bowl; add milk, and let soak about 5 minutes. Squeeze milk from bread; discard milk.

2. Melt butter in a small skillet over medium heat; add onion, and sauté until tender. Combine sautéed onion, bread, ground chuck, and next 8 ingredients in a large bowl. Shape into 1½-inch meatballs.

3. Cook half of meatballs in 1½ tsp. hot oil in a large nonstick skillet over medium-high heat 5 minutes or until browned, turning once. Transfer to Dutch oven; add 4 cups broth. Bring to a boil; reduce heat to low, and simmer, covered, 15 minutes. Remove meatballs, reserving cooking liquid. Keep meatballs warm. Repeat with remaining meatballs and oil.

4. Whisk together flour and remaining 1 cup broth. Stir flour mixture into cooking liquid. Cook over medium-high heat, stirring constantly, 3 minutes or until thickened and bubbly.

5. Return meatballs to Dutch oven; cook over low heat until meatballs are thoroughly heated. Add sour cream, stirring just until blended. Serve meatballs and sauce over hot cooked noodles. Makes 6 servings.

Note: Use an ice-cream scoop to form meatballs.

STUFFED PEPPERS

Hands-on Time: 30 min.   Total Time: 1 hr., 20 min.

Feel free to add your favorite herb or cheese to this family favorite.

6   medium-size green bell peppers
1¼ lb. ground chuck
½   cup finely chopped celery
½   cup finely chopped green bell pepper
½   cup finely chopped onion
1   garlic clove, minced
1   cup cooked rice
1   tsp. salt
⅛   tsp. freshly ground black pepper
1   (24-oz.) jar pasta sauce, divided
1   cup (4 oz.) shredded sharp Cheddar cheese

1. Preheat oven to 375°. Remove tops and seeds from whole bell peppers.
2. Cook ground chuck and next 4 ingredients in a large skillet over medium-high heat, stirring often, 8 minutes or until vegetables are tender; drain. Stir in rice, salt, black pepper, and 1½ cups pasta sauce.
3. Fill each bell pepper with ¾ cup beef mixture; place in a 13- x 9-inch baking dish. Add water to just cover bottom of baking dish, and tightly cover with aluminum foil. Bake at 375° for 45 minutes; uncover and sprinkle with cheese. Bake 5 more minutes or until cheese melts. Spoon remaining pasta sauce over peppers. Makes 6 servings.

Love It Lighter: Substitute ground turkey breast for the chuck to shave fat and calories.

TASTY TRIVIA

Rice was introduced to the New World by way of South Carolina in 1680, and its ready acclimatization to Southern growing conditions fostered its production throughout the Southern colonies. In Louisiana, rice found a particularly welcoming home: The flatlands were ideal for its growth, and the Acadians and Creoles considered it a basic in their cuisine. So basic is this nutritious grain in the area, it is often served three times a day. No wonder Louisianians are said to consume more rice in one year than most Americans consume in five years.

BOW TO THE KING

by Gene B. Bussell

You could live a hundred years and never see anything more beautiful than the flats off the Florida Keys. The waters are warm, shallow, and clear as gin. Yet somehow—between the sugar sand and a sky filled with clouds you could climb—this watery landscape is transformed into a myriad of colors. One moment it takes on the blue-green of a '57 Chevy, swirled with streaks of lavender. Then its olive-etched turtle grass floor appears from the sand. And somehow the sunlight changes it once again to a tantalizing sapphire blue.

This bright place is full of life and has its own rhythm. A pair of ink black rays glide through the waters like stealth fighters, casting wavy shadows as they silently pass by. Bonefish stir the sand, their tails tipping out of the water in pursuit of shrimp and crab with the changing tide. As I look out across the water to the horizon in the distance, it all seems to merge into one, and with that, the hope of a big fish calls.

I have come to this place for an audience with the king—the "silver king," as tarpon are called. Anybody who grew up reading *Field & Stream* is reverent of this big, powerful fish. Tarpon migrating through the Keys can weigh more than 150 pounds.

Record fish in Florida exceed 200 pounds. Its scientific name, *Megalops atlanticus,* suggests a prehistoric background. It's actually a reference to its large eye. Its back is dark green, bluish, almost black, with a prominent dorsal fin and metallic, silver sides. It has a giant, bony mouth that turns upward. It feeds on crab and fish such as mullet, swallowing them whole.

Sight fishing for tarpon is just that: watching the clear waters for fish and then casting your line in their direction, waiting for their reaction. I know that, even if I catch this silver wonder, we both will win in the end, and I will set him free. Tarpon fishing is primarily catch-and-release. But the wind and clouds have their own agenda now. It's blowing and the clouds make it difficult to see into the waters. The waves created by the wind also don't help.

Still, I am mesmerized watching for tarpon in the water. Standing in the boat, my rod ready to cast, my eyes peeled for rolling or their dark torpedo-like forms moving through the water. I remind myself that, should I be lucky enough to get a strike, I must fight the impulse to pull back on the line when he makes his run into the air. To catch a

tarpon, you must learn to "bow to the king"—bend toward him, giving the line slack as he leaps up in battle to throw the hook. The tarpon's true glory may be in his acrobatic attempts to break free of the line. This fish has more rock 'n' roll than Elvis in one of his rhinestone jumpsuits (Elvis being "The King," of course).

The boat gently sways, the water now kissing the hull. An osprey whistles out from its perch in the pines along the shore. I'm distracted and look up at the sky. It's almost too big to take in. It's quiet, peaceful, almost motionless above. The sunlight streams through the clouds, and the water sparkles. Suddenly, out of nowhere, there they are, within shouting distance—tarpon. I feel a rush of adrenaline as I hold my breath and cast in their direction. He strikes. I have him—but for only a split second. I make one wrong move, and he makes his escape. The silver king has won. He streaks away in a flash of glory. No tarpon today. And with all the respect he is due, I now bow to the silver king. A lesson learned.

CRISPY FRIED CATFISH

Hands-on Time: 40 min.   Total Time: 2 hr., 40 min.

Serve this favorite with Alabama Hush Puppies found on page 49 to round out your fish fry.

12 (6-oz.) catfish fillets
1   tsp. salt
½   tsp. pepper
1   (2-oz.) bottle hot sauce

Vegetable oil
2   cups self-rising
      cornmeal mix

Tartar sauce (optional)
Cocktail sauce (optional)
Garnish: lemon wedges

1. Sprinkle fillets with salt and pepper; place in a shallow dish. Add hot sauce to fillets, turning to coat. Cover and chill 2 hours.

2. Pour oil to a depth of 4 inches into a large deep skillet; heat over medium-high heat to 375°.

3. Place cornmeal mix in a large zip-top plastic freezer bag. Add fillets, 1 at a time; seal bag, and shake until completely coated. Fry fillets, in batches, 4 minutes on each side or until golden brown. Drain on a wire rack over paper towels. Serve with tartar sauce or cocktail sauce, and garnish, if desired. Makes 6 servings.

CLASSIC TROUT AMANDINE

Hands-on Time: 30 min.   Total Time: 2 hr., 30 min.

A perfect pairing—delicate trout with buttery almonds and a rich sauce.

2 cups milk	¾ cup all-purpose flour	½ cup sliced almonds
⅛ tsp. hot sauce	½ tsp. pepper	2 Tbsp. fresh lemon juice
1½ tsp. salt, divided	¾ cup butter, divided	2 tsp. Worcestershire sauce
12 (4-oz.) trout fillets	1 Tbsp. olive oil	¼ cup chopped fresh parsley

1. Stir together milk, hot sauce, and 1 tsp. salt in a 13- x 9-inch baking dish; add fillets, turning to coat. Cover and chill 2 hours. Drain, discarding marinade.

2. Combine flour and pepper in a shallow dish. Dredge fillets in flour mixture.

3. Melt ¼ cup butter with oil in a large skillet over medium heat. Fry fillets, in batches, in butter mixture 2 minutes on each side or until fish flakes with a fork. Transfer to a serving platter; keep warm.

4. Combine remaining ½ cup butter and almonds in a saucepan; cook over medium heat, stirring often, until almonds are lightly browned. Add lemon juice, Worcestershire sauce, and remaining ½ tsp. salt; cook, stirring constantly, 1 minute. Remove from heat; stir in parsley. Pour almond mixture over fillets, and serve immediately. Makes 6 servings.

Note: Trout fillets are sold as single fillets, or sometimes as a "saddle." Be sure to buy the smaller, single fillets, if possible, so that they will fit in your skillet with ease.

SALMON CROQUETTES

Hands-on Time: 35 min.   Total Time: 2 hr., 35 min.

Croquettes can be formed into various shapes. Maybe you remember your mom forming them into oblong shapes. Salmon croquettes made from canned salmon were popular to make because the salmon was readily available when fresh seafood wasn't.

1 (15½-oz.) can pink salmon, drained, skinned, bones removed, and flaked
½ tsp. salt
¼ tsp. paprika
1 Tbsp. butter
1 Tbsp. all-purpose flour
1 cup milk
1 large egg
About 1¼ cups fine, dry breadcrumbs
2 large eggs, lightly beaten
Vegetable oil
Lemon wedges

1. Stir together salmon, salt, and paprika in a medium bowl.

2. Melt butter in a medium saucepan over low heat; whisk in flour until smooth. Cook 1 minute, whisking constantly. Gradually whisk in milk; cook over medium heat, whisking contantly until mixture is thickened and bubbly.

3. Beat 1 egg until thick and just until yellow disappears. Gradually stir about one-fourth of hot mixture into egg; add to remaining hot mixture, stirring constantly. Cook over medium-low heat, stirring constantly, 2 minutes or until slightly thickened. Remove from heat, and add to salmon mixture. Chill 1 hour.

4. Shape ¼ cup chilled mixture with floured hands into 12 (3-inch) patties; dredge each croquette in breadcrumbs, and dip in beaten eggs. Dredge again in breadcrumbs. Chill 1 hour.

5. Pour oil to a depth of ¼ inch into a large skillet. Fry croquettes, in batches, 2 minutes on each side until golden brown; drain on paper towels. Transfer croquettes to a serving platter. Serve immediately with lemon wedges. Makes 8 servings.

"I was a fool for the salmon croquettes that my mother served hot from a butter-sputtering skillet. Bound with butter, her pucks of canned salmon gained textural complexity by way of crushed saltine crackers. They reached their apogee when she set them awash in a puddle of stone-ground grits. In the years since I left home, I've learned to love all manner of fish, from gigged flounder to sea urchin roe, but what I crave are her salmon croquettes."

—John T. Edge

HOT TUNA MELTS

Hands-on Time: 15 min.   Total Time: 18 min.

The tuna salad sandwich was a staple for lunch on every table in the 1950s and 1960s. If you're hooked on coffee shop tuna salad sandwiches, you'll love these heated versions. But don't limit yourself to Cheddar cheese. Experiment with some of the flavored and smoked cheeses available today.

⅓ cup mayonnaise

¼ cup sliced pimiento-stuffed Spanish olives, drained

3 hard-cooked eggs, chopped

3 Tbsp. sweet pickle relish

2 Tbsp. finely chopped onion

1 (5-oz.) can solid white tuna in spring water, drained and flaked

2 English muffins, split and lightly toasted

4 sharp Cheddar cheese slices

1. Preheat broiler with oven rack 5½ inches from heat. Stir together first 5 ingredients in a medium bowl; add tuna, stirring gently to blend. Spoon on muffin halves; place on a baking sheet.

2. Broil 2 minutes. Top each with a cheese slice; broil 1 more minute or until cheese melts. Makes 4 servings.

Note: You can find hard-cooked eggs in the deli department of your local grocery store.

CRAB-STUFFED FLOUNDER

Hands-on Time: 15 min.   Total Time: 40 min.

If you'd rather, use regular crabmeat. Just be sure to pick thoroughly to discard any bits of shell.

2 (2-lb.) whole flounder	¼ cup chopped fresh parsley	Vegetable cooking spray
½ cup butter	1 Tbsp. fresh lemon juice	Melted butter
⅓ cup minced onion	¾ tsp. salt, divided	Fresh lemon juice
⅓ cup minced green bell pepper	¾ tsp. freshly ground black pepper, divided	Lemon wedges
1 lb. fresh lump crabmeat, drained	Dash of hot sauce	

1. Lay each fish flat on a cutting board, light side of flesh down; split lengthwise, beginning ¾ inch from head and cutting down center of fish to tail. Make a crosswise slit in flounder near head, intersecting with first cut to make a "T." Cut flesh along both sides of backbone to the tail, allowing the knife to run over the rib bones to form a pocket for stuffing.

2. Melt ½ cup butter in a large skillet over medium heat; add onion and bell pepper, and sauté until onion is transparent. Remove from heat. Add crabmeat, parsley, 1 Tbsp. lemon juice, ¼ tsp. salt, ¼ tsp. black pepper, and a dash of hot sauce; stir gently to blend.

3. Preheat oven to 350°. Brush pocket of fish with melted butter, and sprinkle with remaining ½ tsp. salt and ½ tsp. pepper. Stuff fish loosely with crabmeat mixture; place fish on a lightly greased jelly-roll pan. Bake at 350° for 25 minutes (depending on size of fish) or until fish flakes easily with a fork; baste frequently with melted butter and lemon juice as fish bakes.

4. Remove fish to a serving platter; serve with lemon wedges. Makes 6 to 8 servings.

SHRIMP DESTIN

Hands-on Time: 24 min.   Total Time: 24 min.

Read about Marian's fondness for this recipe on pg. 77. This may be served over hot cooked rice instead of rolls.

2   lb. unpeeled, large raw shrimp (21/25 count)
1   cup butter
¼   cup chopped green onions
2   tsp. minced garlic

1   Tbsp. dry white wine
1   tsp. fresh lemon juice
⅛   tsp. salt
⅛   tsp. coarsely ground pepper

1   tsp. dried dill weed
1   tsp. chopped fresh parsley
6   French rolls, split lengthwise and toasted

1. Peel shrimp; devein, if desired.

2. Melt butter in a large skillet over medium-high heat; add green onions and garlic, and sauté until onions are tender. Add shrimp, wine, and next 3 ingredients; cook over medium heat, stirring occasionally, 3 to 5 minutes or just until shrimp turn pink. Stir in dill weed and parsley. Spoon shrimp mixture over toasted rolls, and serve immediately. Makes 6 servings.

SHRIMP CREOLE

Hands-on Time: 20 min.   Total Time: 45 min.

For a spicier version of this Louisiana favorite, add hot sauce or more crushed red pepper.

3   Tbsp. butter
2   medium-size green bell peppers, finely chopped
1   medium onion, minced (1½ cups)
¼   cup chopped celery

1   bay leaf
1   tsp. chopped fresh parsley
¾   tsp. salt
¼   tsp. ground black pepper
⅛   tsp. dried crushed red pepper

2   (14.5-oz.) cans diced tomatoes
1   lb. peeled and deveined medium-size raw shrimp (26/30 count)
Hot cooked rice

Melt butter in a small Dutch oven over medium heat; add bell pepper and next 7 ingredients, and sauté 7 minutes or until vegetables are tender. Stir in tomatoes; bring to a boil, reduce heat to low, and simmer, stirring occasionally, 20 minutes. Increase heat to medium. Add shrimp; cook, stirring occasionally, 4 minutes or just until shrimp turn pink. Remove and discard bay leaf. Serve immediately over rice in shallow bowls. Makes 4 servings.

ADAMS' RIBS

Hands-on Time: 45 min.   Total Time: 5 hr., 15 min.

Adams' Ribs is the hot and spicy product of a marriage. It is said that the wife's Cajun background is the source of the spicy heat, while her husband's commitment to the best equipment and a perfectly built fire contributes the smoky tenderness. A spice rub and two adapted sauces give the ribs their signature taste and texture.

BASTING SAUCE

3 cups red wine vinegar
1 cup dry white wine
¾ cup ketchup
¼ cup firmly packed light brown sugar
¼ cup Worcestershire sauce
¼ cup yellow mustard
2 Tbsp. freshly ground black pepper
1 to 2 Tbsp. ground red pepper or dried crushed red pepper

RIBS

1 Tbsp. garlic powder
1 Tbsp. Creole seasoning
2 Tbsp. freshly ground black pepper
1 Tbsp. Worcestershire sauce
8 lb. pork spareribs

SERVING SAUCE

1 Tbsp. butter
1 medium onion, finely chopped

1½ tsp. minced garlic
1 cup ketchup
½ cup white vinegar
¼ cup fresh lemon juice
¼ cup steak seasoning
2 Tbsp. light brown sugar
1 Tbsp. Cajun seasoning
2 Tbsp. hickory liquid smoke

1. Prepare Basting Sauce: Combine all ingredients and 1 cup water in a saucepan; bring to a boil over medium-high heat. Reduce heat to medium, and simmer 1 hour.

2. Prepare Ribs: Combine garlic powder and next 3 ingredients; rub on all sides of ribs.

3. Light 1 side of grill, heating to 300° to 350° (medium) heat; leave other side unlit. Arrange ribs over unlit side, and grill, covered with grill lid, 2 to 3 hours, turning and basting with Basting Sauce every hour. (The longer the ribs cook, the more tender they will be.)

4. Increase heat to 350° to 400° (medium-high) heat; grill, covered with grill lid, 1 more hour, basting with Basting Sauce every 10 minutes.

5. Meanwhile, prepare Serving Sauce: Melt butter in a large skillet over medium heat; add onion and garlic, and sauté 5 minutes or until onion is tender. Add ketchup and remaining ingredients; bring to a simmer. Simmer 15 minutes. Cool completely (about 1 hour). Serve ribs with Serving Sauce. Makes 8 to 10 servings.

Note: We tested with Dale's Steak Seasoning sauce and Luzianne Cajun Seasoning.

Makeover in Minutes: When you have a hankering for 'cue but not the time to do it all from scratch, substitute store-bought barbecue sauce for the Serving Sauce.

Southern Living

FOLLOWING
THE FOLIAGE TRAIL
IN THE
GREAT SMOKIES

PORK CHOPS WITH CREAM GRAVY

Hands-on Time: 50 min.   Total Time: 50 min.

Serve these delicious pork chops with mashed potatoes, and use the gravy to top both the chops and the potatoes.

½   cup cracker meal*
1   tsp. poultry seasoning
¼   tsp. salt
⅛   tsp. pepper
6   (½-inch-thick) bone-in pork chops
4   bacon slices
1   Tbsp. all-purpose flour
1   cup milk
½   tsp. salt
¼   tsp. pepper

1. Stir together first 4 ingredients in a medium bowl. Dredge pork chops in cracker meal mixture.
2. Cook bacon in a large skillet over high heat until crisp; remove bacon, and drain on paper towels, reserving drippings in skillet. Cook pork chops in hot drippings 4 minutes on each side or until browned; drain on paper towels; reserving drippings in skillet. Transfer pork chops to a serving platter; keep warm.
3. Add flour to reserved drippings, stirring until well blended. Cook over medium heat, stirring constantly, 1 minute. Gradually add milk; cook over medium heat, stirring constantly, 18 minutes or until thickened. Stir in ½ tsp. salt and ¼ tsp. pepper.
4. Serve pork chops immediately with gravy. Makes 6 servings.

* Cracker meal can be found with the flour and cornmeal at your grocery store. You can also make your own by finely crushing saltine crackers.

TASTY TRIVIA

Pork chops received short shrift in the old cookbooks as a rule. One recipe from 1893 says only, "Fry or stew pork chops, after taking off the rind or skin, the same as for veal." One suspects the pork chop was lost in the shuffle at butchering time, perhaps when the tenderloin and rib roasts were cut. One matter has remained the same, however: With pork of every cut, the accompaniments of choice have mostly been applesauce and sauerkraut.

mama's way or your way

Country music star Miranda Lambert can't live without her mama's meatloaf. She asked us to make a healthier version for her to take on the road.

MAMA'S WAY:
- Irresistible home-cooked flavor
- Ground beef-and-pork combination
- Tender texture

YOUR WAY:
- Uses leaner meats
- Contains fiber-rich oats
- Rich tomato topping

mama's way

BEV'S FAMOUS MEATLOAF

Hands-on Time: 15 min. Total Time: 1 hr., 50 min.

2 lb. lean ground beef
1 lb. ground pork sausage
18 saltine crackers, crushed
½ medium-size green bell
    pepper, diced
½ medium onion, finely chopped

2 large eggs, lightly beaten
1 Tbsp. Worcestershire sauce
1 tsp. yellow mustard
½ cup firmly packed light brown
    sugar, divided
½ cup ketchup

1. PREHEAT oven to 350°. Combine first 8 ingredients and ¼ cup brown sugar in a medium bowl just until blended. Place mixture in a lightly greased 11- x 7-inch baking dish, and shape mixture into a 10- x 5-inch loaf.
2. BAKE at 350° for 1 hour. Remove from oven, and drain. Stir together ketchup and remaining ¼ cup brown sugar; pour over meatloaf. Bake 15 more minutes or until a meat thermometer inserted into thickest portion registers 160°. Remove from oven; let stand 20 minutes. Remove from baking dish before slicing. Makes 10 servings.

> "My mom and I have cooked together as far back as she could bring a stool to the kitchen counter, and her meatloaf has always been my favorite recipe."
>
> —Miranda Lambert

BETTER-FOR-YOU TURKEY MEATLOAF

Hands-on Time: 15 min.   Total Time: 2 hr., 10 min.

¾ cup uncooked quick-cooking oats
¾ cup diced green bell pepper
¾ cup finely chopped onion
¾ cup milk
1 large egg, lightly beaten
1 Tbsp. Worcestershire sauce
1 tsp. salt
1 tsp. yellow mustard
2 lb. lean ground turkey
1 (16-oz.) package reduced-fat ground turkey sausage
1 (15.5-oz.) can stewed tomatoes with green peppers and onions, drained
1½ Tbsp. light brown sugar

1. Preheat oven to 350°. Combine first 8 ingredients in a medium bowl. Add ground turkey and sausage; combine mixture just until blended, using hands. Place mixture on a lightly greased rack in an aluminum foil-lined broiler pan; shape mixture into a 10- x 5-inch loaf. Top with stewed tomatoes, and sprinkle with brown sugar.

2. Bake at 350° for 1 hour and 35 minutes or until a meat thermometer inserted into thickest portion registers 165°. Remove from oven; let stand 20 minutes. Makes 10 servings.

ALL THE FIXIN'S

sumptuous side dishes
that also make great
veggie plate medleys

It's difficult to grow up in the South without adopting some favorite side-dish picks found at the local meat-and-three. My entire family often passed on the meat altogether because we simply couldn't resist a loaded veggie plate when our favorites were on the menu.

a note from
Marian

In summer, especially, the options might number in the dozens—fried green tomatoes, squash casserole, turnip greens, cornbread, simple sliced tomatoes, black-eyed peas, fresh corn, and everything in between. At home, Mom would

make these same side dishes for us from scratch.

It would all start with a trip to Murphree's, a produce stand we frequented, or, sometimes more spontaneously, when we passed a temporary roadside stand or pickup truck selling fresh-from-the-field goodness on our way home from church on Sunday. I looked forward to those meals more than Thanksgiving. The leftovers were always just as good, too.

SUMMER FRUIT SALAD

Hands-on Time: 20 min.   Total Time: 20 min.

½ cup bottled poppy-seed dressing

2 tsp. grated fresh ginger

2 avocados, thinly sliced

4 cups loosely packed arugula

2 cups halved seedless green grapes

1 mango, julienned

1 cup sliced fresh strawberries

¼ cup thinly sliced green onions

¼ cup fresh cilantro leaves

Whisk together dressing and grated ginger in a large bowl. Cut avocado slices in half crosswise; gently toss with dressing mixture. Add arugula and remaining ingredients; gently toss to coat. Serve immediately. Makes 8 to 10 appetizer servings.

BEST WALDORF SALAD

Hands-on Time: 15 min.   Total Time: 15 min.

For added flavor, toast the pecans at 350° for 6 to 8 minutes.

2   large Gala apples, diced
1   large Granny Smith apple, diced
1½   cups halved seedless green grapes
½   cup coarsely chopped pecans
½   cup diced celery
⅓   cup raisins
⅓   cup mayonnaise

Stir together all ingredients. Makes 6 to 8 servings.

Chunky Tomato-Fruit Gazpacho

CHUNKY TOMATO-FRUIT GAZPACHO

Hands-on Time: 30 min.   Total Time: 2 hr., 30 min.

This no-cook side soup makes use of all of the fresh produce sold at roadside stands, and promises refreshment for hot summer days. The original recipe specifies to use salad cucumbers instead of pickling cucumbers.

2	cups finely diced cantaloupe	1	jalapeño pepper, seeded and finely chopped	¼	cup chopped fresh basil
2	cups finely diced honeydew melon	1	cup finely diced peaches	3	Tbsp. chopped fresh mint
2	cups finely diced tomatoes	2	cups fresh orange juice	3	Tbsp. fresh lemon juice
1	mango, finely diced	½	cup finely chopped sweet onion	1	tsp. sugar
2	medium cucumbers, finely diced			½	tsp. salt
					Garnish: fresh basil sprigs

Combine first 14 ingredients in a large bowl. Cover and chill 2 to 24 hours. Garnish, if desired. Makes about 9 cups.

MARINATED VEGETABLE SALAD

Hands-on Time: 13 min.   Total Time: 13 min., plus 8 hr. for chilling

Marinating makes for no waste from the garden and helps tenderize those end-of-the-season crops.

½	lb. fresh broccoli, trimmed	4	celery ribs, cut into ½-inch pieces	1½	cups tarragon vinegar
½	medium cauliflower, trimmed	1	small zucchini, halved lengthwise and cut into ¼-inch slices	¼	cup olive oil
½	lb. carrots, diagonally cut into ¼-inch pieces			¼	cup vegetable oil
¾	lb. sliced fresh mushrooms	1	medium cucumber, peeled, halved, seeded, and cut into ¼-inch slices	¼	cup sugar
2	small green bell peppers, cut into 1-inch pieces			½	Tbsp. yellow mustard
				2	garlic cloves, minced
				1½	tsp. salt
				1	tsp. dried tarragon

1. Cut broccoli and cauliflower into bite-size pieces.

2. Combine broccoli, cauliflower, and next 6 ingredients in a large serving bowl; toss well.

3. Stir together vinegar and next 7 ingredients. Pour over vegetables, and toss well. Cover and chill 8 hours or overnight. Makes 9 servings.

TOMATO ASPIC WITH
BLUE CHEESE DRESSING

Hands-on Time: 15 min.   Total Time: 1 hr., 45 min., plus 8 hr. for chilling

Make individual aspics by pouring chilled mixture into lightly greased ½-cup aspic molds or 6-oz. punch cups. Cover and chill until firm. Unmold onto salad plates and serve dressing on the side.

3   envelopes unflavored
    gelatin
1   (46-oz.) can tomato juice,
    chilled and divided
2   Tbsp. grated onion
½   tsp. salt

1   cup chopped green bell
    pepper
1   cup chopped celery
    Green leaf lettuce leaves
1   (3-oz.) package cream
    cheese, softened

¼   cup milk
1   (4-oz.) package crumbled
    blue cheese
    Garnish: cooked shrimp

1. Sprinkle gelatin over 1½ cups cold tomato juice in a large saucepan; let stand 1 minute. Cook over medium heat, stirring until gelatin dissolves (about 3 minutes). Remove from heat; stir in onion, salt, and remaining tomato juice. Chill 1½ to 2 hours until consistency of unbeaten egg white.

2. Fold in bell pepper and celery; spoon mixture into a lightly greased 6-cup ring mold. Cover and chill 8 hours or until firm. Unmold onto a lettuce-lined serving plate.

3. Combine cream cheese and milk; beat at medium speed with an electric mixer until blended. Add blue cheese; beat until blended. Spoon dressing into center of mold. Garnish, if desired. Makes 10 to 12 servings.

GREEN GODDESS SALAD

Hands-on Time: 20 min.   Total Time: 20 min.

This creamy herb dressing, known as green goddess, was popular in the 1950s and 1960s. It gets its pale green hue from minced parsley. Iceberg was the lettuce of choice.

2   heads iceberg lettuce, torn into coarse chunks (about 13 cups)
1   cup mayonnaise
½   cup sour cream
⅓   cup minced fresh flat-leaf parsley
¼   cup minced onion
2   Tbsp. tarragon vinegar
2   Tbsp. garlic wine vinegar
2   Tbsp. white wine vinegar
2   Tbsp. anchovy paste
1   Tbsp. fresh lemon juice

Place lettuce in a large bowl. Process mayonnaise and remaining ingredients in a blender or food processor until smooth. Cover and chill 2 hours, if desired. Pour desired amount of dressing over lettuce, and toss gently. Store leftover dressing in refrigerator up to a week. Makes 10 to 12 servings.

SIMPLE BEET SALAD

Hands-on Time: 20 min.   Total Time: 2 hr., 5 min.

2 lb. assorted medium beets	⅓ cup bottled balsamic vinaigrette	½ cup chopped walnuts
		Garnish: fresh parsley leaves

1. Preheat oven to 400°. Divide beets between 2 large pieces of heavy-duty aluminum foil; drizzle with balsamic vinaigrette, and sprinkle with salt and pepper to taste. Seal foil, making 2 loose packets.
2. Bake at 400° for 45 to 55 minutes until fork-tender.
3. Let cool 1 hour in packets, reserving accumulated liquid.
4. Bake walnuts at 400° in a single layer in a shallow pan 8 to 10 minutes or until toasted and fragrant, stirring halfway through.
5. Peel beets, and cut into slices or wedges. Arrange beets on a serving platter or in a bowl. Drizzle with reserved liquid, and sprinkle with walnuts. Garnish, if desired. Makes 6 to 8 servings.

ASPARAGUS WITH LEMON SAUCE

Hands-on Time: 20 min.   Total Time: 20 min.

While making the lemon sauce, bring a large pot of water to a boil for the asparagus. Just as the sauce begins to thicken, drop the asparagus into the boiling water. They will be finished at the same time, and the asparagus will remain crisp-tender for serving.

2   lb. fresh asparagus
¼   cup butter
¼   cup all-purpose flour
2   cups milk

2   egg yolks, beaten
½   tsp. lemon zest
3   Tbsp. fresh lemon juice
1   tsp. salt

¼   tsp. freshly ground pepper
Lemon wedges (optional)

1. Snap off and discard tough ends of asparagus.

2. Melt butter in a medium saucepan over medium heat. Add flour; cook, whisking constantly, 1 minute. Add milk; cook, whisking constantly, 8 minutes or until thickened. Gradually stir about one-fourth of hot milk mixture into egg yolks; add yolk mixture to remaining hot milk mixture, and cook, whisking constantly, 1 minute. Remove from heat; stir in lemon zest and next 3 ingredients.

3. Cook asparagus in boiling water to cover 3 minutes or until crisp-tender; drain and keep warm. Serve lemon sauce over hot asparagus with lemon wedges, if desired. Makes 8 servings.

FRESH GREEN BEANS AMANDINE

Hands-on Time: 20 min.   Total Time: 45 min.

This dish is often mispronounced as "AL-mandine." There is no "L" in the pronunciation.

⅔ cup slivered almonds
2 lb. fresh green beans

4 thick hickory-smoked
bacon slices, cooked
and crumbled

2 Tbsp. butter
⅓ cup finely chopped onion
½ tsp. salt

1. Preheat oven to 350°. Bake almonds in a single layer in a shallow pan 5 to 7 minutes or until lightly toasted, stirring halfway through.

2. Rinse beans, trim, and remove strings, if necessary. Cut beans in half diagonally. Place in a 5-qt. Dutch oven; add bacon and 1 cup water. Bring to a boil over medium-high heat; cover, reduce heat, and simmer 15 minutes. Drain.

3. Melt butter in a medium skillet over medium heat. Add onion; sauté over medium-high heat 3 minutes or until tender. Add onion and salt to beans; toss well to coat.

4. Add almonds to skillet; toss well to coat. Sprinkle over beans. Serve immediately. Makes 4 to 6 servings.

BAKED BEANS

Hands-on Time: 20 min.   Total Time: 9 hr.

These beans follow the rule for the best barbecue: Cook them low and slow for great flavor.

1   (16-oz.) package dried
    navy beans
10 bacon slices, cut into
    ⅓-inch pieces
1   medium onion, chopped

¼   cup molasses
½   cup ketchup
3   Tbsp. sugar
1   Tbsp. Worcestershire
    sauce

1   Tbsp. dry mustard
1½ tsp. salt
¼   tsp. pepper

1. Rinse and sort beans according to package directions. Place in a large Dutch oven; cover with water 2 inches above beans, and let soak 1 hour. Drain.
2. Place beans and bacon in Dutch oven; cover with water 2 inches above beans, and bring to a boil. Cover, reduce heat, and simmer 30 minutes. Drain, reserving 3 cups liquid.
3. Combine onion and next 7 ingredients; stir well. Add onion mixture and reserved liquid to bean mixture. Pour into a 5-qt. slow cooker. Cook on LOW 7 hours. Makes 10 to 12 servings.

ORANGE-GLAZED CARROTS

Hands-on Time: 30 min.   Total Time: 45 min.

If you love carrots, double this recipe as it only makes 2 cups.

1   lb. carrots, peeled and
    sliced

¼   cup butter, melted
1   cup fresh orange juice

1   tsp. sugar
⅛   tsp. salt

Combine all ingredients in a medium saucepan; bring to a boil. Cover, reduce heat, and simmer 10 to 15 minutes or until carrots are crisp-tender. Uncover and cook, stirring occasionally, 13 to 15 minutes or until most of liquid evaporates. Makes 4 servings.

SOUTHERN-STYLE CREAMED CORN

Hands-on Time: 15 min. Total Time: 28 min.

Sprinkle crumbled bacon or chopped fresh basil over this classic summer dish, if you'd like.

6 ears fresh corn, husks removed	2 tsp. cornstarch
¼ cup butter	½ tsp. salt
½ cup half-and-half or milk	¼ tsp. freshly ground pepper

1. CUT tips of corn kernels into a large bowl; scrape milk and remaining pulp from cobs into bowl.
2. COMBINE corn, butter, and ¼ cup water in a large skillet or saucepan. Cover and cook over medium heat, stirring occasionally, 10 minutes.
3. COMBINE half-and-half and next 3 ingredients, whisking until blended. Gradually add cream mixture to corn, stirring well. Cover and cook 3 minutes or until thickened, stirring often. Makes 4 to 6 servings.

Note: Puree half of the corn for even creamier results.

Fried Okra

Hands-on Time: 10 min.   Total Time: 52 min.

Soaking the fresh okra in salt water eliminates the need to salt it after frying.

2   lb. fresh okra
¾   cup salt
2   cups plain yellow or white cornmeal
Canola oil

1. CUT off and discard tip and stem ends of okra; cut okra crosswise into ½-inch-thick slices. Place in a large bowl.
2. COMBINE 3 qt. water and salt; pour over okra. Soak 30 minutes; drain, rinse well, and drain again. Dredge okra, in batches, in cornmeal.
3. POUR oil to a depth of 2 inches into a Dutch oven; heat to 375°. Fry okra, in batches, 4 minutes or until golden. Drain on paper towels. Serve immediately. Makes 8 to 10 servings.

GRANDMOTHER'S GARDEN

by Chef Frank Stitt

Highlands Bar and Grill, Bottega Restaurant & Café, and Chez Fonfon

Summertime lunch at my Grandmother White's kitchen table meant an overload of dishes from her "kitchen" garden right outside her back door.

Up above the small chicken house and just beyond where the old smokehouse used to be and beyond the biggest holly tree anyone had ever seen, was the garden that she tended with meticulous care, rich with aged mule manure. This garden produced the most amazing green beans, shell beans, tomatoes, onions, squash, cucumbers, corn, asparagus, fat fordhook lima beans, and so much more. Not that I didn't love the creamed corn, the new potatoes cooked with big green pole beans and onions, or the cucumber and tomato salad with vinegar and fresh dill, but it was the stewed okra that brought me back for second or third helpings. Most other cousins and guests would ooh and aah about the fried okra, but my mom, grandmother, and I knew that the combination of sliced sweet onions cooked down in a little bacon drippings with her put-up canned tomatoes, simmering good and long with the tiniest baby okra, was what really made us smile.

BAKED CHEESE GRITS

Hands-on Time: 10 min.   Total Time: 1 hr., 20 min.

Make these grits for a special brunch. Your guests will enjoy the wonderful cheesy flavor. For a little kick, sprinkle smoked paprika over the top of the grits.

1 tsp. salt	½ cup butter, cut up	3 large eggs, lightly beaten
1½ cups uncooked regular grits	4 cups (16 oz.) shredded sharp Cheddar cheese	Smoked paprika (optional)

1. Preheat oven to 350°. Lightly grease a 2½-qt. baking dish.

2. Bring salt and 6 cups water to a boil. Stir in grits, and reduce heat to low. Cover and cook, stirring occasionally, 15 to 20 minutes or until thickened. Remove from heat.

3. Add butter and cheese, stirring until blended. Gradually stir about one-fourth of hot grits into eggs; add egg mixture to remaining hot grits, stirring constantly. Pour grits into prepared baking dish.

4. Bake at 350° for 45 minutes or until slightly firm. Sprinkle with paprika, if desired. Makes 6 to 8 servings.

SQUASH CASSEROLE

Hands-on Time: 15 min.   Total Time: 1 hr., 7 min.

Slightly sweet yellow squash is paired with tangy Cheddar and buttery crackers—what's not to love? This casserole is at its best in the summer when yellow squash is in season.

8 large yellow squash, cut into ½-inch-thick slices	2 cups (8 oz.) shredded sharp Cheddar cheese, divided	¼ cup milk
1 tsp. salt		¼ cup butter, cut into pieces
¼ tsp. pepper		
1½ cups round buttery cracker crumbs		

1. Preheat oven to 350°. Lightly grease a 2-qt. baking dish.

2. Combine squash and water to cover in a medium saucepan; bring to a boil. Cover, reduce heat, and simmer 12 minutes or until tender; drain. Mash squash.

3. Combine squash, salt, and pepper; stir well. Spoon half of mixture into prepared dish. Sprinkle ¾ cup cracker crumbs and 1½ cups cheese over squash. Repeat layers with remaining squash and cracker crumbs. Pour milk over top, and dot with butter.

4. Bake, uncovered, at 350° for 30 minutes.

5. Sprinkle remaining ½ cup cheese over top; bake 5 minutes or until cheese melts. Makes 6 to 8 servings.

CREAMED SPINACH

Hands-on Time: 35 min.   Total Time: 45 min.

This rich side dish received our Test Kitchens' highest rating. We especially loved it served over creamy grits.

¼ cup pine nuts
2 cups whipping cream
½ cup butter
⅔ cup grated Parmesan
   cheese

½ tsp. salt
½ tsp. freshly grated nutmeg
½ tsp. freshly ground pepper

2 (9-oz.) packages fresh
   spinach, thinly sliced
Hot cooked grits (optional)

1. Preheat oven to 350°. Bake pine nuts in a single layer in a shallow pan 5 minutes or until lightly toasted, stirring halfway through.

2. Combine whipping cream and butter in a large saucepan. Bring to a boil over medium-high heat; reduce heat to medium, and cook, stirring often, 15 minutes or until thickened.

3. Stir in cheese and next 3 ingredients. Add spinach; cook over low heat, stirring often, 3 minutes or until spinach has wilted. Serve over grits, if desired; sprinkle with pine nuts. Makes 4 servings.

Love It Lighter: Trade the whipping cream for half-and-half to reduce the fat from this ultra-rich side dish.

Crusty Broiled Tomatoes

CRUSTY BROILED TOMATOES

Hands-on Time: 15 min.   Total Time: 17 min.

To boost flavor, toss breadcrumbs with finely chopped fresh basil or your favorite fresh herb.

4 medium tomatoes	⅛ tsp. ground red pepper	1 cup freshly grated
1 Tbsp. Dijon mustard	6 Tbsp. butter, melted	Parmesan cheese
¼ tsp. salt	1 cup soft, fresh	
¼ tsp. freshly ground black pepper	breadcrumbs	

1. Preheat broiler with oven rack 5½ inches from heat. Cut tomatoes in half. Spread cut sides with mustard; sprinkle with salt, black pepper, and red pepper.
2. Place tomato halves on oven rack. Combine butter, breadcrumbs, and cheese. Spoon crumb mixture on top of each tomato half.
3. Broil 2 minutes or until crumbs are golden brown and tomatoes are thoroughly heated. Makes 8 servings.

FRIED GREEN TOMATOES

Hands-on Time: 30 min.   Total Time: 35 min.

For a crowd, double or triple this versatile recipe, which can be served as a side dish or appetizer.

¾ cup plain yellow or white cornmeal	½ tsp. pepper	Vegetable oil
1½ tsp. salt	4 large green tomatoes, cut into ¼-inch-thick slices	

1. Combine cornmeal, salt, and pepper in a shallow bowl. Dredge tomatoes in cornmeal mixture.
2. Pour oil to a depth of ½ inch into a large cast-iron skillet or Dutch oven; heat to 375°.
3. Fry tomatoes, in batches, 3 minutes on each side or until golden. Drain on paper towels. Season with salt to taste. Serve immediately. Makes 14 servings.

AND ME WITHOUT MY CAST-IRON SKILLET

by Amy Bickers

As summer draws near, many Southerners wax eloquent about the fresh-from-the-vine appeal of a fat red tomato, sliced and sandwiched between two pieces of mayonnaise-laden bread. I am not one of those people. I'll say "y'all" all day long. I'll say "git" instead of "get" and turn "nine" into a two-syllable word. But I will never, ever eat a soggy tomato sandwich.

Before I get carted across the Mason-Dixon Line, I might as well confess a few more Southern food crimes. I don't have a clue what's in a mint julep. I don't make pimiento cheese (the pimientos weird me out). I've never made a pound cake, and I wouldn't even attempt pralines. I also don't have the urge to fry anything. I do love bacon, but I often cook it in the microwave.

My kitchen is ill-equipped. There are probably freshmen at LSU with better-stocked cabinets. I don't own a cast-iron skillet, but I've heard that if you do have one, it needs to be well seasoned. For all I know, this involves pouring a lot of Tony Chachere's Creole Seasoning on it. There are no Mason jars in my kitchen in which to store whatever it is Southern women are expected to grow in their backyards and then shove into glass. If you asked me to do some canning, I'd assume you wanted me to fire somebody.

Let's blame my mother. The few lessons she taught me in the kitchen didn't come from a Junior League cookbook.

Lesson No. 1: Sandwiches should be cut in half diagonally because "they just taste better that way."

Lesson No. 2: Set the table every night, forks to the left, knives to the right.

Lesson No. 3: Sit still during supper and make interesting conversation.

As a working, single mother of two, Mom was and still is a great believer in simple sustenance. Prep time was minimal. Lemon pepper chicken, a side of white rice, and a small green salad were enough to satisfy us at day's end. As we sat at the table, Mom would have my younger brother and me tell her the most exciting thing that happened that day. Sometimes Mom would say, "If we had a million dollars, what would we do with it?" and we would launch into lively debate.

Rather than teaching us to cook, my mom taught us lessons passed down by a long line of talkers. The most important is this: If you aren't going to say something entertaining, why would you speak aloud?

My children are growing up much like I did. They have witnessed food crimes for which I should be tried in the court of chef John Besh. I frequently make chicken-and-sausage gumbo, and it's delicious. Ask my Louisiana-born children how to make it, and they will tell you to pour a mix from a package into a pot and add water and meat. It's true. I've never made a roux in my life. I have more interest in bringing back regular use of the word "rue"—as in "I rue the day I spent an entire hour

stirring roux in a pot nonstop."

This is not to say I don't admire Southern cooks. I am in awe of people who make meal prep look effortless while they chat with guests and fill wineglasses in between stirring and mixing and popping things in and out of the oven. I will never be one of those people. I count on them to invite me over to dinner.

What my mother taught me—and what I can teach my own children—is the delicious joy in sitting at the table and talking, even if the biscuits you're buttering came from a can. Because the most important part of the meal is not the food that's being served but the stories being told. There's nothing more Southern than that.

MACARONI AU GRATIN

Hands-on Time: 15 min.   Total Time: 1 hr., 25 min.

The secrets to this divine recipe: Use block cheese and shred it yourself; also, let the dish stand for 15 minutes before serving for a texture that's heavenly.

2 cups uncooked elbow macaroni	4 large eggs, lightly beaten	4 cups (16 oz.) shredded New York sharp Cheddar cheese
1½ tsp. salt	2 cups milk	
	¼ tsp. pepper	

1. Preheat oven to 300°. Lightly grease a 13- x 9-inch baking dish.

2. Cook macaroni according to package directions, adding 1 tsp. salt; drain well. Combine eggs, milk, pepper, and remaining ½ tsp. salt in a large bowl; add cooked macaroni, and stir well.

3. Spoon half of macaroni mixture into prepared dish. Sprinkle with half of cheese. Repeat layers with remaining macaroni mixture and cheese, ending with cheese.

4. Bake at 300° for 30 minutes; increase temperature to 400°, and bake 10 minutes or until lightly browned. Let stand 15 minutes before serving. Makes 8 to 10 servings.

Note: Use 10 (6-oz.) ramekins or ovenproof dishes for individual macaroni au gratins.

CHEESY SCALLOPED POTATOES

Hands-on Time: 25 min.   Total Time: 1 hr., 10 min.

Letting the potatoes stand for 15 minutes helps the sauce continue to thicken.

2½ lb. red potatoes, peeled	¼ tsp. ground red pepper	1 cup (4 oz.) shredded Swiss cheese
3 Tbsp. butter	2 cups whipping cream	
⅓ cup chopped green onions	¾ cup milk	¼ cup freshly grated Parmesan cheese
⅓ cup chopped red bell pepper	¾ tsp. salt	
1 garlic clove, minced	¼ tsp. freshly ground black pepper	

1. Preheat oven to 350°. Lightly grease an 11- x 7-inch baking dish. Cut potatoes into ⅛-inch-thick slices.

2. Melt butter in a Dutch oven over medium-high heat; add green onions and next 3 ingredients. Cook, stirring constantly, 2 minutes. Stir in whipping cream and next 3 ingredients.

3. Add potato slices; bring to a boil over medium heat, and cook, stirring gently, 10 minutes or until potato slices are tender. Spoon potatoes and sauce into prepared dish; sprinkle with cheeses.

4. Bake at 350° for 25 minutes or until bubbly and golden. Let stand 15 minutes before serving. Makes 8 servings.

Makeover in Minutes: In a hurry? Buy bags of precut home-style sliced potatoes in your grocer's refrigerated section to save a step.

Macaroni au Gratin

Sweet Potato Casserole

SWEET POTATO CASSEROLE

Hands-on Time: 15 min.   Total Time: 1 hr., 20 min.

Sweet potato casserole is a favorite Thanksgiving side dish, but you don't have to wait until then for it. It teams well with turkey, but it's also perfect with pork or chicken.

6 medium-size sweet potatoes	2 large eggs	2 Tbsp. all-purpose flour
½ cup butter, melted	1 tsp. vanilla extract	2 Tbsp. butter, softened
½ cup sugar	½ cup firmly packed light brown sugar	
⅓ cup milk	½ cup finely chopped pecans	

1. Preheat oven to 350°. Lightly grease an 11- x 7-inch baking dish.

2. Bring sweet potatoes and water to cover to a boil, and cook 30 to 35 minutes or until tender. When cool enough to handle, peel potatoes, place in a bowl, and mash.

3. Combine mashed sweet potatoes, melted butter, and next 4 ingredients; beat at medium speed with an electric mixer until smooth. Spoon into prepared baking dish.

4. Combine brown sugar and remaining ingredients; sprinkle over sweet potato mixture.

5. Bake at 350° for 30 minutes. Makes 8 servings.

HASH BROWN POTATOES

Hands-on Time: 15 min.   Total Time: 15 min.

The key to the best hash brown potatoes is to avoid over-stirring them while they brown. And the secret to flavor is cooking them in bacon drippings.

¼ cup bacon drippings	2 Tbsp. minced fresh parsley	2 garlic cloves, minced
2 Tbsp. butter	½ tsp. dried oregano	¼ tsp. salt
⅔ cup minced onion		¼ tsp. pepper
1 (20-oz.) package refrigerated diced potatoes		

1. Melt bacon drippings and butter in a 9-inch skillet over medium heat. Add onion to skillet, and sauté 4 to 5 minutes or until tender. Add potatoes and remaining ingredients, stirring gently to coat.

2. Cook over medium-high heat, stirring occasionally, 5 minutes or until browned on all sides. Makes 4 servings.

PICNIC POTATO SALAD

Hands-on Time: 20 min.   Total Time: 1 hr., 15 min.

This best-loved potato salad serves a crowd. It's perfect to bring to a potluck.

4 lb. Yukon gold potatoes	½ cup sour cream	1 Tbsp. spicy brown mustard
3 hard-cooked eggs, peeled and grated	⅓ cup finely chopped sweet onion	1 tsp. salt
1 cup mayonnaise	¼ cup sweet pickle relish	¾ tsp. freshly ground pepper
½ cup diced celery		Garnish: fresh parsley leaves

1. Cook potatoes in boiling water to cover 40 minutes or until tender; drain and cool 15 minutes. Peel potatoes, and cut into 1-inch cubes.

2. Combine potatoes and eggs.

3. Stir together mayonnaise and next 7 ingredients; gently stir into potato mixture. Serve immediately, or cover and chill 12 hours. Garnish, if desired. Makes 8 servings.

FOOD FOR THOUGHT—
ONE WORLD TRAVELER FINDS
HER SOUTHERN ROOTS IN A
PLATE OF GREENS

by Marti Buckley Kilpatrick

My plate, overflowing with fried chicken, collards, and peas, should have produced an immediate feeling of comfort. But it didn't. Instead, I was distracted by an uninvited dinner guest—a very un-Southern craving for just a bit of imported cheese and crusty bread.

I think it all began with the several months I spent living in Europe—and ended with me feeling that I had outgrown the South of my childhood. It made me into a wannabe expatriate, with a body in Alabama and a mind halfway across the world. My recent marriage, however, planted me firmly in the red dirt of my home state.

Prodding at some collard greens with a fork, I was struck by the fact that I could either continue on this gloomy path to certain cultural identity crisis or reconcile myself with who and where I am. Maybe this very vegetable I was maiming with my flatware was a chance to redeem myself. If collards couldn't be incorporated into my global worldview, then did I really have hope as a Southerner?

At that moment, my quest for self-discovery began in an unlikely place: The kitchen.

Reactions varied: If you want to get a Southerner impassioned, ask him or her about the "correct" way to cook collard greens. When I described my venture to my grandma, she just laughed and shook her head. But in the end, it was just me, my identity, and that quintessential leafy green.

Before I knew it, I was chopping, baking, and sautéing. An invitation to prepare dinner for my mother resulted in collard-and-ham croquetas. The crunchy exterior revealed a warm, creamy filling, straight out of a tapas bar in Spain, with a little pop of slightly bitter greens. Then the cuisine moved north with a collard quiche, a simple and homey version of the French pie. I was cooking my way across the globe. The rigorous washing of the thick leaves became a routine and their almost rubbery texture a familiar feel under my fingers.

I continued to push collards to the limits, incorporating them into dishes they never dreamed of in their quiet vegetable lives. Cooked and pureed, collards transformed into a bright, creamy pesto. I journeyed east on the culinary map, wrapping and frying them into collard wontons. Perhaps the most surprising success was the collard green ice cream, a velvety vanilla semifreddo featuring sweet and salty almonds and, of course, caramelized collards. Good? Let's just say this time Grandma's mouth was too full of greens to do any laughing.

Faced with the last leafy bunch, I decided to get back to basics. After a couple hours of simmering, I settled onto the sofa with a bowl of slow-cooked collards. I realized that everything I love about the South was contained in this steaming mess o' greens—the simplicity, the straight-forwardness of the flavor, the comfort and warmth that flooded my mouth and throat after every spoonful. I may go far and wide, fall in love with faraway cuisines, people, and places, but it's a relief to know that all it will take to remind me of my roots is a simple stewed vegetable.

HOPPIN' JOHN

Hands-on Time: 20 min.   Total Time: 2 hr., 35 min.

You'll want to pass the hot sauce when you serve this traditional Southern dish so that everyone can select their own heat level.

1   (16-oz.) package dried
    black-eyed peas
½   lb. salt pork, chopped
2   medium-size green bell
    peppers, chopped

2   medium onions, chopped
1½ cups uncooked regular
    rice
2   Tbsp. butter
¼   tsp. ground red pepper

1¼ tsp. hot sauce
4   tsp. salt

1. Rinse and sort peas according to package directions. Place in a large Dutch oven; cover with water 2 inches above peas. Bring to a boil. Boil 1 minute; cover, remove from heat, and soak 1 hour. Remove from Dutch oven, and drain.

2. Sauté salt pork in Dutch oven over medium-high heat 6 minutes or until crisp. Remove with a slotted spoon, reserving drippings in pan. Add bell peppers and onions; sauté 5 minutes. Add 7 cups water; return peas and salt pork to pan, and bring to a boil. Reduce heat; partially cover, and simmer 30 minutes.

3. Add rice; cover and cook, stirring occasionally, 30 minutes or until peas are tender and rice is done. Remove from heat; stir in butter and remaining ingredients. Serve immediately. Makes 10 to 12 servings.

DELICIOUS BLACK-EYED PEAS

Hands-on Time: 16 min.   Total Time: 2 hr., 50 min.

These black-eyed peas are a great side dish for any traditional Southern meal. Serve alongside fried chicken and cooked greens.

1 (16-oz.) package dried black-eyed peas	3 garlic cloves, crushed	1 bay leaf
1 Tbsp. salt	3 medium-size green bell peppers, chopped	3 Tbsp. white vinegar
1 garlic clove, halved	3 medium onions, chopped	1 tsp. salt
4 to 6 bacon slices		¼ tsp. ground black pepper

1. Rinse and sort peas according to package directions. Place in a Dutch oven; cover with water 2 inches above peas. Bring to a boil. Boil 1 minute; cover, remove from heat, and soak 1 hour. Drain.

2. Add boiling water to cover. Add 1 Tbsp. salt and garlic halves; cover and simmer, stirring occasionally, 1½ hours, adding 1½ cups boiling water as needed. Discard garlic halves.

3. Cook bacon in a large skillet over medium-high heat 5 to 6 minutes or until crisp; remove bacon, and drain on paper towels, reserving 2 Tbsp. drippings in skillet. Crumble bacon.

4. Sauté crushed garlic, bell peppers, onions, and bay leaf in hot drippings 10 minutes or until tender. Remove from heat, and stir in vinegar, 1 tsp. salt, and ¼ tsp. black pepper. Discard bay leaf. Stir onion mixture into peas. Add crumbled bacon just before serving. Makes 20 servings.

"Widespread Panic takes the Southern New Year's tradition of collard greens and black-eyed peas very seriously. No matter where we are playing for New Year's Eve, on January 1st we take time out to eat collard greens for money and black-eyed peas for health in the New Year."

—Domingo "Sunny" Ortiz of Widespread Panic

BING CHERRY SALAD

Hands-on Time: 15 min.   Total Time: 1 hr., 50 min., plus 8 hr. for chilling

1   (15-oz.) can dark, sweet
     pitted cherries
2   (8-oz.) cans crushed
     pineapple in juice

1   (6-oz.) package
     cherry-flavored gelatin
1   cup cold water

Garnishes: mayonnaise,
     poppy seeds,
     arugula leaves

1. Drain cherries and pineapple, reserving 1½ cups juice in a saucepan. (If necessary, add water to equal 1½ cups.) Bring juice mixture to a boil over medium heat; stir in gelatin, and cook, stirring constantly, 2 minutes or until gelatin dissolves. Remove from heat, and stir in 1 cup cold water. Chill until consistency of unbeaten egg whites (about 1½ hours).

2. Gently stir in drained cherries and pineapple. Pour mixture into an 8-inch-square baking dish or 8 (⅔-cup) molds. Cover and chill 8 hours or until firm. Garnish, if desired. Makes 8 servings.

mama's way or your way

Simmered with pork or sautéed and meatless, collards are a Southern favorite.

MAMA'S WAY:
- Smoky pork flavor
- Tender texture
- Delicious pot likker

YOUR WAY:
- Speedy preparation
- Better for you
- On the table in 26 minutes

SOUTHERN-STYLE COLLARD GREENS

Hands-on Time:1 hr., 4 min. Total Time: 3 hr., 4 min.

12 hickory-smoked bacon
  slices, finely chopped
2 medium-size sweet onions,
  finely chopped
¾ lb. smoked ham, chopped
6 garlic cloves, finely chopped
3 (32-oz.) containers chicken
  broth

3 (1-lb.) packages fresh collard
  greens, washed and trimmed
⅓ cup cider vinegar
1 Tbsp. sugar
1 tsp. salt
¾ tsp. pepper

COOK bacon in a 10-qt. stockpot over medium heat 10 to 12 minutes or until almost crisp. Add onion, and sauté 8 minutes; add ham and garlic, and sauté 1 minute. Stir in broth and remaining ingredients. Cook 2 hours or to desired degree of tenderness. Makes 10 to 12 servings.

mama's way

SAUTÉED GREENS

Hands-on Time: 26 min.   Total Time: 26 min.

½ cup chopped onion
3 garlic cloves, minced
1 Tbsp. chopped fresh ginger
1 serrano pepper, split*
1 Tbsp. sesame oil

1 tsp. salt
½ tsp. black pepper
1 (1-lb.) package fresh collard greens, washed, trimmed, and coarsely chopped

1 Tbsp. sugar
1 Tbsp. rice vinegar

Sauté onion and next 3 ingredients in hot oil in a large skillet or wok 1 minute. Stir in salt and black pepper. Add greens; sauté 2 minutes. Add sugar and vinegar; cover and cook 3 minutes or until wilted. Remove and discard serrano pepper before serving. Makes 4 to 6 servings.

* ½ jalapeño pepper, split, may be substituted.

your way

Try Sautéed Greens with Pork: Stir in ½ lb. chopped smoked pork with greens.

COVERED DISH CLASSICS

one-dish favorites
for family dinners
and potlucks

Growing up, I was a bit suspicious of casseroles at potlucks or church suppers. They were mysterious things and I didn't know what might be inside, from whose kitchen they came, or whether I wanted to risk sampling such vague concoctions.

a note from
Marian

Mom made classic luncheon fare such as a warm chicken casserole, side salad, and roll. That was an easy standby for daytime gatherings. For parties, she might spoon creamed chicken or seafood into puff pastry cups for an elegant entrée that was simple to make and always the crowd pleaser. Most of all, Mom had a knack for elevating a basic dish. She might spike the turkey tetrazzini with flavorful sherry or sprinkle sliced almonds to add crunch to the crust of a gratin. Embellishing every-day recipes to make them special was truly her signature, whether she was serving just our family at home or taking a dish to share with a new neighbor or a friend in need.

I share Mom's philosophy in my food styling for *Southern Living*. I strive to do justice to the foods that make our region special so that they look as delicious in photos as they have tasted through the generations.

CHEESY CHICKEN TETRAZZINI

Hands-on Time: 30 min.   Total Time: 1 hr., 25 min.

Tetrazzini is said to be named for the opera singer Luisa Tetrazzini. And it's a dish worth singing about! Often made with turkey, this cheesy chicken version is a great addition to a buffet. Just add a simple side salad and...bravo!

½ cup sliced almonds
¾ tsp. salt, divided
⅛ tsp. black pepper
4 skinned and boned chicken breasts, cut into ½-inch cubes
1 Tbsp. olive oil
7 oz. uncooked spaghetti
¼ cup butter

1 medium-size green bell pepper, chopped
2½ Tbsp. all-purpose flour
1 cup milk
¼ cup dry white wine
1 (10¾-oz.) can cream of mushroom soup
1 (8-oz.) package sliced fresh mushrooms

1 (2-oz.) jar diced pimiento, drained
⅛ tsp. garlic powder
½ cup grated Parmesan cheese
3 cups (12 oz.) shredded sharp Cheddar cheese, divided

1. Preheat oven to 350°. Lightly grease a 13- x 9-inch baking dish.
2. Bake almonds in a single layer in a shallow pan 4 to 6 minutes or until lightly toasted, stirring halfway through.
3. Combine 1 cup water, ¼ tsp. salt, and ⅛ tsp. black pepper in a large saucepan; bring to a boil over medium-high heat. Add chicken to pan; cover, reduce heat to low, and simmer 10 minutes or until done. Drain chicken, discarding liquid.
4. Combine olive oil, 6 cups water, and remaining ½ tsp. salt in a Dutch oven; bring to a boil over medium-high heat. Add spaghetti, and cook 10 minutes or until almost tender. Drain well.
5. Melt butter in a Dutch oven over medium heat; add bell pepper, and sauté until tender. Gradually whisk in flour until blended. Gradually whisk in milk, next 6 ingredients, and 2 cups Cheddar cheese until blended. Cook over medium heat, stirring constantly, 10 minutes or until thoroughly heated. Stir in chicken.
6. Spread half of spaghetti into prepared baking dish; spread half of chicken mixture over spaghetti. Repeat layers.
7. Bake at 350° for 15 minutes. Sprinkle with remaining 1 cup cheese and almonds; bake 5 more minutes or until cheese is melted and bubbly. Makes 6 to 8 servings.

CHICKEN DIVAN

Hands-on Time: 25 min.   Total Time: 35 min.

This signature 1950s classic from New York's Divan Parisienne is made ultra-rich by folding in whipped cream. Don't be tempted to leave it out! The rich elegance of this dish made it a dinner party favorite across the country.

½ cup butter
½ cup all-purpose flour
2 cups milk
2 egg yolks, lightly beaten
2 Tbsp. dry sherry
½ tsp. Worcestershire sauce

2 tsp. grated Parmesan cheese
½ tsp. salt
½ cup whipping cream, whipped

2 (10-oz.) packages frozen broccoli spears
3 cups chopped cooked chicken (about 1 lb.)
Grated Parmesan cheese (optional)

1. Preheat oven to 450°. Lightly grease an 11- x 7-inch baking dish.
2. Melt butter in a heavy saucepan over low heat; whisk in flour. Gradually add milk, and cook, whisking constantly, until thickened. Remove from heat.
3. Gradually stir about one-fourth of hot mixture into egg yolks; add yolk mixture to remaining hot mixture, stirring constantly. Stir in sherry and next 3 ingredients. Fold in whipped cream.
4. Microwave broccoli according to package directions; drain. Arrange in prepared baking dish. Cover with chopped chicken. Pour sauce over chicken, and sprinkle with additional cheese, if desired.
5. Bake at 450° for 10 to 12 minutes or until bubbly and browned. Makes 6 to 8 servings.

Note: Use steamed fresh or frozen cooked broccoli florets if you'd like in place of the broccoli spears, and substitute Cheddar for the Parmesan.

MY CASSEROLE CRISIS

by Kim Cross

I confess: It took me nearly 30 years to learn how to make this Southern dish.

My next-door neighbor had to throw out his back to bring me to terms with my gravest shortcoming as a Southerner. What do we do to help a friend faced with death, disaster, or back surgery? Make casseroles, of course. I was mortified to realize that I'd never made one. And I didn't have the foggiest notion where to begin. I know, I know. Bless my heart.

Now, before I get myself in trouble with Mom, let me affirm that my mother is an extraordinary cook. Her culinary prowess is praised in hushed tones by anyone who has tasted her chili. My most fastidious foodie friend calls every Thanksgiving to get my mom's recipe for candied yams. Mom can fry fish and boil collards with the best—but she never did make a casserole.

So I consulted my girlfriends for advice. They seemed mildly shocked, as if I'd admitted I wasn't sure exactly how to operate a toothbrush. "It's so easy," they said, reciting recipes from memory, "and they are really good."

I scribbled notes on a napkin and rushed to the store, ticking off each ingredient with growing apprehension. Rotisserie chicken... check. Cream of mushroom soup... check. Grated cheese...check. Frozen broccoli...hmm, why not fresh? Mayonnaise...really? Corn flakes... seriously?

I assembled the casserole with mounting anxiety. It didn't look right. It didn't even look edible. I called my friend and left a panicked message. "Help! I'm having a casserole crisis! Should I dilute the cream of mushroom soup? Am I supposed to defrost the broccoli?" She didn't return my call in time, so I gathered my wits and just guessed.

As I folded mayonnaise into cold cream of mushroom soup—ew!— I wondered if this was all a very mean joke. The cold mushroom-mayo porridge looked like wallpaper paste and smelled decidedly less appetizing. I dutifully followed my girlfriends' instructions and pictured them sharing a belly laugh. Then I imagined my poor neighbor doubled over with food poisoning or just plain disgust. That wouldn't be good for his back.

After much deliberation, I decided to take my chances. I plodded across the front yard and sheepishly presented the casserole with a million apologies for how bad it was likely to taste. If it was good, I'd take the

credit. If it was awful, we could blame my friends.

The neighbors peeked under the foil and inquired what was in it. Cringing, I told them, half expecting them to recoil in horror. Instead, their eyebrows raised in interest and they cooed approval. "That sounds delicious!" Surely they were just being nice.

The next day, I left town on a business trip. As I hopped on the plane, I wondered with dread if I'd delivered a ticking food bomb. Whenever I'm on the road, the neighbors invite my husband to dinner. He'd likely partake of the casserole, and I knew he'd give me a brutally honest report. That is, if he could speak between the dry heaves.

"It was good," he said. That's a rave review from a man whose most enthusiastic assessment is, "That's neat!" The neighbors confirmed his appraisal, reassuring me that my casserole had caused them no gastrointestinal woes. I asked my husband to elaborate. "It wasn't gourmet," he said. "It was a casserole."

KING RANCH CHICKEN

Hands-on Time: 13 min.   Total Time: 1 hr., 43 min.

This is the true definition of comfort food: soft, warm, cheesy layers of chicken and tortillas with a subtle hint of chiles. It's no wonder Southern Living *has run several versions of this recipe through the decades, including quick and lightened variations. Resist the temptation to dip the tortillas longer than five seconds, or they will break down and dissolve in the broth.*

1 (3½- to 4-lb.) whole chicken, cut up
1 (16-oz.) package corn tortillas
1 large onion, thinly sliced or chopped
1 large green bell pepper, chopped
2 cups (8 oz.) shredded Cheddar cheese
1½ tsp. chili powder
½ tsp. garlic salt
1 (10¾-oz.) can cream of chicken soup
1 (10¾-oz.) can cream of mushroom soup
1 (10-oz.) can diced tomatoes and green chiles

1. Preheat oven to 350°. Lightly grease a 13- x 9-inch baking dish.
2. Cook chicken in a Dutch oven in boiling water to cover 45 minutes or until tender. Remove chicken, reserving 3 cups broth in pan. Let chicken cool; skin, bone, and shred chicken using 2 forks. Set meat aside.
3. Bring reserved broth to a boil; dip tortillas in broth 5 seconds to soften. Place half of tortillas in prepared baking dish. Layer with half each of chicken, onion, and bell pepper. Repeat layers.
4. Sprinkle with cheese, chili powder, and garlic salt.
5. Combine soups, and spread over cheese; top with tomatoes and green chiles. (Mixture will be wet on top.)
6. Bake at 350° for 45 minutes or until mixture is thoroughly heated. Makes 8 servings.

Makeover in Minutes: Try this all-time favorite casserole using one of the following twists.

Variation 1: Substitute a mojo-flavored deli-roasted chicken and nacho cheese soup for the chicken and soups called for in the original recipe.

Variation 2: Substitute 2 cups (8 oz.) shredded Monterey Jack cheese for Cheddar cheese. Decrease chili powder to 1 tsp., and add 1 tsp. ground cumin.

Variation 3: Substitute 6 skinned, bone-in chicken breasts for whole chicken. Add 1 large red bell pepper, chopped, in addition to the green bell pepper.

Variation 4: Substitute 2 cups (8 oz.) shredded Monterey Jack cheese for Cheddar cheese. Add 1 large red bell pepper, chopped, and sauté with onion and green bell pepper in 2 Tbsp. butter until tender.

CHICKEN-WILD RICE CASSEROLE

Hands-on Time: 25 min.   Total Time: 3 hr.

If you don't have dry sherry on hand, you can substitute dry white wine or chicken stock.

2   (3-lb.) whole chickens
1   cup dry sherry
1½ tsp. salt
½   tsp. curry powder
1   medium onion, sliced
½   cup sliced celery

¼   cup butter
2   (8-oz.) containers sliced fresh mushrooms
2   (6-oz.) packages long-grain and wild rice mix

1   (8-oz.) container sour cream
1   (10¾-oz.) can cream of mushroom soup

1. Preheat oven to 350°. Lightly grease a 2½-qt. baking dish.

2. Place chickens in a large Dutch oven; add sherry, next 4 ingredients, and 1 cup water. Cover and bring to a boil over medium-high heat; reduce heat to low, and simmer 1 hour. Remove from heat; pour broth through a wire-mesh strainer into a bowl, discarding solids. Let chicken cool; reserve broth for cooking rice.

3. Skin and bone chicken; cut chicken into pieces. Melt butter in Dutch oven over medium-high heat; add mushrooms, and sauté 5 minutes or until golden. Drain mushrooms, discarding liquid. Reserve ¼ cup mushrooms.

4. Cook rice according to package directions, substituting reserved broth for water. Combine chicken, remaining mushrooms, and rice in prepared baking dish. Stir together sour cream and mushroom soup; add to chicken mixture, stirring to blend. Arrange reserved mushrooms in a circle around edges of dish. (Casserole can be prepared ahead up to this point and frozen, or cover and chill for 8 hours or overnight, if desired.)

5. Bake, covered, at 350° for 1 hour or until bubbly. Makes 8 to 10 servings.

Note:
To save prep time, substitute rotisserie chickens for whole chickens. One rotisserie chicken yields about 3 cups chopped chicken. This dish can be prepared ahead if you wish.

COUNTRY CAPTAIN

Hands-on Time: 20 min.   Total Time: 1 hr., 15 min.

Country Captain is an iconic Lowcountry classic. Legend has it that a ship's captain who ferried spices from the Far East brought this chicken curry recipe to this country. Rice is the traditional side dish.

½ cup slivered almonds
½ cup all-purpose flour
1¾ tsp. salt, divided
½ tsp. ground black pepper
1 (3½-lb.) whole chicken, cut up
Vegetable oil
2 medium onions, chopped
2 medium-size green bell peppers, chopped
1 garlic clove, minced
2 (14.5-oz.) cans diced tomatoes
¼ cup currants
2 tsp. curry powder
½ tsp. ground white pepper
½ tsp. ground thyme
2 cups hot cooked rice

1. Preheat oven to 350°. Bake almonds in a single layer in a shallow pan 5 to 7 minutes or until lightly toasted, stirring halfway through.
2. Combine flour, 1 tsp. salt, and ½ tsp. black pepper. Dredge chicken in flour mixture.
3. Pour oil to a depth of ½ inch into a large skillet. Heat oil over medium-high heat. Fry chicken, in batches, 2 to 3 minutes or until browned on all sides; drain, reserving 2 Tbsp. drippings in skillet. Place chicken in a 13- x 9-inch baking dish.
4. Sauté onion, green pepper, and garlic in reserved drippings until tender. Add tomatoes, next 4 ingredients, and remaining ¾ tsp. salt; stir well. Spoon over chicken.
5. Bake, covered, at 350° for 55 minutes to 1 hour or until done.
6. Transfer chicken to a large serving platter, and spoon rice around chicken. Spoon sauce over rice, and sprinkle with almonds. Makes 4 servings.

COUNTRY COOKING...

CREAMED CHICKEN

Hands-on Time: 25 min.   Total Time: 30 min.

A popular alternative to serving this dish in pastry shells or over rice was spooning it over toast points.

½ cup sliced almonds
¼ cup butter
1 (8-oz.) package sliced fresh mushrooms
⅓ cup chopped green bell pepper
1 medium onion, chopped

⅓ cup all-purpose flour
2 cups chicken broth
1 cup half-and-half
2 cups chopped cooked chicken or turkey
½ tsp. ground nutmeg
⅛ tsp. ground black pepper

3 Tbsp. dry sherry
1 (2-oz.) jar diced pimiento, drained
8 frozen puff pastry shells, baked, or hot cooked rice

1. Preheat oven to 350°. Bake almonds in a single layer in a shallow pan 4 to 6 minutes or until lightly toasted, stirring halfway through. Set aside.

2. Melt butter in a Dutch oven over medium-high heat; add mushrooms, bell pepper, and onion, and sauté until tender. Add flour, stirring until smooth. Cook, stirring constantly, 1 minute. Gradually add chicken broth and half-and-half; cook over medium heat, stirring constantly, until thickened and bubbly. Stir in chicken, next 4 ingredients, and almonds; cook until thoroughly heated.

3. Spoon mixture into pastry shells, or serve over rice. Makes 8 servings.

OLD-FASHIONED CHICKEN AND DUMPLINGS

Hands-on Time: 45 min.   Total Time: 2 hr., 30 min.

This popular comfort food is also known as chicken and sliders in some parts of the country.

1 (3- to 3¾-lb.) whole chicken	6 Tbsp. butter	¾ cup buttermilk
1½ tsp. salt, divided	6 Tbsp. all-purpose flour	Garnishes: chopped
½ tsp. freshly ground black pepper	2 cups all-pupose flour	hard-cooked egg,
	½ tsp. baking soda	chopped fresh flat-leaf
	3 Tbsp. shortening	parsley

1. Bring chicken, water to cover, and 1 tsp. salt to a boil in a Dutch oven over medium heat. Cover, reduce heat to medium-low, and simmer 1 hour or until tender. Remove chicken, reserving broth in Dutch oven. Let chicken cool.

2. Skin and bone chicken; shred meat with 2 forks. Skim fat from broth. Add chicken and pepper to broth, and bring to a boil over medium-high heat. Reduce heat to medium-low, and simmer.

3. Meanwhile, melt butter in a small saucepan over medium heat; whisk in 6 Tbsp. flour. Cook, whisking constantly, 1 minute; stir flour mixture into broth mixture, and cook 1 to 2 minutes or until thickened.

4. Combine 2 cups flour, baking soda, and remaining ½ tsp. salt; cut in shortening with a pastry blender until crumbly. Add buttermilk, stirring with a fork just until dry ingredients are moistened. Turn dough out onto a well-floured surface; knead lightly 4 or 5 times.

5. Pat dough to ¼-inch thickness. Pinch off dough in 1½-inch pieces, and drop pieces, 1 at a time, into simmering broth. Cook, stirring occasionally, 3 to 4 minutes or to desired consistency. Garnish, if desired. Makes 4 to 6 servings.

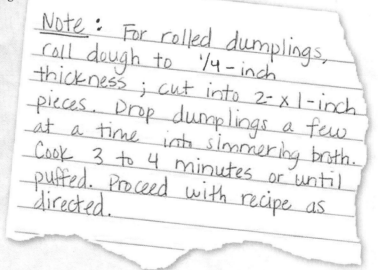

Note: For rolled dumplings, roll dough to ¼-inch thickness; cut into 2- x 1-inch pieces. Drop dumplings a few at a time into simmering broth. Cook 3 to 4 minutes or until puffed. Proceed with recipe as directed.

CHICKEN CACCIATORE

Hands-on Time: 45 min.   Total Time: 1 hr., 30 min.

Cacciatore means "hunter's style," and this rustic Italian favorite was born out of the sporting pastime of the well-to-do. Thighs are typically a cheaper part of the chicken but are perfect here because they add extra juiciness to the dish.

6 skin-on, bone-in chicken thighs (2½ to 3 lb.)
2 Tbsp. olive oil
2 medium onions, cut into ¼-inch slices
2 garlic cloves, minced
1 (14.5-oz.) can petite diced fire-roasted tomatoes with roasted garlic

1 (26-oz.) jar tomato-and-basil pasta sauce
1 tsp. salt
1 tsp. dried Italian seasoning
½ tsp. celery seeds
¼ tsp. freshly ground pepper
2 bay leaves
¼ cup dry white wine

Hot cooked spaghetti
Freshly grated Parmesan cheese

1. Brown chicken, in batches, in hot oil in a large Dutch oven over medium-high heat 3 minutes on each side; remove chicken, reserving drippings in pan.

2. Add onion and garlic to pan drippings; sauté over medium heat until tender.

3. Combine tomatoes and next 6 ingredients in a large bowl, stirring well. Add to onion mixture in skillet; add chicken to skillet. Cover and cook over medium-low heat 45 minutes; uncover and stir in wine. Reduce heat to low, and cook, uncovered, 20 minutes or until chicken is tender, turning chicken occasionally. Skim off excess fat. Discard bay leaves.

4. Serve chicken and sauce over hot cooked spaghetti; sprinkle with Parmesan cheese. Makes 6 servings.

CHICKEN-PECAN QUICHE

Hands-on Time: 20 min.   Total Time: 2 hr., 7 min.

You'll love this delectable quiche with its creamy chicken-pecan filling and savory Cheddar crust.

1½ cups (6 oz.) shredded
     sharp Cheddar cheese,
     divided
1   cup all-purpose flour
¾   cup chopped pecans
½   tsp. salt

¼   tsp. paprika
⅓   cup vegetable oil
1   cup sour cream
½   cup chicken broth
¼   cup mayonnaise
3   large eggs, lightly beaten

2   cups finely chopped
     cooked chicken
¼   cup minced onion
3   drops of hot sauce
¼   cup pecan halves

1. Preheat oven to 350°. Combine 1 cup shredded cheese and next 4 ingredients in a medium bowl; stir well. Add oil; stir well. Firmly press mixture in bottom and up sides of a 9-inch deep-dish pie plate. Bake at 350° for 12 minutes. Cool completely (about 30 minutes).

2. Whisk together sour cream and next 3 ingredients until smooth. Stir in chicken, next 2 ingredients, and remaining ½ cup cheese. Pour chicken mixture into prepared crust. Arrange pecan halves on top of chicken mixture.

3. Bake at 350° for 55 minutes or until set. Let stand 10 minutes before serving. Makes 8 servings.

"Every person who loves food should invest in a cast-aluminum pot. They are indestructible and can be thrown directly into the fire. You always want to burn hardwood on the fire. Don't burn any trash or plastic or any other substances in the fire that you're cooking on. Build up some good coals. Move some of the burning wood with a shovel and make a nice flat bed to lay your pot on. Enjoy."

—from *Southern Ground* by Zac Brown

BEEF STROGANOFF

Hands-on Time: 30 min.   Total Time: 50 min.

Stirring in the sour cream at the end gives the sauce its creamy tanginess.

1½ lb. boneless sirloin steak, trimmed
1   tsp. salt
2   Tbsp. olive oil, divided
2   Tbsp. butter
1   (8-oz.) package sliced fresh mushrooms
1¼ cups beef broth
1   Tbsp. Worcestershire sauce
2   tsp. Dijon mustard
2   Tbsp. all-purpose flour
1   (8-oz.) container sour cream
Hot cooked, buttered egg noodles
Garnish: chopped fresh parsley

1. Slice steak across the grain into 2- x ⅛-inch strips; sprinkle with salt.
2. Heat 1 Tbsp. oil in a large skillet over high heat. Add steak, and cook until browned, turning once. Remove steak from skillet, and keep warm.
3. Melt butter with remaining 1 Tbsp. oil in skillet over medium-high heat; add mushrooms, and cook 6 minutes or until liquid is almost absorbed, stirring occasionally to loosen particles from bottom of skillet.
4. Combine beef broth, Worcestershire sauce, and mustard in a small bowl; whisk in flour. Add mixture to skillet; stir well. Reduce heat to medium, and cook, stirring constantly, 6 minutes or until thickened. Stir in steak.
5. Reduce heat to medium-low; cover and cook 20 minutes or until steak is tender. Just before serving, stir in sour cream; cook 1 minute or just until thoroughly heated. Serve over hot cooked egg noodles. Garnish, if desired. Makes 4 to 6 servings.

TASTY TRIVIA

stroganoff (STRAW-guh-noff)

Thought to be named after a 19th-century Russian diplomat named Count Paul Stroganov, beef stroganoff made its way to the United States with servicemen who had sampled it on tours of duty in Europe.

This rich main dish calls for thin strips of tender, lightly floured beef, onions, and sliced mushrooms quickly sautéed in butter until golden brown, combined with a sour cream sauce, and served over hot wide noodles or rice pilaf. Stroganoff can be made with different cuts of beef, but the tenderloin or top loin is preferred.

GOING HOME AGAIN

by Amy Bickers

"You can never go home again, but the truth is you can never leave home, so it's all right."

—Maya Angelou

My homesickness flutters with uneasy irony. I live in Alabama now, but whispers and echoes tell me Louisiana is home. When I visit Louisiana, I do a tour of old haunts and former homes. I drive by my high school. I pick up a Humphrey—a yogurt-granola-and-fruit concoction from a sandwich shop called Counter Culture. The sign outside, despite regular repainting, is cracked and peeling. The soda fountain dispenses Diet Coke in foamy bursts. I was 21 when I worked here. Most of my paychecks went to happy hours. Some of my bills didn't get paid. Each morning, I walked in the back door of this shop, watered the sprouts for the sandwiches, cut up chicken, and made egg salad. I'm just a customer now, and I come and go through the front door. I pay with my credit card, and I don't get a discount.

I drive by the first house I ever purchased. The front door is still the bold red I painted it five years ago. I carried groceries in that side door. I sat on the front steps with my neighbor, borrowing and lending books. My son learned to ride his bike in the yard. In my new city, I seek out gray cottages with red front doors. I imagine my furniture inside, even if reality can't yet afford the high mortgage of this fantasy.

They're doing construction on one of the main thoroughfares. On a long-ago Sunday drive, my great-uncle took us by these formerly empty fields. He drove so slowly that the driver behind us threw up his arms in frustration. My brother and I sat in the backseat and giggled and rolled our eyes, not yet old enough to appreciate a meandering tour. My great-uncle used to own the property and wondered what would be done with it. That was two decades ago. He has since passed away. The land is now parking lots and big-box stores. These familiar sights dot the landscape of every other growing city in America and, thus, make my hometown unrecognizable to me.

The slow drivers aren't slow because they have stories to tell or because memories cloud their vision. Progress is to blame.

My mother moved away more than 15 years ago. My brother headed west to Arizona, while I took I-20 east. There is no childhood home to return to for holidays or

long weekends. My mother long ago packed my bedroom items into a box marked "Amy" and brought it to me in Birmingham. Letters from old boyfriends, photos from school dances, moody poems I wrote at 13—I keep them safe. I am the caretaker of my own past now.

I turn right at the light to avoid traffic. LSU flags line the streets of my childhood. When the Iron Bowl rolls around and Alabama schoolchildren wear the colors of AU or UA, I defiantly send mine out in purple and gold. I feed them crawfish. I season evening meals with Tony Chachere's and insist they build a tolerance for spicy foods. Homesickness is the taskmaster.

Yet when I travel to the place I call home, this flighty creature turns on its wing and floats upside down before landing in the cage of the heart. Its beak closes on the bittersweet flavor of expectations unmet. And like a migratory bird at season's end, I am pulled in a different direction. The easterly wind shifts and pushes me on my way again.

Shepherd's Pie

SHEPHERD'S PIE

Hands-on Time: 35 min.   Total Time: 1 hr., 35 min.

Lamb is the traditional meat used in shepherd's pie, a dish originally created to use leftovers from a roast. It's a one-dish meal filled with vegetables and topped with a crust of mashed potatoes.

1½ lb. ground lamb
¼   cup chopped onion
2   Tbsp. butter
3   Tbsp. all-purpose flour
1   (14.5-oz) can beef broth
1   large egg, lightly beaten
½   cup milk

½   cup soft, fresh breadcrumbs
1   cup frozen peas and carrots
½   tsp. salt
¼   tsp. freshly ground pepper

2   (24-oz.) containers refrigerated garlic mashed potatoes
1½ cups (6 oz.) shredded white Cheddar cheese

1. Preheat oven to 350°. Lightly grease a 9-inch deep-dish pie plate.
2. Cook lamb and onion in a large skillet over medium heat 10 minutes or until browned, stirring to crumble. Drain well.
3. Melt butter in a medium saucepan over medium heat. Add flour; cook, whisking constantly, 1 minute or until golden brown. Gradually add broth; cook, stirring constantly, 10 to 12 minutes or until thickened.
4. Combine lamb mixture, broth mixture, egg, and next 5 ingredients in a large bowl, mixing well.
5. Spread half of potatoes into prepared pie plate. Spoon lamb mixture over potatoes. Spread remaining potatoes over top. Sprinkle with cheese. Place pie plate on a baking sheet.
6. Bake at 350° for 1 hour or until cheese is melted and lightly browned. Makes 6 to 8 servings.

RED BEANS AND RICE

Hands-on Time: 20 min.   Total Time: 3 hr., 20 min.

This Louisiana Creole dish has become an icon of New Orleans cuisine. Look for small red beans, rather than kidney beans. Serve with crusty French bread and a green salad with vinaigrette.

1   lb. dried red beans
1   (¾-lb.) smoked ham hock
1   large onion, chopped
1   large garlic clove, chopped

1   bay leaf
¼   tsp. ground red pepper
1   lb. smoked mild or hot link sausage

¼   tsp. salt
Hot cooked rice

1. Rinse and sort beans according to package directions. Place beans in a Dutch oven; cover with water 2 inches above beans. Bring to a boil. Boil 1 minute; cover, remove from heat, and soak 1 hour.
2. Drain beans, and return to Dutch oven. Add 6 cups water, ham hock, and next 4 ingredients; bring to a boil over medium-high heat. Reduce heat to low; cover and simmer 1 hour or until beans are tender.
3. Cut sausage in half lengthwise; cut into 1-inch pieces. Add sausage and salt to beans; simmer, uncovered, stirring often, 1 hour or until a thick gravy forms. Discard bay leaf. Serve over hot cooked rice. Makes 6 servings.

ITALIAN SAUSAGE LASAGNA

Hands-on Time: 27 min.   Total Time: 1 hr., 22 min.

Lasagna is an all-time family favorite. Convenience foods streamline prep time in this recipe, keeping it less than 30 minutes.

1   lb. Italian sausage, casings removed
1   medium onion, chopped
1   garlic clove, minced
1   (14.5-oz.) can diced tomatoes with basil, garlic, and oregano
2   cups tomato-and-basil pasta sauce

1   tsp. sugar
1   Tbsp. chopped fresh basil
¼   tsp. salt
3   Tbsp. chopped fresh parsley, divided
12 lasagna noodles
1   (15-oz.) container ricotta cheese

2   tsp. chopped fresh oregano
¾   cup freshly grated Parmesan cheese, divided
3   cups (12 oz.) Italian six-cheese shredded blend

1. Preheat oven to 350°. Lightly grease a 13- x 9-inch baking dish.

2. Cook sausage, onion, and garlic in a large skillet over medium heat, stirring until sausage crumbles and is no longer pink.

3. Stir in tomatoes, next 4 ingredients, and 2 Tbsp. parsley; bring to a boil over medium-high heat. Cover, reduce heat to low, and simmer, stirring occasionally, 10 minutes or until sauce is slightly thickened.

4. Meanwhile, cook lasagna noodles according to package directions; drain.

5. Combine ricotta cheese, oregano, ¼ cup Parmesan cheese, and remaining 1 Tbsp. parsley.

6. Spread 2 cups meat mixture into prepared baking dish. Top with 4 noodles, 1 cup ricotta cheese mixture, 1 cup Italian cheese, and 4 more noodles. Spread remaining ricotta cheese mixture over noodles, and top with 2 cups meat mixture, 1 cup Italian cheese, and remaining 4 noodles. Top with remaining meat mixture and Italian cheese.

7. Bake at 350° for 45 minutes or until bubbly. Let stand 10 minutes before serving. Makes 8 to 10 servings.

SPAGHETTI WITH MEATBALLS

Hands-on Time: 30 min.   Total Time: 45 min.

Sure to become a weeknight favorite, these meatballs are simmered in a simple tomato sauce enhanced with fresh herbs. Shape the meatballs a day in advance, if desired.

2 Tbsp. butter	2 Tbsp. chopped fresh basil	½ tsp. salt
½ cup chopped onion	1 Tbsp. chopped fresh parsley	2 Tbsp. vegetable oil
2 garlic cloves, minced		Hot cooked spaghetti
1 (28-oz.) can diced tomatoes	1 Tbsp. chopped fresh oregano	Freshly grated Parmesan cheese
½ tsp. pepper, divided	1 lb. ground beef	
1 (6-oz.) can tomato paste	2 Tbsp. grated onion	

1. Melt butter in a large skillet over medium heat. Add onion and garlic; sauté 5 minutes or until tender. Add tomatoes, ¼ tsp. pepper and next 4 ingredients. Reduce heat to medium-low, and cook, uncovered, stirring occasionally, 20 minutes.

2. Meanwhile, combine ground beef, grated onion, salt, and remaining ¼ tsp. pepper. Shape into 12 (1½-inch) meatballs.

3. Heat oil in a large skillet over medium heat. Cook meatballs in hot oil, turning occasionally, until no longer pink; drain. Add meatballs to sauce; cook over low heat 15 minutes. Serve over spaghetti; sprinkle with Parmesan cheese. Makes 4 servings.

JAMBALAYA

Hands-on Time: 45 min.   Total Time: 1 hr., 15 min.

This recipe originated at the famous Bon Ton Café in New Orleans.

1½ lb. unpeeled, medium-size raw shrimp (31/35 count)
1 Tbsp. canola oil
1 lb. andouille sausage, cut diagonally into ¼-inch-thick slices
2 Tbsp. butter
3 cups chopped onion (2 medium)
3 cups chopped green bell pepper (3 medium)
1½ cups chopped celery (3 large ribs)
1 tsp. minced garlic
1½ cups converted rice
2½ cups chicken broth
2 Tbsp. chopped fresh parsley
2 tsp. salt
½ tsp. dried thyme
¼ tsp. ground red pepper
2 (14.5-oz.) cans diced tomatoes, drained

1. Peel shrimp; devein, if desired.
2. Heat oil in a large Dutch oven over medium heat. Add sausage, and cook 8 minutes. Remove sausage, reserving drippings in Dutch oven.
3. Melt butter with drippings in Dutch oven over medium heat. Add onion and next 3 ingredients; sauté 15 minutes or until vegetables are tender. Stir in rice and next 5 ingredients; bring to a boil. Reduce heat to medium-low, and simmer, covered, 20 minutes or until rice is tender and liquid is almost absorbed.
4. Stir in shrimp and tomatoes; cook, stirring occasionally, 3 to 5 minutes or just until shrimp turn pink. Stir in sausage. Makes 8 servings.

Tuna Casserole

Hands-on Time: 20 min.   Total Time: 50 min.

This retro recipe, also known as "Tuna Wiggle," was the quintessential 1950s dish, popular because the ingredients were easy to find and it was quick to prepare. In our version, crushed kettle-cooked potato chips offer a delicious update.

1   (5-oz.) package medium-size egg noodles
1   (10¾-oz.) can cream of
     mushroom soup
¾   cup milk
½   cup sour cream
½   cup finely chopped onion
1   (5-oz.) can solid white tuna in spring
     water, drained and flaked
1   cup (4 oz.) shredded sharp
     Cheddar cheese
1   cup frozen petite English peas, thawed
½   tsp. freshly ground black pepper
1   cup crushed kettle-cooked
     potato chips

1. PREHEAT oven to 350°. Lightly grease an 8-inch square baking dish.
2. COOK noodles according to package directions; drain. Stir in soup and next 7 ingredients; pour into prepared baking dish. Sprinkle with crushed chips.
3. BAKE, uncovered, at 350° for 30 minutes or until bubbly. Makes 6 servings.

CRAB IMPERIAL

Hands-on Time: 20 min.   Total Time: 30 min.

For a seaworthy presentation, serve Crab Imperial in natural baking shells. Look for them at specialty cooking supply stores. Otherwise, shallow individual ramekins will work as a substitute.

4 natural baking shells	2 Tbsp. dry sherry	1 lb. fresh lump crabmeat,
5 Tbsp. butter, divided	½ cup mayonnaise	drained
1 Tbsp. all-purpose flour	1 Tbsp. fresh lemon juice	¼ cup freshly grated
½ cup milk	½ tsp. salt	Parmesan cheese
1 tsp. dried minced onion	¼ tsp. freshly ground pepper	⅛ tsp. paprika (optional)
1½ tsp. Worcestershire sauce		

1. Preheat oven to 450°. Lightly grease 4 natural baking shells.

2. Melt 1 Tbsp. butter in a small heavy saucepan over low heat; add flour, whisking until smooth. Cook, whisking constantly, 1 minute. Gradually add milk and onion; cook over medium heat, stirring constantly, 2 minutes or until thickened and bubbly. Remove sauce from heat.

3. Stir in Worcestershire sauce and sherry. Stir in mayonnaise and next 3 ingredients.

4. Melt remaining 4 Tbsp. butter in a medium-size heavy skillet over medium heat. Add crabmeat, and sauté 1 to 2 minutes. Remove from heat. Stir in sauce.

5. Spoon mixture into prepared baking shells (about ¾ cup each). Sprinkle with cheese, and, if desired, paprika.

6. Bake at 450° for 10 minutes or until hot and bubbly. Serve immediately. Makes 4 servings.

KENTUCKY BURGOO

Hands-on Time: 1 hr., 45 min.   Total Time: 5 hr., plus 8 hr. for chilling

A Southern staple, Kentucky Burgoo is a thick stew of assorted meats such as beef, chicken, and veal, and just about every vegetable on the planet. Like Brunswick stew, it's served as a side with a hearty plate of barbecue. Leftover burgoo freezes well for a make-ahead option.

1 (4- to 5-lb.) chicken	1 Tbsp. fresh lemon juice	2 green bell peppers,
1 lb. beef chuck roast	1 Tbsp. Worcestershire	chopped
1 lb. veal stew meat	sauce	2 cups frozen butter beans
1½ to 2 lb. beef marrow bones	1 Tbsp. sugar	or baby lima beans
1 celery rib	1½ tsp. ground black pepper	2 cups sliced celery
1 carrot	1 tsp. ground red pepper	2 cups finely chopped
1 small onion, quartered	3 onions, chopped	cabbage
6 fresh parsley sprigs	4 tomatoes, chopped	2 cups sliced fresh okra
1 (12-oz.) can tomato paste	1 turnip, peeled and	2 cups fresh corn kernels
2 Tbsp. salt	finely chopped	½ lemon, seeded

1. Combine 4 qt. water, chicken, and next 14 ingredients in a large heavy stockpot; bring to a boil over medium-high heat. Cover, reduce heat to low, and simmer 1 hour; cool. Remove meat, reserving liquid in pot; discard vegetables. Skin, bone, and chop meat; return to pot. Cover and chill 8 hours or overnight.

2. Skim fat from liquid, and discard. Add onion and remaining ingredients; cover and simmer 1 hour, stirring often to prevent sticking. Makes 32 cups.

CASSOULET

Hands-on Time: 30 min.   Total Time: 3 hr., 45 min., plus 8 hr. for soaking beans

French in origin, a cassoulet is a stew of white beans and meats such as sausage and pork. It's covered and cooked slow to marry the flavors.

1	lb. dried great Northern beans	1	(6- to 7-lb.) whole chicken	1	(14.5-oz.) can diced tomatoes
1	lb. ham hock	2	tsp. salt, divided	½	tsp. dried thyme
3	garlic cloves, crushed	4	tsp. freshly ground pepper, divided	1	cup fresh French bread breadcrumbs
1	onion, halved	1	lb. andouille sausage, cut into 1-inch pieces	¼	cup chopped fresh parsley
2	carrots, cut in half	1	medium onion, chopped		
2	celery ribs, cut in half	4	garlic cloves, minced		
1	tsp. dried thyme	1	cup dry white wine		
1	bay leaf				

1. Rinse and sort beans according to package directions; place in an 8-qt. ovenproof Dutch oven. Cover with water 2 inches above beans; soak 8 hours. Drain.

2. Add 2½ qt. water to beans; stir in ham hock and next 6 ingredients. Bring to a boil; cover and cook 2 hours or until beans are tender. Remove and discard ham hock, onion, carrots, celery, and bay leaf.

3. Preheat oven to 350°. Place chicken in a roasting pan; sprinkle with 1 tsp. salt and 2 tsp. pepper.

4. Bake at 350° for 2 hours or until a meat thermometer inserted in meaty portion of thigh registers 160°; cool, reserving 3 Tbsp. drippings. Remove chicken from bone, and cut into serving-size pieces. Reduce oven temperature to 325°.

5. Cook sausage in a large skillet over medium-high heat until browned; remove sausage, reserving drippings in skillet.

6. Add reserved chicken drippings to drippings in skillet. Add chopped onion, and cook over medium-high heat, stirring constantly, until tender. Add minced garlic, and cook, stirring constantly 1 minute. Add wine, and cook 5 minutes or until reduced by half.

7. Add tomatoes, ½ tsp. thyme, remaining 2 tsp. pepper, and remaining 1 tsp. salt; stir into beans.

8. Spoon half each of beans, sausage, and chicken into Dutch oven; repeat layers. Sprinkle with breadcrumbs.

9. Bake at 325° for 1½ hours. Sprinkle with parsley just before serving. Makes 8 to 10 servings.

Note: Substitute any spicy smoked sausage for andouille.

SMOKY MOUNTAIN BRUNSWICK STEW

Hands-on Time: 30 min.
Total Time: 1 hr., 15 min.

Virginia and Georgia compete for the claim to Brunswick stew, and the rivalry is fierce. A Southern classic, the tomato-based stew originally contained squirrel, but we prefer chicken and hearty vegetables.

1   (3-lb.) whole chicken, cut up
1   tsp. salt
½   tsp. paprika
1   Tbsp. butter
1   Tbsp. canola oil
2   medium onions, chopped
1   medium-size green bell pepper, chopped
3   cups chicken broth
1   (14.5-oz.) can diced tomatoes
1   tsp. Worcestershire sauce
1   cup barbecue sauce
½   tsp. hot sauce
2   cups frozen whole kernel corn
1   (10-oz.) package frozen baby lima beans
1   (0.75-lb.) package barbecued pork
2   Tbsp. chopped fresh parsley

1. Sprinkle chicken with salt and paprika. Melt butter with oil in a large Dutch oven over medium-high heat; add chicken, and cook, turning occasionally, 6 minutes or until browned on all sides. Remove chicken, reserving drippings in Dutch oven. Skin and bone chicken. Cut meat into bite-size pieces.
2. Add onion and green pepper to reserved drippings in Dutch oven; sauté until tender. Add chicken, chicken broth, next 4 ingredients, and 1 cup water; partially cover, and bring to a boil over medium-high heat. Add corn and next 3 ingredients; cover, reduce heat to low, and simmer 30 minutes. Makes 13 cups.

TASTY TRIVIA

Where Brunswick stew originated causes heated discussions in the South. Depending on which story you accept, it was created either in Brunswick County, Virginia, in 1828, or on St. Simons Island, Georgia, in 1898. Supporters on both sides hotly dispute which state possesses bragging rights.

In Virginia, the basic ingredients are boiled chicken, potatoes, onions, butter beans, corn, and tomatoes. Huge batches simmer for hours, resulting in a thick stew that's eaten with a fork. Virginians serve it as a main dish with bread on the side. In Georgia, the stew is more tomato- and barbecue-based, and usually includes barbecued pork and chicken. There, it's a prized side dish of the best barbecue joints, and real aficionados order it by the bowlful. Most Georgians laugh at the Virginia version that adds butter beans.

BEEF STEW

Hands-on Time: 45 min.   Total Time: 2 hr., 45 min.

To cut down on prep time, buy 2 lb. of stew meat instead of a roast.

1   (2¾-lb.) boneless chuck roast, trimmed
5   Tbsp. all-purpose flour, divided
3   Tbsp. vegetable oil
1   Tbsp. Worcestershire sauce
2   tsp. salt
1   tsp. garlic salt

¾   tsp. freshly ground black pepper
⅛   tsp. ground allspice
2   bay leaves
4   carrots, peeled and cut into 1-inch pieces
2   celery ribs, cut into 1-inch pieces

2   large red potatoes, peeled and cut into 1-inch pieces
3   small onions, each cut into 6 wedges
1   small green bell pepper, cut into 1-inch pieces

1. Cut roast into 1-inch cubes. Place beef and ¼ cup flour in a zip-top plastic bag; seal bag, and shake vigorously to coat.

2. Heat oil in a large Dutch oven over medium-high heat. Add beef, and cook, stirring occasionally, until browned. Add Worcestershire sauce, next 5 ingredients, and 4 cups water; bring to a boil. Cover, reduce heat to low, and simmer 1 hour.

3. Add carrots and next 4 ingredients to beef mixture; bring to a boil over medium-high heat, stirring occasionally. Reduce heat to low; cover and simmer 1 hour or until vegetables and beef are tender, stirring occasionally. Discard bay leaves.

4. Combine remaining 1 Tbsp. flour and 3 Tbsp. water, stirring well; stir into stew. Bring to a boil over medium-high heat; boil, stirring constantly, 5 minutes or until thickened and bubbly. Makes 11½ cups.

CURRIED CREAM OF TOMATO SOUP

Hands-on Time: 25 min.   Total Time: 55 min.

Curry powder adds a bit of fire, but don't worry—the soup is tempered by the creaminess of half-and-half.

¼   cup butter
1   large onion, minced
3   carrots, shredded
2   Tbsp. chopped pitted black olives
1   Tbsp. curry powder

1   (28-oz.) can whole San Marzano tomatoes in puree, coarsely chopped
3   Tbsp. chopped fresh parsley
1   (14-oz.) can chicken broth

¼   tsp. ground allspice
¼   tsp. ground cumin
1   cup half-and-half
1   tsp. salt
1   tsp. sugar
    Croutons

1. Melt butter in large saucepan over medium heat. Add onion, carrots, and olives; cook, stirring occasionally, 10 minutes. Sprinkle vegetables with curry powder; cook, stirring often, 2 minutes. Reduce heat to low; stir in tomatoes and next 4 ingredients. Cook, covered, 30 minutes.

2. Process mixture in 2 batches in a blender until smooth, stopping to scrape down sides as needed. Return soup to saucepan; stir in half-and-half, salt, and sugar. Cook over low heat until thoroughly heated. Serve hot topped with croutons. Makes 7 cups.

Cold Cucumber Soup

COLD CUCUMBER SOUP

Hands-on Time: 10 min.   Total Time: 1 hr., 10 min.

This delicious cucumber soup was all the rage in our Test Kitchen. Cool and refreshing, it is the perfect starter course for summer entertaining or as a light meal on a hot afternoon.

1½ cups sour cream
1   tsp. dried dill weed
1   Tbsp. Worcestershire
     sauce
½   tsp. celery salt

1   Tbsp. fresh lemon juice
¼   tsp. pepper
¾   tsp. salt
2   green onions, coarsely
     chopped

3   medium cucumbers,
     peeled, seeded, and
     coarsely chopped
Garnish: thinly sliced
     cucumber half moons

Combine first 9 ingredients in a blender; process until smooth. Chill 1 hour before serving. Garnish, if desired. Makes 4¼ cups.

VEGETABLE-CHEDDAR CHOWDER

Hands-on Time: 45 min.   Total Time: 45 min.

Warm and comforting, this thick and creamy chowder is perfect for a winter day. One notion regarding the origin of "chowder" is the possibility that it is a derivation of the French word chaudière, *which is a type of pot such stews are cooked in.*

3   cups chicken broth
4   medium potatoes, peeled
     and diced
1   medium onion, chopped
1   cup thinly sliced carrots
½   cup diced green bell
     pepper

⅓   cup butter
⅓   cup all-purpose flour
3½   cups milk
4   cups (16 oz.) shredded
     sharp Cheddar cheese

¼   cup chopped jarred
     roasted red bell peppers
¼   tsp. hot sauce (optional)
½   cup chopped green onions

1. Bring chicken broth to a boil in a large Dutch oven. Add potatoes and next 3 ingredients. Bring to a boil over medium-high heat; reduce heat to low, and simmer 10 minutes or until vegetables are tender. Drain vegetables, and return to Dutch oven.

2. Melt butter in a heavy saucepan over low heat; add flour, whisking until smooth. Cook, whisking constantly, 1 minute. Gradually add milk; cook over medium heat, whisking constantly, 19 minutes or until thickened and bubbly. Add cheese, stirring until melted.

3. Stir cheese sauce; red peppers; and, if desired, hot sauce into vegetable mixture. Cook over low heat, stirring contantly, until thoroughly heated (do not boil). Sprinkle with chopped green onions. Makes 10½ cups.

CHICKEN AND SEAFOOD GUMBO

Hands-on Time: 1 hr., 40 min.   Total Time: 3 hr., 40 min.

This gumbo really serves a crowd. The main rule in making gumbo: Allow plenty of time. You can't rush this dish. The roux, or foundation, of gumbo takes time and hands-on stirring for just the right color, flavor, and thickness.

1 cup vegetable oil
1 cup all-purpose flour
3 large onions, chopped
8 celery ribs, chopped
1 green bell pepper, chopped
2 garlic cloves, minced
½ cup chopped fresh parsley (optional)
2 Tbsp. vegetable oil
1 lb. fresh okra, sliced

2 qt. chicken broth
½ cup Worcestershire sauce
½ cup ketchup
1 large tomato, chopped
1 Tbsp. salt
½ tsp. hot sauce
4 bacon slices or 1 large ham slice, chopped
¼ tsp. dried thyme leaves
¼ tsp. dried rosemary leaves
2 bay leaves

4 lb. unpeeled, medium-size raw shrimp (31/35 count)
2 cups chopped cooked chicken
1 lb. fresh crabmeat, drained
1 pt. fresh oysters
1 tsp. molasses
Lemon juice (optional)
Hot cooked rice

1. Heat 1 cup oil in large heavy stockpot over medium heat. Add flour, stirring constantly with a wooden spoon, until roux is milk chocolate or dark caramel colored (about 15 to 20 minutes).
2. Add onions; celery; bell pepper; garlic; and, if desired, parsley. Cook, stirring often, 30 minutes or until tender.
3. Heat 2 Tbsp. oil in a large skillet. Fry okra 5 minutes or until browned. Add to vegetable mixture, and cook over low heat 5 minutes. (Mixture may be cooled, packaged, and frozen or refrigerated for later use at this point.)
4. Add chicken broth, next 9 ingredients, and 1 qt. water. Cook over medium heat 2 hours.
5. Peel shrimp; devein, if desired. Add shrimp; chicken; crabmeat; and, if desired, oysters. Cook 10 minutes.
6. Stir in molasses and desired amount of lemon juice. Discard bay leaves.
7. Spoon hot cooked rice into soup bowls; ladle gumbo over rice, and serve immediately. Makes 32 cups.

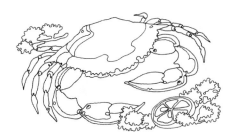

SHE-CRAB SOUP

Hands-on Time: 22 min.   Total Time: 22 min.

It's traditional to serve this rich and decadent soup with a
drizzle of sherry at the table.

6	Tbsp. butter
3	Tbsp. all-purpose flour
2	cups milk
2	cups half-and-half
½	tsp. Worcestershire sauce
1	tsp. lemon zest
1	tsp. salt
¼	tsp. freshly ground white pepper
¼	tsp. ground mace
1	lb. fresh crabmeat, drained
2	Tbsp. dry sherry
½	cup whipping cream, whipped
Ground red pepper	

Melt butter in a large saucepan over medium-low heat. Whisk
in flour until smooth. Cook, stirring constantly, 1 minute.
Add milk and next 7 ingredients, gently stirring until blended.
Increase heat to medium, and cook, stirring often, 5 minutes.
Remove from heat. Stir in sherry. Top each serving with
a dollop of whipped cream, and sprinkle with ground red
pepper. Makes 6 cups.

mama's way or your way

Rediscover an old-fashioned favorite baked with a rich puff pastry crust, or spoon a deliciously quick stovetop twist over buttermilk biscuits.

MAMA'S WAY:
- Made-from-scratch cream sauce
- Deluxe double crust
- Sautéed leeks and seasoned potatoes

YOUR WAY:
- Weeknight easy
- Buttermilk biscuits sub for crust
- Sautéed mushrooms and baby peas

mama's way

DOUBLE-CRUST CHICKEN POT PIE

Hands-on Time: 31 min.   Total Time: 1 hr., 41 min.

½ cup butter
2 medium leeks, sliced
½ cup all-purpose flour
1 (14.5-oz.) can chicken broth
3 cups chopped cooked chicken
1½ cups frozen cubed hash browns
   with onions and peppers
1 cup matchstick carrots

⅓ cup chopped fresh flat-leaf
   parsley
½ tsp. salt
½ tsp. freshly ground pepper
1 (17.3-oz.) package frozen puff
   pastry sheets, thawed
1 large egg

1. PREHEAT oven to 375°. Melt butter in a large skillet over medium heat; add leeks, and sauté 3 minutes. Sprinkle with flour; cook, stirring constantly, 3 minutes. Whisk in chicken broth; bring to a boil, whisking constantly. Remove from heat; stir in chicken and next 5 ingredients.

2. ROLL each pastry sheet into a 12- x 10-inch rectangle on a lightly floured surface. Fit 1 sheet into a 9-inch deep-dish pie plate; spoon chicken mixture into pastry. Place remaining pastry sheet over filling in opposite direction of bottom sheet; fold edges under, and press with tines of a fork, sealing to bottom crust. Whisk together egg and 1 Tbsp. water, and brush over top of pie.

3. BAKE at 375° on lower oven rack 55 to 60 minutes or until browned. Let stand 15 minutes. Makes 6 to 8 servings.

STOVETOP CHICKEN PIE

Hands-on Time: 35 min.   Total Time: 35 min.

8 frozen buttermilk biscuits
1 small sweet onion, diced
1 Tbsp. canola oil
1 (8-oz.) package sliced
   fresh mushrooms
4 cups chopped cooked
   chicken

1 (10¾-oz.) can reduced-fat
   cream of mushroom soup
1 cup low-sodium chicken
   broth
½ cup dry white wine
½ (8-oz.) package ⅓-less-
   fat cream cheese, cubed

½ (0.7-oz.) envelope
   Italian dressing mix
   (about 2 tsp.)
1 cup frozen baby sweet
   peas, thawed

1. Bake biscuits according to package directions.

2. Meanwhile, sauté onion in hot oil in a large skillet over medium-high heat 5 minutes or until golden. Add mushrooms, and sauté 5 minutes or until tender. Stir in chicken and next 5 ingredients; cook, stirring frequently, 5 minutes or until cheese is melted and mixture is thoroughly heated. Stir in peas, and cook 2 minutes. Spoon chicken mixture over hot split biscuits. Makes 6 to 8 servings.

BLUE-RIBBON DESSERTS

no Southern sit-down
is ever complete without
something sweet to eat

Some people are famous for their cornbread or homemade barbecue sauce, but my mom was known for her gorgeous meringues and the dense and rich chocolate mousse cake. She even made the cakes during certain times of the year, like at Easter or around the holidays, when she knew she could sell them.

She would take orders from neighbors, colleagues at work, or members of our church, and then for a few frantic weeks she would carefully craft such beautiful desserts that she developed quite a following over the years. The money she made selling them was her "play money" to spend on gifts or something we needed at home. She provided countless sweet endings to the meals of so many families over the years. Ours, too, for sure.

PERFECT CHOCOLATE CAKE

Hands-on Time: 45 min.   Total Time: 2 hr., 40 min., including Whipped Cream
Filling and Rich Chocolate Frosting

This cake is appropriately named for its towering layers, whipped cream filling, and luscious frosting.

Wax paper
1   cup unsweetened cocoa
2   cups boiling water
1   cup butter, softened
2½ cups sugar

4   large eggs
2¾ cups all-purpose flour
2   tsp. baking soda
½   tsp. baking powder

½   tsp. salt
1½ tsp. vanilla extract
Whipped Cream Filling
Rich Chocolate Frosting

1. Preheat oven to 350°. Line 3 (9-inch) round cake pans with wax paper. Lightly grease wax paper. Combine cocoa and boiling water, stirring until smooth. Let cool completely (about 30 minutes).
2. Beat butter at medium speed with an electric mixer until creamy. Gradually add sugar, beating well. Add eggs, 1 at a time, beating just until yellow disappears.
3. Combine flour, baking soda, baking powder, and salt; add to butter mixture alternately with cocoa mixture, beating at low speed after each addition and beginning and ending with flour mixture. (Do not overbeat.) Stir in vanilla. Pour batter into prepared cake pans.
4. Bake at 350° for 22 minutes or until a wooden pick inserted in center comes out clean. Cool in pans on wire racks 10 minutes; remove from pans, and cool completely on wire racks (about 1 hour).
5. Spread Whipped Cream Filling between layers; spread Rich Chocolate Frosting on top and sides of cake. Chill until ready to serve. Store in refrigerator. Makes 12 servings.

WHIPPED CREAM FILLING

Hands-on Time: 10 min.   Total Time: 10 min.

1   cup whipping cream

1   tsp. vanilla extract

2   to 4 Tbsp. powdered
    sugar

Beat whipping cream and vanilla until foamy; gradually add desired amount of powdered sugar, beating until soft peaks form. Cover and chill until ready to assemble. Makes 2 cups.

RICH CHOCOLATE FROSTING

Hands-on Time: 15 min.   Total Time: 15 min.

1   cup semisweet chocolate
    morsels

½   cup half-and-half
1   cup butter

2⅓ cups powdered sugar

Combine first 3 ingredients in a saucepan; cook over medium heat, stirring until chocolate melts. Remove from heat; add powdered sugar, stirring until blended. Place saucepan in a large bowl of ice; beat at low speed with an electric mixer until frosting holds its shape and loses its gloss. Add additional half-and-half, 1 tsp. at a time, if necessary, to reach desired spreading consistency. Makes 2½ cups.

Southern Living®

1990 ANNUAL RECIPES

Every single recipe
month-by-month

plus indexes
charts and tips
color photographs
menus
and more

LANE CAKE

Hands-on Time: 30 min.   Total Time: 3 hr., 20 min., including Lane Cake Filling and Seven-Minute Frosting

1	cup butter, softened	¾	tsp. salt	Lane Cake Filling
2	cups sugar	1	cup milk	Seven-Minute Frosting
3¼	cups all-purpose flour	1	tsp. vanilla extract	Garnish: whole maraschino
1	Tbsp. baking powder	8	egg whites, stiffly beaten	cherries

1. Preheat oven to 325°. Grease and flour 3 (9-inch) round cake pans. Beat butter at medium speed with an electric mixer until creamy; gradually add sugar, beating well. Combine flour, baking powder, and salt; add to butter mixture alternately with milk, beating well after each addition and beginning and ending with flour mixture. Stir in vanilla. Fold in egg whites. Pour batter into prepared cake pans.

2. Bake at 325° for 25 minutes or until a wooden pick inserted in center comes out clean. Cool in pans on wire racks 10 minutes; remove from pans to wire racks, and cool completely (about 1 hour).

3. Spread Lane Cake Filling between layers and on top of cake; spread Seven-Minute Frosting on sides. Garnish, if desired. Makes 12 servings.

LANE CAKE FILLING

Hands-on Time: 30 min.   Total Time: 1 hr.

8	egg yolks	1	cup raisins	½	cup sliced maraschino
1½	cups sugar	1	cup sweetened flaked	cherries
½	cup butter		coconut	
1	cup chopped pecans	½	cup bourbon	

Combine first 3 ingredients in a heavy saucepan. Cook over medium heat, stirring constantly, 20 minutes or until thickened. Remove from heat, and stir in pecans and remaining ingredients. Cool completely (about 30 minutes). Makes 3½ cups.

SEVEN-MINUTE FROSTING

Hands-on Time: 15 min.   Total Time: 15 min.

This frosting gets its name because the beating process usually takes about seven minutes.

¾	cup sugar	1	egg white	Dash of salt
2	Tbsp. plus 1½ tsp. cold water	1½	tsp. light corn syrup	½	tsp. vanilla extract

1. Combine first 5 ingredients in top of a large double boiler. Beat at low speed with an electric mixer 30 seconds or just until blended.

2. Place over boiling water; beat at high speed 7 minutes or until stiff peaks form. Remove from heat. Add vanilla; beat 2 minutes or until frosting is thick enough to spread. Makes 4 cups.

HUMMINGBIRD CAKE

Hands-on Time: 30 min.   Total Time: 2 hr., 15 min.,
including Cream Cheese Frosting

Since it originally ran in 1978, this recipe has become the most requested recipe in Southern Living *history. Submitted by Mrs. L.H. Wiggins of Greensboro, North Carolina, this cake is known to have won numerous blue ribbons at county fairs. The first time it ran in the magazine it had 1½ cups of oil and double the frosting. We much prefer this version today; it's every bit as yummy as the original, higher-fat version.*

Shortening

Wax paper

3   cups all-purpose flour

2   cups sugar

1   tsp. baking soda

1   tsp. salt

1   tsp. ground cinnamon

3   large eggs

1   cup vegetable oil

2   cups mashed bananas

1   cup chopped pecans

1   (8-oz.) can crushed
    pineapple

1½ tsp. vanilla extract

Cream Cheese Frosting

1. Preheat oven to 350°. Grease 3 (9-inch) round cake pans; line pans with wax paper, and grease paper. Dust with flour, shaking out excess.

2. Combine 3 cups flour and next 4 ingredients in a large bowl; add eggs and oil, stirring until dry ingredients are moistened. (Do not beat.) Stir in bananas, 1 cup pecans, pineapple, and vanilla. Pour batter into prepared pans.

3. Bake at 350° for 25 to 30 minutes or until a wooden pick inserted in center comes out clean. Cool layers in pans on wire racks 10 minutes; remove from pans to wire racks, and cool completely (about 1 hour).

4. Spread Cream Cheese Frosting between layers and on top and sides of cake. Store in refrigerator. Makes 12 servings.

CREAM CHEESE FROSTING

Hands-on Time: 10 min.   Total Time: 10 min.

1   (8-oz.) package cream
    cheese, softened

½   cup butter, softened

1   (16-oz.) package
    powdered sugar

1   tsp. vanilla extract

Beat cream cheese and butter at medium speed with an electric mixer until smooth. Gradually add powdered sugar, beating at low speed until light and fluffy. Stir in vanilla. Makes about 3 cups.

MILLION DOLLAR POUND CAKE

Hands-on Time: 15 min.   Total Time: 3 hr., 10 min.

The secret to success when baking this classic is not to open the oven door during baking; this could cause the cake to fall.

2   cups butter, softened
3   cups sugar
6   large eggs
4   cups all-purpose flour
¾   cup milk
1   tsp. almond extract
1   tsp. vanilla extract

1. Preheat oven to 300°. Grease and lightly flour a 10-inch tube pan.

2. Beat butter at medium speed with an electric mixer until creamy. Gradually add sugar, beating well. Add eggs, 1 at a time, beating just until yellow disappears. Gradually add flour to butter mixture alternately with milk, beating well after each addition and beginning and ending with flour. Stir in extracts. Pour batter into prepared pan.

3. Bake at 300° for 1 hour and 40 minutes or until a long wooden pick inserted in center comes out clean. Cool in pan on a wire rack 15 minutes; remove from pan to wire rack, and cool completely (about 1 hour). Makes 12 servings.

TASTY TRIVIA

Although debate remains today as to the genesis of the pound cake (particularly among Virginians), it is thought to be of British origin. Despite the questions over development, the cake nonetheless receives its name from the original ingredient measurements: a pound of sugar, a pound of flour, a pound of butter, and a pound of eggs. While the amounts of ingredients have changed over time, the sturdy, classic cake remains a favorite. Some Southerners even confess to toasting it for breakfast.

FIFTEEN WAYS TO CHARM HER

by Amy Bickers

Number one. We still expect you to give up your seat for a lady. On a bus, at a bar, on a train...we don't care where you are. Unless you are at a restaurant and the only lady in sight is the one taking your order, stand up. Now.

On a recent Friday night at a bustling restaurant bar, two friends and I waited for our table to be called. The barstools were occupied, so we stood patiently, sipping wine and chatting about the workweek. When a couple nearby stood up, another woman— who had been there less time than we had—swooped in, reaching across us to put her purse on the stool. This isn't the worst part. It's what happened next: Her male companion then slid onto the other barstool.

Hang on while I do a geography check. Are we not in the South? If ladies are waiting for a seat and you have a Y chromosome, do you sit down? No, sir. No, you do not.

We know modern life is confusing. The roles of men and women have evolved over the years. As Pink once sang, "Shorty got a job, Shorty got a car, Shorty can pay her own rent."

But come on, let's keep some things old-school. My late grandfather—he of the East Texas upbringing, U.S. Navy captain status, and Cary Grant good looks—would never have allowed a woman to stand while he sat. And if you want a Southern woman to love you, neither will you. So, men, here's a short list of things Southern girls still expect from you.

We still expect you to...
1. Stand up for a lady. Actually, this doesn't just involve chairs.
2. Know that the SEC has the best football teams in the nation. Big 12 fan? Hmm, perhaps you should keep walking.
3. Kill bugs. Delta Burke as Southern belle Suzanne Sugarbaker on *Designing Women* said, "...Ya know,... when men use Women's Liberation as an excuse not to kill bugs for you. Oh, I just hate that! I don't care what anybody says, I think the man should have to kill the bug!"
4. Hold doors open.
5. Fix things or build stuff. I once watched in awe as my step-father built a front porch on the house he shares with my mother. He knew just what to do, cutting every notch, hammering every nail. The project was complete by sunset.
6. Wear boots occasionally. Not the fancy, I-paid-$1,000-for-these kind. We're talking about slightly mud-crusted, I-could-have-just-come-

in-from-the-field boots.

7. Take off your hat inside.

8. Grill stuff.

9. Call us. If you want to ask us out, don't text and don't email. Pick up the phone and use your voice.

10. Stand when we come back to the dinner table. "Just a little half-stand is enough to make me melt," my friend Stephanie says.

11. Pull out our chairs. Wait, that's not all. Scoot them back in before we hit the floor.

12. Pay the tab on the first few dates. "If you ask me out, you pay," Stephanie says. "If I ask you out, you should still pay." Listen, guys, it's just simpler this way.

13. Don't show up in a wrinkled, untucked shirt. Care about your appearance but not too much. Don't smell better than we do. Don't use mousse or gel. You shouldn't look like you spend more time in front of the mirror than we do.

14. Never get in bar fights. Patrick Swayze might look cool in *Road House*, but in reality, bar fights are stupid and embarrassing. You don't look tough. You look like an idiot.

15. Know how to mix our favorite cocktail just the way we like it. Fix your favorite, too. Sit down on the porch (it's okay if you didn't build it), tell us how your day went, and we'll tell you about ours. We'll leave the long list to the girl who falls in love with you.

PINEAPPLE UPSIDE-DOWN CAKE

Hands-on Time: 20 min.   Total Time: 1 hr., 30 min.

While upside-down cakes baked in cast-iron skillets had been common for a while, it wasn't until the 1920s and 30s, when pineapple was sliced into rings and canned, that this sweet cake became a pop icon. With the additional creation of vibrant maraschino cherries, every housewife around the country had a copy of this recipe in her repertoire.

¼ cup butter
1 cup firmly packed light brown sugar
½ cup chopped pecans
2 (8-oz.) cans sliced pineapple

6 to 8 maraschino cherries (without stems)
3 large eggs, separated
1 cup granulated sugar

1 cup all-purpose flour
1 tsp. baking powder
½ tsp. salt

1. Preheat oven to 350°. Melt butter in a lightly greased 9-inch cast-iron skillet over low heat. Remove from heat. Sprinkle with brown sugar and pecans.

2. Drain pineapple, reserving ¼ cup plus 1 Tbsp. pineapple juice. Arrange pineapple slices in a single layer over brown sugar mixture. Place 1 cherry in center of each pineapple slice.

3. Beat egg yolks at medium speed with an electric mixer until thick and pale; gradually add granulated sugar, beating well. Combine flour, baking powder, and salt; gradually add to sugar mixture, beating at low speed just until blended. Stir in reserved pineapple juice.

4. Beat egg whites at high speed until stiff peaks form; fold into batter. Spoon batter over pineapple slices.

5. Bake at 350° for 40 to 45 minutes or until a wooden pick inserted in center comes out clean. Cool in skillet on a wire rack 30 minutes; carefully run a knife around edge of cake to loosen. Invert cake onto a serving plate, spooning any topping in skillet over cake. Makes 8 servings.

STRAWBERRY SHORTCAKE

Hands-on Time: 30 min.   Total Time: 2 hr., 8 min.

Whipped cream and sliced fresh strawberries crown each layer of this delectable shortcake.

2   (16-oz.) containers fresh strawberries, sliced
¼   to ½ cup granulated sugar
½   cup butter, softened and divided
2   cups all-purpose flour

1   Tbsp. plus 1 tsp. baking powder
¼   tsp. salt
¼   cup granulated sugar
Dash of ground nutmeg
½   cup milk

2   large eggs, separated
¼   cup granulated sugar
1   cup whipping cream
¼   cup powdered sugar
Garnish: sliced fresh strawberries

1. Combine sliced strawberries and desired amount of granulated sugar; stir gently, and chill 1 to 2 hours. Drain.

2. Preheat oven to 450°. Butter 2 (9-inch) round cake pans with ½ tsp. butter each.

3. Combine flour and next 4 ingredients in a large bowl; cut in remaining butter with a pastry blender until mixture is crumbly.

4. Whisk together milk and egg yolks. Add to flour mixture; stir with a fork until a soft dough forms. Pat dough out into prepared cake pans. (Dough will be sticky; moisten fingers with water as necessary.)

5. Beat egg whites at medium speed with an electric mixer just until stiff peaks form. Brush surface of dough with beaten egg white; sprinkle with ¼ cup granulated sugar.

6. Bake at 450° for 8 to 10 minutes or until layers are golden brown. (Layers will be thin.) Remove from pans to wire racks, and let cool completely (about 30 minutes).

7. Beat whipping cream until foamy; gradually add powdered sugar, beating until soft peaks form.

8. Place 1 cake layer on a serving plate. Spread half of whipped cream over layer, and arrange half of sweetened strawberries on top. Repeat procedure with remaining layer, whipped cream, and sweetened strawberries, reserving a small amount of whipped cream. Top cake with remaining whipped cream, and garnish, if desired. Store in refrigerator. Makes 8 servings.

CHOCOLATE MOUSSE CAKE

Hands-on Time: 31 min.   Total Time: 3 hr., 23 min., including Chocolate Crust
and Whipped Cream Topping, plus 8 hr. for chilling

Love cheesecake? Adore mousse? This dense cake capped with whipped cream combines both. For a special touch, top the cake with a paper doily, and sift cocoa over it. Carefully remove the doily. Pure bliss!

1   (8-oz.) package cream
     cheese, softened
1   (3-oz.) package cream
     cheese, softened
⅔   cup sugar
6   large eggs

⅓   cup whipping cream
1   Tbsp. plus 1 tsp. vanilla
     extract
9   (1-oz.) semisweet
     chocolate baking squares,
     melted

Chocolate Crust
Whipped Cream Topping
Unsweetened cocoa

1. Preheat oven to 375°. Beat first 3 ingredients at medium speed with an electric mixer until light and fluffy. Add eggs, 1 at a time, beating well after each addition. Add ⅓ cup whipping cream, vanilla, and melted chocolate; beat at low speed just until blended. Pour into Chocolate Crust.

2. Bake at 375° for 30 to 35 minutes or until edges are firm and center is still soft. Cool to room temperature; cover and chill 8 hours or overnight.

3. Run a knife around edge of chilled cake; remove cake from pan. Spread cake with Whipped Cream Topping; sift cocoa over topping. Store in refrigerator. Makes 10 to 12 servings.

CHOCOLATE CRUST

Hands-on Time: 15 min.   Total Time: 1 hr., 53 min.

⅓   cup butter
2   (1-oz.) semisweet
     chocolate baking squares

1⅓ cups fine, dry
     breadcrumbs

⅓   cup sugar

1. Preheat oven to 350°. Combine butter and chocolate in a small, heavy saucepan; cook over low heat, stirring often until chocolate melts. Remove from heat.

2. Stir breadcrumbs and sugar into chocolate mixture, blending well. Press into bottom and 2 inches up sides of a 9-inch springform pan.

3. Bake at 350° for 8 minutes. Chill thoroughly. Makes 1 (9-inch) crust.

WHIPPED CREAM TOPPING

Hands-on Time: 10 min.   Total Time: 10 min.

1½ cups whipping cream   ¼   cup powdered sugar   ½   tsp. vanilla extract

Beat whipping cream at medium speed with an electric mixer until foamy; gradually add powdered sugar, beating until soft peaks form. Add vanilla, beating just until blended. Makes 3 cups.

COLA CAKE

Hands-on Time: 20 min.   Total Time: 1 hr., 23 min., including Cola Frosting

½   cup chopped pecans
2   cups all-purpose flour
2   cups sugar
1   tsp. baking soda
1   cup cola soft drink
1   cup butter, cut into pieces
2   Tbsp. unsweetened cocoa
½   cup buttermilk
2   large eggs, beaten
1   tsp. vanilla extract
1½ cups miniature marshmallows
Cola Frosting

1. Preheat oven to 350°. Grease a 13- x 9-inch pan.
2. Bake pecans in a single layer in a shallow pan 8 to 10 minutes or until lightly toasted, stirring halfway through.
3. Combine flour, sugar, and baking soda in a large bowl.
4. Combine cola, butter, and cocoa in a heavy saucepan; cook over medium-low heat, stirring often, just until butter melts and starts to bubble. Gradually stir into flour mixture. Combine buttermilk, eggs, and vanilla; add to flour mixture, stirring until blended. Stir in marshmallows. Pour into prepared pan. (Use a spatula to distribute marshmallows, if necessary.)
5. Bake at 350° for 30 to 35 minutes or until a wooden pick inserted in center comes out clean. Remove from oven; cool in pan on a wire rack 10 minutes. Spread Cola Frosting over warm cake; sprinkle with pecans. Makes 15 servings.

Cola Frosting

Hands-on Time: 10 min.
Total Time: 15 min.

½   cup butter
¼   cup cola soft drink
3   Tbsp. unsweetened cocoa
3   cups powdered sugar
1   tsp. vanilla extract

COMBINE first 3 ingredients in a heavy saucepan; cook over medium-low heat, stirring often, just until butter melts and starts to bubble. Remove from heat; whisk in sugar and vanilla, whisking until smooth. Let stand 5 minutes. Makes 1½ cups.

Coca-Cola is a thirst quencher beloved by young and old alike around the world. It would never have come into being were it not for the inspiration of an Atlanta druggist, John S. Pemberton. In 1886, with no thoughts of giving pleasure, he combined coca leaves and kola nuts to make a remedy for hangovers AND for headaches in general. He called it coca-cola. Another Atlanta druggist bought Pemberton out for $2,000. The secret formula was sold and resold. The beverage's real growth began under the leadership of Asa G. Candler, a native of Villa Rica, Georgia. By 1891 he owned the formula outright, and the rest is lucrative history.

Lemon Bars

LEMON BARS

Hands-on Time: 20 min.   Total Time: 1 hr., 58 min.

These luscious bars are as irresistible today as when they debuted in the sixties, likely because they taste so great and they're an easy make-ahead dessert. Just prepare as directed, making sure to use the size pan indicated for best texture, and freeze, covered, up to one month. Thaw, dust with powdered sugar, and enjoy a tangy treat!

2 cups all-purpose flour	2 cups granulated sugar	¼ cup plus 2 Tbsp. fresh
½ cup powdered sugar	2 Tbsp. cornstarch	lemon juice
1 cup butter, softened	5 large eggs, lightly beaten	2 Tbsp. butter, melted
1 tsp. vanilla extract	1 Tbsp. lemon zest	¼ cup powdered sugar

1. Preheat oven to 350°. Grease a 13- x 9-inch baking dish. Beat first 4 ingredients at medium speed with an electric mixer until blended. Pat mixture into bottom of prepared dish.

2. Bake at 350° for 18 minutes or until golden.

3. Meanwhile, combine 2 cups granulated sugar and cornstarch. Add eggs and next 3 ingredients; beat well. Pour mixture over crust.

4. Bake at 350° for 20 to 25 minutes or until set. Let cool completely in pan on a wire rack (about 1 hour).

5. Sift ¼ cup powdered sugar over top. Cut into bars. Makes 1 dozen.

Makeover in Minutes: You can substitute lime juice and lime zest for lemon juice and lemon zest to change up the citrus tang.

HELLO DOLLY BARS

Hands-on Time: 10 min.   Total Time: 1 hr., 40 min.

Hello Dolly Bars are gooey, chewy, and portable! They're also known as seven-layer bars when you use chocolate and butterscotch morsels.

¼ cup butter	1⅓ cups butterscotch	1 (14-oz.) can sweetened
1 cup graham cracker crumbs	morsels	condensed milk
1 (7-oz.) package sweetened flaked coconut	1 cup chopped pecans	

1. Preheat oven to 350°. Melt butter in a 13- x 9-inch pan. Sprinkle cracker crumbs over butter. Layer coconut, morsels, and pecans over cracker crumbs in order listed. Spoon sweetened condensed milk over top of layers. (Do not stir.)

2. Bake at 350° for 30 minutes. Let cool completely in pan on a wire rack (about 1 hour). Cut into bars. Makes 2 dozen.

CONGO SQUARES

Hands-on Time: 15 min.   Total Time: 1 hr., 7 min.

These bars are cut small because they're so deliciously rich.

2½ cups all-purpose flour
1½ tsp. baking powder
½ tsp. salt
⅔ cup butter

2¼ cups firmly packed light
    brown sugar
3 large eggs
2 tsp. fresh lemon juice

1 cup chopped pecans
1 cup semisweet chocolate
    morsels

1. Preheat oven to 350°. Lightly grease a 13- x 9-inch pan. Combine first 3 ingredients.

2. Melt butter in a large saucepan over low heat. Remove from heat, and stir in sugar. Add eggs, 1 at a time, stirring well after each addition. Stir in lemon juice. Add flour mixture, pecans, and chocolate morsels, stirring to blend. Spread mixture into prepared pan.

3. Bake at 350° for 20 to 25 minutes or until set. (Do not overbake; remove as soon as done.) Cool in pan on wire rack 2 minutes. Cut into 1½-inch squares. Let cool completely in pan on wire rack (about 30 minutes). Makes about 3 dozen.

CREAM CHEESE BROWNIES

Hands-on Time: 15 min.   Total Time: 1 hr., 25 min.

The cream cheese mixture adds another dimension of flavor, texture, and richness to these to-die-for brownies.

4 (1-oz.) unsweetened
    chocolate baking squares
4 (1-oz.) semisweet
    chocolate baking squares
⅓ cup butter
2 (3-oz.) packages cream
    cheese, softened

¼ cup butter, softened
2 cups sugar, divided
6 large eggs, divided
1 tsp. vanilla extract
2 Tbsp. all-purpose flour
1½ cups semisweet chocolate
    morsels, divided

2 tsp. vanilla extract
1 cup all-purpose flour
1 tsp. baking powder
1 tsp. salt

1. Preheat oven to 325°. Grease a 13- x 9-inch pan. Microwave first 3 ingredients in a 1-qt. glass bowl at HIGH 1½ to 2 minutes or until melted and smooth, stirring at 30-second intervals. Cool.

2. Beat cream cheese and ¼ cup butter at medium speed with an electric mixer until creamy; gradually add ½ cup sugar, beating well. Add 2 eggs, 1 at a time, beating well after each addition. Stir in 1 tsp. vanilla. Fold in 2 Tbsp. flour and ½ cup chocolate morsels.

3. Beat remaining 4 eggs in a large bowl at medium speed. Gradually add remaining 1½ cups sugar, beating well. Add melted chocolate mixture and 2 tsp. vanilla; beat until well blended.

4. Combine 1 cup flour, baking powder, and salt; fold into chocolate batter until blended. Stir in remaining 1 cup chocolate morsels. Reserve 3 cups chocolate batter; spread remaining batter in prepared pan. Pour cream cheese mixture over batter. Top with reserved 3 cups chocolate batter; swirl mixture with a knife.

5. Bake at 325° for 40 to 45 minutes. Let cool completely in pan on a wire rack (about 30 minutes). Cut brownies into bars. Makes 1½ dozen.

MORAVIAN TEA CAKES

Hands-on Time: 28 min.   Total Time: 3 hr., 55 min.

This simple cookie is soft and airy with a hint of vanilla. The dough is easy to roll, so let the kids join in the cookie baking fun!

Parchment paper	3	large eggs	1	tsp. salt
1	cup butter, softened	2	Tbsp. buttermilk	1	tsp. vanilla extract
2	cups sugar	1	tsp. baking soda	5½	cups all-purpose flour

1. Line baking sheets with parchment paper. Beat butter at medium speed with an electric mixer until creamy; gradually add sugar, beating well. Add eggs, 1 at a time, beating well after each addition.
2. Combine buttermilk and next 3 ingredients; stir well. Add to butter mixture alternately with flour, beginning and ending with flour. Divide dough in half; cover and chill 2 hours.
3. Preheat oven to 375°. Roll 1 portion of dough to ¼-inch thickness on a lightly floured surface; cut out with a 2½-inch heart-shaped or round cookie cutter. Place 1 to 1½ inches apart on prepared baking sheets. Repeat procedure with remaining half of dough.
4. Bake at 375° for 10 minutes or until lightly browned. Cool on baking sheets 5 minutes. Remove to wire racks to cool completely (about 30 minutes). Makes about 5 dozen.

THUMBPRINT COOKIES

Hands-on Time: 20 min.   Total Time: 1 hr., 20 min.

These little cookies are beautiful displayed in decorative paper cups on a tray of assorted sweets. As an added bonus, you can make them ahead because they freeze well.

½	cup butter, softened	½	tsp. vanilla extract	Finely ground pecans or
¼	cup firmly packed light	1	cup all-purpose flour	walnuts (or mixed)
	brown sugar	¼	tsp. salt	Seedless raspberry jam
1	large egg, separated			

1. Preheat oven to 350°. Beat butter at medium speed with an electric mixer until creamy; gradually add brown sugar, beating well. Add egg yolk and vanilla, beating until blended.
2. Combine flour and salt; add to butter mixture, beating at low speed until blended.
3. Shape dough into 1-inch balls. Lightly beat egg white. Dip each dough ball into egg white; roll in nuts. Place 2 inches apart on ungreased baking sheets. Press thumb or end of a wooden spoon into each ball, forming an indentation.
4. Bake at 350° for 15 minutes. Cool 1 minute on baking sheets; remove to wire racks. Press centers again with thumb while cookies are still warm; fill center of each cookie with jam. Cool completely on wire racks (about 30 minutes). Makes about 2 dozen.

ICEBOX COOKIES

Hands-on Time: 23 min.   Total Time: 1 hr., 41 min., plus 8 hr. for chilling

Think of these as cookies on demand! You can make the dough ahead, store it in the refrigerator or freezer, and, when the need arises, just slice the dough and bake only the number you want. Chill or freeze any remaining dough for later use.

1 cup finely chopped pecans	1 cup firmly packed light brown sugar	2 large eggs
1 cup unsalted butter, softened	1 cup granulated sugar	1 tsp. vanilla extract
		3½ cups self-rising flour

1. Preheat oven to 350°. Bake pecans in a single layer in a shallow pan 8 to 10 minutes or until lightly toasted, stirring halfway through.

2. Beat butter and sugars at medium speed with an electric mixer until light and fluffy. Add eggs, 1 at a time, beating well after each addition. Add vanilla, beating until blended. Gradually add flour to butter mixture, beating just until blended. Stir in pecans.

3. Divide dough into 3 equal portions; roll each portion into a 12-inch log. Cover and chill 8 to 24 hours.

4. Preheat oven to 350°. Cut each log into ¼-inch slices; place slices on ungreased baking sheets.

5. Bake at 350° for 10 minutes or until lightly browned. Transfer to wire racks to cool completely (about 30 minutes). Store cookies in an airtight container, or freeze. Makes about 7 dozen.

CHOCOLATE CHIP FORGOTTEN COOKIES

Hands-on Time: 15 min.   Total Time: 15 min., plus 12 hr. for standing

These cookies are baked the old "baking day" way, when kisses were baked last as the oven cooled. They're best eaten the same day or within five days.

2 egg whites, at room temperature	⅔ cup sugar	1 cup chopped pecans
⅛ tsp. salt	1 cup semisweet chocolate morsels	½ tsp. vanilla extract

1. Preheat oven to 350°. Line baking sheets with aluminum foil.
2. Beat egg whites in a large mixing bowl at high speed with an electric mixer until foamy; add salt. Add sugar, 1 Tbsp. at a time, beating 2 to 4 minutes or until stiff peaks form and sugar dissolves. Fold in chocolate morsels, pecans, and vanilla.
3. Drop by heaping teaspoonfuls 2 inches apart onto prepared baking sheets. Place in oven, and immediately turn off heat. Do not open oven door for at least 12 hours. Gently remove cookies from foil, and store in an airtight container. Makes about 2½ dozen.

MONSTER COOKIES

Hands-on Time: 20 min.   Total Time: 1 hr., 30 min.

Big in size and in flavor! These cookies contain oats, peanut butter, and chocolate. More stunning than that is their size—they're dropped from ¼-cup measures rather than teaspoons.

½ cup butter, softened	¾ tsp. light corn syrup	¼ tsp. salt
1 cup granulated sugar	¼ tsp. vanilla extract	1 cup candy-coated milk chocolate pieces
1 cup plus 2 Tbsp. firmly packed light brown sugar	4½ cups uncooked regular oats	1 (6-oz.) package semisweet chocolate morsels
3 large eggs	2 tsp. baking soda	
2 cups peanut butter		

1. Preheat oven to 350°. Lightly grease baking sheets.
2. Beat butter and sugars at medium speed with an electric mixer until light and fluffy. Add eggs, 1 at a time, beating well after each addition. Add peanut butter, corn syrup, and vanilla, beating until blended. Stir together oats, soda, and salt; gradually add to butter mixture, beating well. Stir in candy and chocolate morsels. (Dough will be stiff.)
3. Pack dough into a ¼-cup measure. Drop dough 4 inches apart onto prepared baking sheets. Lightly press each cookie into a 3½-inch circle with fingertips.
4. Bake at 350° for 12 to 15 minutes (centers of cookies will be slightly soft). Cool slightly on baking sheets; remove to wire racks to cool completely (about 30 minutes). Makes 2½ dozen.

SOUTH CAROLINA COCONUT CREAM PIE

Hands-on Time: 22 min.   Total Time: 1 hr., 22 min.

Coconut cream pie is the perfect closer to a cookout. And the whipped cream topping takes it over the top!

¾   cup granulated sugar
2½   Tbsp. all-purpose flour
1½   cups milk
3   egg yolks
2   Tbsp. butter, cut up
1   cup sweetened flaked coconut
1   tsp. vanilla extract, divided
1   (9-inch) baked piecrust shell
1   cup whipping cream
¼   cup powdered sugar
Garnish: toasted sweetened flaked coconut

1. Combine granulated sugar and flour in a heavy saucepan. Whisk together milk and egg yolks. Gradually whisk egg mixture into sugar mixture; bring to a boil over medium heat, whisking constantly. Boil 3 minutes or until thickened; remove from heat.

2. Stir in butter, 1 cup coconut, and ½ tsp. vanilla. Cover with plastic wrap, placing plastic wrap directly on surface of filling in pan; let stand 30 minutes. Spoon custard into prepared crust; cover and chill 30 minutes or until set.

3. Meanwhile, beat whipping cream at high speed with an electric mixer until foamy; gradually add powdered sugar and remaining ½ tsp. vanilla, beating until soft peaks form. Spread or pipe whipped cream over pie filling. Store in refrigerator. Garnish, if desired. Makes 6 to 8 servings.

CHOCOLATE CREAM PIE

Hands-on Time: 25 min.   Total Time: 2 hr., 35 min., including Meringue

This decadent pie is reminiscent of those you find at local barbecue restaurants.

½ (14.1-oz.) package refrigerated piecrusts
1¼ cups sugar
3 Tbsp. cornstarch
⅛ tsp. salt
4 egg yolks

2 cups milk
2 Tbsp. butter
2 (1-oz.) unsweetened chocolate baking squares, melted

1 tsp. vanilla extract
Meringue

1. Preheat oven to 350°. Fit piecrust into a 9-inch pie plate according to package directions; fold edges under, and crimp. Bake at 350° according to package directions. Let cool completely (about 30 minutes). Reduce oven temperature to 325°.

2. Whisk together sugar and next 2 ingredients in a large heavy saucepan. Whisk together egg yolks and milk. Gradually whisk egg mixture into sugar mixture; add butter.

3. Cook over medium heat, stirring constantly, 8 to 10 minutes or until mixture thickens and boils. Boil 3 minutes. Remove from heat. Stir in melted chocolate and vanilla. Spoon into prepared piecrust.

4. Spread Meringue over hot filling, sealing edges.

5. Bake at 325° for 18 to 20 minutes or until meringue peaks are lightly browned. Let cool completely on a wire rack (about 1 hour). Store in refrigerator. Makes 8 servings.

MERINGUE

Hands-on Time: 10 min.   Total Time: 10 min.

5 egg whites
½ tsp. cream of tartar

¾ cup sugar

½ tsp. vanilla extract

1. Beat egg whites and cream of tartar at high speed with an electric mixer just until foamy.

2. Gradually add sugar, 1 Tbsp. at a time, beating until stiff peaks form and sugar dissolves (2 to 4 minutes). Add vanilla, beating well. Makes enough for 1 (9-inch) pie.

Tips for perfect meringue pies:

• Make sure the filling is very hot when you top it with the meringue to prevent "weeping."

• Spread meringue quickly onto hot filling, and anchor it to the edge of the crust to seal and keep it from shrinking.

BEST-EVER LEMON MERINGUE PIE

Hands-on Time: 26 min.   Total Time: 2 hr., including Mile-High Meringue

1½ cups sugar
⅓ cup cornstarch
⅛ tsp. salt
4 egg yolks

1¾ cups milk
½ cup fresh lemon juice
3 Tbsp. butter
1 tsp. lemon zest

1 (9-inch) baked piecrust
   shell
Mile-High Meringue

1. Preheat oven to 325°. Whisk together first 3 ingredients in a medium-size heavy nonaluminum saucepan.
2. Whisk together egg yolks and next 2 ingredients in a large bowl; whisk into sugar mixture in pan over medium heat. Bring to a boil, and boil, whisking constantly, 1 minute. Remove from heat. Stir in butter and zest until smooth. Spoon into piecrust.
3. Spread Mile-High Meringue over hot filling, sealing edges.
4. Bake at 325° for 20 to 25 minutes or until meringue peaks are lightly browned. Let cool completely on a wire rack (about 1 hour). Store in refrigerator. Makes 8 servings.

MILE-HIGH MERINGUE

Hands-on Time: 10 min.   Total Time: 10 min.

6 egg whites
½ tsp. cream of tartar

½ cup sugar

½ tsp. vanilla extract

1. Beat egg whites and cream of tartar at high speed with an electric mixer just until foamy.
2. Gradually add sugar, 1 Tbsp. at a time, beating until stiff peaks form and sugar dissolves (2 to 4 minutes). Add vanilla, beating well. Makes enough for 1 (9-inch) pie.

KEY LIME PIE

Hands-on Time: 20 min.   Total Time: 2 hr., plus 8 hr. for chilling

Give thanks to the early Bahamian settlers who gave us Key lime pie. This tangy-sweet pie made with Key limes is Florida's official pie. And it's never green, but a natural creamy yellow color.

1¼ cups graham cracker crumbs
1½ Tbsp. sugar
5 Tbsp. butter, melted
4 egg yolks

1 (14-oz.) can sweetened condensed milk
½ cup fresh Key lime juice*
2 tsp. Persian lime zest
2 Tbsp. granulated sugar

1 cup whipping cream
1 Tbsp. powdered sugar
½ tsp. vanilla extract

1. Preheat oven to 350°. Combine first 3 ingredients; press in bottom and up sides of a 9-inch pie plate. Bake 5 minutes. Cool on a wire rack 20 minutes.

2. Meanwhile, whisk egg yolks; add condensed milk and next 3 ingredients, whisking until smooth. Spoon into prepared crust.

3. Bake at 350° for 15 minutes or until set. Cool completely on a wire rack (about 1 hour). Cover and chill 8 hours.

4. Beat whipping cream at high speed with an electric mixer until slightly thickened; add powdered sugar and vanilla, beating until stiff peaks form.

5. Spread whipped cream over top of pie. Store in refrigerator. Makes 10 servings.

* Persian lime juice may be substituted.

REBECCA BOONE'S CHESS PIE

Hands-on Time: 10 min.   Total Time: 1 hr., 50 min.

We're not exactly sure how chess pie arrived at its name. One theory is that gentlemen wanted a sweet dessert to enjoy over a game of chess. Another suggests that because it's so high in sugar, it kept well in a pie chest ("chess pie") at room temperature. We just know it's legendary for its simplicity and appeal.

½ (14.1-oz.) package refrigerated piecrusts
5 large eggs, lightly beaten
1½ cups sugar

1 Tbsp. plain yellow or white cornmeal
¼ cup plus 2 Tbsp. butter, softened

1 Tbsp. white vinegar
1 tsp. vanilla extract

1. Preheat oven to 350°. Fit piecrust into a 9-inch pie plate according to package directions; fold edges under, and crimp.

2. Stir together eggs, and next 2 ingredients until blended. Add butter and remaining ingredients, stirring well. Pour into piecrust.

3. Bake at 350° for 40 minutes, shielding edges with aluminum foil after 10 minutes to prevent excessive browning. Cool completely on a wire rack (about 1 hour). Makes 6 to 8 servings.

CRUNCH-TOP APPLE PIE

Hands-on Time: 20 min.   Total Time: 4 hr., 20 min., including Pastry and Crunch Topping

This pie showcases the best of both worlds—double piecrust and streusel topping. Braeburn apples work well in this pie because they hold their shape when cooked and provide contrast to the soft applesauce.

Pastry, divided	⅛ tsp. salt	1 Tbsp. fresh lemon juice
¾ cup sugar	4½ cups peeled and chopped	1 Tbsp. butter, cut up
1 Tbsp. all-purpose flour	cooking apples (about 4)	Crunch Topping
½ tsp. ground cinnamon	1 (16-oz.) jar applesauce	

1. Preheat oven to 425°. Roll half of Pastry to ⅛-inch thickness on a lightly floured surface; fit piecrust into a 9-inch pie plate, and trim off excess piecrust along edges. Combine sugar and next 3 ingredients; stir in apples and next 2 ingredients. Spoon apple mixture into prepared pie plate, and dot with butter.
2. Roll out remaining Pastry to ⅛-inch thickness on a lightly floured surface. Using the width of a ruler as a guide, cut piecrust into 9 (1-inch-wide) strips. Arrange strips in a lattice design over filling; gently press ends of strips, sealing to bottom piecrust. Prepare Crunch Topping, and sprinkle over lattice crust.
3. Bake at 425° for 10 minutes (place foil on rack beneath pie to catch drips, if necessary); reduce oven temperature to 350°, and bake 1 hour and 5 minutes or until crust is golden brown. Cool 2 hours. Makes 8 to 10 servings.

PASTRY

Hands-on Time: 10 min.   Total Time: 40 min.

2½ cups all-purpose flour	⅔ cup plus 2 Tbsp.	½ cup ice water
1 tsp. salt	shortening	

Combine flour and salt; cut in shortening with a pastry blender until mixture is crumbly. Sprinkle ice water, 1 Tbsp. at a time, evenly over surface; stir with a fork until dry ingredients are moistened. Shape into 2 balls; wrap in plastic wrap, and chill 30 minutes. Makes enough for 1 double-crust 9-inch pie.

CRUNCH TOPPING

Hands-on Time: 5 min.   Total Time: 5 min.

3 Tbsp. all-purpose flour	⅛ tsp. salt	1 Tbsp. butter, cut up
1 Tbsp. sugar		

Combine first 3 ingredients; cut in butter with a fork until mixture is crumbly. Makes about ¼ cup.

SOUTHERN STRAWBERRY PIE

Hands-on Time: 15 min.   Total Time: 1 hr., 45 min.

You might recognize this luscious dessert as the signature pie from a restaurant chain.

¾ cup sugar
2 Tbsp. cornstarch
2 Tbsp. light corn syrup
3 Tbsp. strawberry-flavored gelatin

1 qt. fresh strawberries, trimmed
1 (9-inch) baked piecrust shell

Sweetened whipped cream

1. Combine first 3 ingredients and 1 cup water in a saucepan; bring to a boil. Cook, stirring constantly, 1 minute or until clear and thickened. Remove from heat. Add gelatin, stirring until dissolved. Cool 30 minutes.

2. Place strawberries, trimmed sides down, in piecrust shell; pour gelatin mixture over strawberries. Chill 1 hour or until firm. Dollop each serving with whipped cream. Store in refrigerator. Makes 6 servings.

Makeover in Minutes: Swap the crust for parfait glasses, and enjoy this refreshing dessert by the spoonful.

"Growing up, I was an admitted mama's boy. Without realizing the uniqueness of it at the time, I recall how my mom, Angelica, so often talked about food, planned family trips around food, sought out that perfect ingredient, or just spent time chatting with me and letting me taste her creations while she cooked. Every year during the spring berry season, Mom organized a family trip to a 'U-pick' strawberry farm. It was a family ritual to bring home overflowing baskets of plump, ripe berries and to hull them to use in all manners of ways—from strawberry ice cream to strawberry shortcakes. If it could be done with strawberries, Mom most likely attempted it."

—Chef Chris Hastings
Hot and Hot Fish Club

PEACH FRIED PIES

Hands-on Time: 20 min.   Total Time: 2 hr., 50 min., including pastry

You can use dried apples or apricots in place of peaches if you'd like. Freezing the pies before frying helps prevent the crust from falling apart in the hot oil.

1 (16-oz.) package dried peaches	2 Tbsp. fresh lemon juice	Egg Pastry
½ cup sugar	½ tsp. ground cinnamon	Vegetable oil
	¼ tsp. ground nutmeg	Powdered sugar

1. Place peaches in water to cover in a large saucepan, and bring to a boil; cook, covered, over medium heat until very tender (about 30 minutes). Drain, reserving ¼ cup liquid; cool to room temperature. Chop peaches, and combine with sugar, lemon juice, spices, and reserved liquid.

2. Roll out Egg Pastry to ⅛-inch thickness, using one-third of pastry at a time. Cut each portion into 5-inch circles, rerolling pastry scraps if necessary.

3. Moisten edges of circles with water. Spoon about 2 Tbsp. peach mixture in center of each pastry circle; fold over, pressing edges to seal. Crimp edges with a fork dipped in flour. Repeat with remaining pastry and peach mixture.

4. Pour oil to a depth of 1½ inches into a Dutch oven; heat to 375°. Fry pies, in batches, 2 minutes on each side or until golden, turning once. Drain well on paper towels. Sprinkle with powdered sugar. Makes about 15 pies.

EGG PASTRY

Hands-on Time: 10 min.   Total Time: 1 hr., 10 min.

3 cups all-purpose flour	¼ cup ice water
½ tsp. salt	1 tsp. white vinegar
¾ cup cold shortening	Wax paper
1 large egg, lightly beaten	

1. COMBINE flour and salt; cut in shortening with a pastry blender until mixture is crumbly. Combine egg, ice water, and vinegar; add to flour mixture, stirring until mixture forms a ball.

2. WRAP pastry in wax paper; chill at least 1 hour or until ready to use. Makes enough for 15 fried pies.

BLACKBERRY COBBLER

Hands-on Time: 15 min.   Total Time: 1 hr., including Crust

Served warm or cold, mounded with ice cream or drenched in cream, fruit cobblers are a favorite summertime dessert, dear to any Southerner's heart.

1 cup sugar	1 Tbsp. fresh lemon juice	1 tsp. sugar
¼ cup all-purpose flour	Crust	Ice cream (optional)
5 cups fresh blackberries*	2 Tbsp. butter, melted	

1. Preheat oven to 425°. Combine 1 cup sugar and ¼ cup flour; add berries, and toss well. Sprinkle with lemon juice. Spoon into lightly greased 8- or 9-inch baking dish.

2. Prepare Crust, and spoon 9 mounds over blackberries. Brush with butter, and sprinkle with 1 tsp. sugar.

3. Bake at 425° for 30 minutes or until browned and bubbly. Serve warm with ice cream, if desired. Makes 9 servings.

* 2 (14-oz.) packages frozen blackberries, thawed and drained, may be substituted. Increase flour to ⅓ cup.

CRUST

Hands-on Time: 5 min.   Total Time: 5 min.

1¾ cups all-purpose flour	¾ tsp. salt	½ cup whipping cream
3 Tbsp. sugar	¼ cup shortening	½ cup buttermilk
1½ tsp. baking powder		

Combine first 4 ingredients; cut in shortening with a pastry blender until mixture is crumbly. Stir in whipping cream and buttermilk just until blended. Makes enough for 1 cobbler.

APPLE DUMPLINGS WITH MAPLE-CIDER SAUCE

Hands-on Time: 30 min.   Total Time: 1 hr., 35 min., including Maple-Cider Sauce

Dessert dumplings are comfort food at its best. This fall favorite features apples accented with aromatic spices encased in pastry and baked.

1½ cups sugar	¼ cup butter	½ cup milk
½ tsp. ground cinnamon, divided	2½ cups all-purpose flour	6 small Braeburn apples
	2 tsp. baking powder	⅓ cup sugar
½ tsp. ground nutmeg, divided	½ tsp. salt	¼ cup butter, cut into pieces
	⅔ cup shortening	Maple-Cider Sauce

1. Preheat oven to 375°. Lightly grease a 13- x 9-inch baking dish.
2. Bring 1½ cups sugar, ¼ tsp. cinnamon, ¼ tsp. nutmeg, and 2 cups water to a boil in a saucepan. Reduce heat; simmer 5 minutes. Remove syrup from heat; stir in ¼ cup butter.
3. Combine flour and next 2 ingredients. Cut in shortening with a pastry blender until crumbly. Add milk, stirring just until dry ingredients are moistened. Shape into a ball. Turn dough out onto a lightly floured surface, and roll into an 18- x 12-inch rectangle. Cut into 6 (6-inch) squares. Place 1 apple in center of each square.
4. Combine ⅓ cup sugar, remaining ¼ tsp. cinnamon, and remaining ¼ tsp. nutmeg; sprinkle over apples. Top evenly with ¼ cup butter cut into pieces.
5. Moisten dough edges with water; pull corners over apples, pinching to seal. Place dumplings in prepared baking dish. Pour syrup over dumplings.
6. Bake at 375° for 50 minutes or until golden brown. Serve with Maple-Cider Sauce. Makes 6 servings.

MAPLE-CIDER SAUCE

Hands-on Time: 5 min.   Total Time: 5 min.

2 tsp. cornstarch	¼ cup firmly packed light brown sugar	¼ cup fresh lemon juice
1½ cups apple cider		
⅔ cup maple syrup		

Combine cornstarch and cider in a saucepan, stirring until smooth; add maple syrup and remaining ingredients. Bring to a boil over medium-high heat; boil 1 minute. Serve warm. Makes 2 cups.

CHARLOTTE RUSSE

Hands-on Time: 1 hr., 10 min.   Total Time: 3 hr., 25 min.,
including Ladyfingers, plus 8 hr. for chilling

You may have never enjoyed Charlotte Russe the original way it was made using homemade ladyfingers. They make the classic dish extra light and lovely. If you're short on time, buy 2 (3-oz.) packages of ladyfingers from your supermarket deli.

1 envelope unflavored gelatin	1 cup sugar	1 tsp. vanilla extract
¼ cup cold milk	2 cups milk	2 cups whipping cream, whipped
2 large eggs	¼ tsp. salt	Ladyfingers
	3 Tbsp. cream sherry	

1. Sprinkle gelatin over ¼ cup cold milk; stir and let stand 1 minute.

2. Whisk together eggs and sugar in top of a double boiler until thick and pale. Stir in 2 cups milk and ¼ tsp. salt. Bring water to a light boil in bottom pan; reduce heat. Cook egg mixture, whisking often, until thickened. Remove from heat; stir in sherry, vanilla, and gelatin mixture. Let cool completely (about 1 hour). Fold in whipped cream.

3. Stand Ladyfingers around edge of a 9- x 3-inch springform pan, rounded sides against sides of pan, trimming to fit, if necessary. Line bottom of pan with remaining Ladyfingers. Pour custard into prepared pan; cover and chill 8 hours or overnight. Unmold from pan. Store in refrigerator. Makes 8 to 10 servings.

LADYFINGERS

Hands-on Time: 30 min.   Total Time: 1 hr. 55 min.

Don't worry if your ladyfingers are longer than 3 inches—you can trim them to fit the springform pan.

Parchment paper	½ cup sugar, divided	⅔ cup all-purpose flour
4 large eggs, separated	½ tsp. vanilla extract	2 Tbsp. powdered sugar

1. Preheat oven to 350°. Line 2 large baking sheets with parchment paper.

2. Beat egg yolks, ¼ cup sugar, and vanilla at high speed with an electric mixer 3 to 5 minutes or until thick and pale.

3. Beat egg whites and remaining ¼ cup sugar at medium-high speed with an electric mixer until stiff peaks form. Fold half of egg white mixture into yolk mixture. Sift flour over mixture, and gently fold in. Fold in remaining half of egg white mixture.

4. Spoon batter into a large decorating bag fitted with a plain metal tip (½- to ¾-inch). Pipe or form 3-inch-long "fingers" of batter on prepared baking sheets. Sift powdered sugar over top.

5. Bake at 350° on bottom oven rack for 15 minutes or until light golden. (These do not brown.) Cool on pans 10 minutes. Remove to wire racks to cool completely (about 1 hour). Makes about 4 dozen.

BANANAS FOSTER

Hands-on Time: 15 min.   Total Time: 15 min.

You can thank Richard Foster and Brennan's Restaurant for this timeless treat. The dessert is named for Foster, a frequent diner at the famed New Orleans eatery.

¼ cup butter	4 barely ripe bananas,	¼ cup dark rum
½ cup firmly packed light	peeled and halved	¼ cup banana liqueur
brown sugar	lengthwise	4 cups vanilla ice cream
¼ tsp. ground cinnamon		

1. Combine butter and next 2 ingredients in a large flat skillet over low heat; cook, stirring until sugar dissolves. Add banana halves; heat 1 to 2 minutes, basting constantly with sauce.
2. Place rum and liqueur in a small pan; heat 1 to 2 minutes or just until warm. Pour over bananas, and carefully ignite with a long match. Let flames die down; baste bananas with sauce. Serve immediately over ice cream. Makes 4 servings.

CARAMEL FLAN

Hands-on Time: 13 min.   Total Time: 1 hr., 15 min., plus 8 hr. for chilling

Baked custards, such as this French variety, gained popularity in the United States when famed chef Alain Sailhac brought back the idea from a trip to Europe and began serving the dish at Le Cirque in New York.

1⅓ cups sugar, divided	5 large eggs, lightly beaten	¼ tsp. salt
3 cups milk	½ tsp. vanilla extract	

1. Preheat oven to 350°. Place oven rack in center of oven.
2. Sprinkle 1 cup sugar evenly into a medium-size heavy saucepan; add ⅓ cup water, and cook over medium-high heat 5 minutes. (Do not stir.) Using a pastry brush dipped in hot water, brush down any sugar crystals on sides of pan. Swirl pan gently when mixture begins to turn golden around the edges. Cook 5 minutes or until dark amber in color. Remove from heat, and pour caramelized syrup into a 9-inch round cake pan. Carefully tilt pan to spread caramelized syrup evenly. Let cool.
3. Bring milk just to a boil. Whisk together eggs and remaining ⅓ cup sugar; stir in vanilla and salt. Gradually stir about one-fourth of hot milk into egg mixture. Add egg mixture to remaining hot milk mixture, stirring constantly. Pour into cake pan, being careful not to disturb the caramelized syrup in the bottom.
4. Place cake pan in a 15- x 10-inch pan. Add hot water to a depth of 1 inch.
5. Bake at 350° for 35 to 40 minutes or until top puffs slightly and a knife inserted near edge of mold comes out clean.
6. Remove from oven, and transfer to a wire rack. Cool to room temperature.
7. Cover loosely, and chill 8 hours or overnight. Run a knife around edge of flan, and invert onto a serving platter. Serve immediately. Makes 8 to 10 servings.

Note: To make ahead, prepare recipe through Step 6. Cover flan with plastic wrap, and store in refrigerator up to 2 days. Once unmolded, serve immediately.

BANANA CUSTARD PUDDING

Hands-on Time: 45 min.   Total Time: 2 hr., 45 min.

For an over-the-top touch, crown this creamy confection with sweetened whipped cream.

4   egg yolks
2½   cups sugar
½   cup all-purpose flour
¼   cup cornstarch
7   cups milk
¼   cup butter, softened
1   tsp. vanilla extract
1   (12-oz.) package vanilla wafers
9   medium bananas, peeled and sliced
Sweetened whipped cream (optional)

1. Place egg yolks in a medium bowl; whisk until thick and pale. Whisk together sugar and next 2 ingredients in a separate medium bowl.

2. Pour milk into a large Dutch oven; cook over medium heat, whisking often, until a candy thermometer registers 160°. Gradually stir about one-fourth of hot milk into yolks; add yolk mixture to remaining hot milk mixture, whisking constantly. Whisk in sugar mixture until blended.

3. Cook over medium heat, whisking constantly, until mixture is thickened and bubbly and coats a spoon. Remove from heat; stir in butter and vanilla. Pour into a bowl; place plastic wrap directly onto warm custard (to prevent a film from forming), and chill 1 hour. (Mixture will thicken as it cools.)

4. Line bottom and sides of a 13- x 9-inch baking dish with one-third of wafers. Arrange half of banana slices over wafers; top with half of chilled custard. Repeat layers once. Crumble remaining one-third of wafers and sprinkle over custard. Chill 1 hour. Top with sweetened whipped cream, if desired. Makes 20 to 25 servings.

TASTY TRIVIA

Several different types of desserts are classified as puddings. One is a soft, creamy boiled pudding made with eggs, milk, sugar, and flavoring. Boiled pudding is thickened with flour, cornstarch, or tapioca, and is usually flavored with chocolate, vanilla, butterscotch, banana, or coconut. Rice puddings are thickened, custard-style, with egg or the starch from the rice. Bread puddings start with firm bread soaked in milk and eggs, and sweetened with sugar; most are baked. Other starchy, cake-like puddings may also be baked, such as Indian pudding or steamed pudding.

CRÊPES SUZETTE

Hands-on Time: 30 min.   Total Time: 1 hr., 50 min., including Dessert Crêpes

Keep a batch of Dessert Crêpes in the freezer like so many ladies did in the 1970s, and you'll always be ready to serve this dramatic dessert. Or if you prefer, you can find premade crêpes in the produce department or deli of the supermarket.

⅓ cup butter	1 Tbsp. fresh lemon juice	3 Tbsp. Grand Marnier
¼ cup sugar	⅓ cup fresh orange juice	Dessert Crêpes
½ cup orange marmalade	3 Tbsp. Curaçao,	¼ cup brandy
1 Tbsp. lemon zest	Cointreau, or Triple Sec	

1. Combine butter and sugar in a large skillet or chafing dish; cook over medium heat until mixture is lightly browned. Stir in marmalade and next 5 ingredients; cook until bubbly. Dip both sides of each crêpe in orange sauce; fold in half and then in quarters. Push to side of pan. Repeat procedure with remaining crêpes.

2. Pour brandy in a small saucepan; heat just until warm. Pour over crêpes, and ignite with a long match. Allow flames to die down, and serve immediately. Makes 12 servings.

DESSERT CRÊPES

Hands-on Time: 20 min.   Total Time: 1 hr., 20 min.

⅓ cup all-purpose flour	1 large egg	1 Tbsp. butter, melted
1 Tbsp. sugar	1 egg yolk	1 Tbsp. Grand Marnier
Dash of salt	¾ cup milk	Wax paper

1. Process first 8 ingredients in a blender 2 minutes or until smooth. Cover and chill 1 hour. (This allows flour particles to swell and soften so that the crêpes are light in texture.)

2. Place a lightly greased crêpe pan or 8-inch nonstick skillet over medium heat until hot. Pour 2 Tbsp. batter into pan; quickly tilt in all directions so that batter covers bottom of pan with a thin film. Cook crêpe 45 seconds. Carefully lift edge of crêpe with a spatula to test for doneness. (The crêpe is ready to turn when it can be shaken loose from pan.) Turn crêpe over, and cook 15 to 30 seconds or until done. Repeat procedure with remaining batter. Stack crêpes between sheets of wax paper to prevent sticking. Makes 12 (6-inch) crêpes.

Note: To make ahead, prepare crêpes as directed, and freeze, separated by wax paper, up to 1 month in a zip-top plastic freezer bag.

BREAD PUDDING WITH WHISKEY SAUCE

Hands-on Time: 20 min.   Total Time: 1 hr., 35 min., including Whiskey Sauce

Old World frugal cooks created bread pudding as a way of using stale bread so it wouldn't go to waste. The heady sauce in this version crowns this New World classic with richness.

1   (16-oz.) day-old French bread loaf, cubed
1   qt. milk
3   large eggs, lightly beaten
2   cups sugar
2   Tbsp. vanilla extract
1   cup raisins
3   Tbsp. butter, melted
Whiskey Sauce

1. Preheat oven to 350°. Place bread in a large, shallow bowl. Add milk, and let soak 10 minutes. Add eggs and next 3 ingredients.
2. Pour butter into a 13- x 9-inch baking dish. Spoon pudding mixture into dish.
3. Bake at 350° for 35 to 45 minutes or until set. Serve warm with Whiskey Sauce. Makes 15 servings.

WHISKEY SAUCE

Hands-on Time: 40 min.   Total Time: 40 min.

1   cup butter, softened
2   cups sugar
2   large eggs, lightly beaten
¼   to ½ cup whiskey

1. Beat butter and sugar at medium speed with an electric mixer until light and fluffy; place in top of a double boiler. Bring water to a light boil in bottom pan; reduce heat to low, and cook, stirring often, about 20 minutes or until very hot. Stir a small amount of hot mixture into eggs; add eggs to hot mixture, stirring constantly.
2. Cook, stirring constantly, 3 minutes or until sauce is thick enough to coat a spoon; remove from heat, and cool. Stir in whiskey to taste. Makes 2 cups.

TASTY TRIVIA

Bread pudding is a baked dessert made with stale French bread cubes or slices that have been soaked in a mixture of eggs, milk, sugar, and flavorings. Chopped fruits or nuts are sometimes added. The pudding may be served hot or cold and is often drenched with whiskey sauce. The bread pudding we know today is derived from England's famous hasty pudding, made from flour, milk, eggs, butter, and spices. Today's Southern bread puddings often show up as savory dishes with cheese, onion, garlic, and other herbs.

PEACH ICE CREAM

Hands-on Time: 35 min.   Total Time: 9 hr., 35 min.,
not including freezing time

Prepare the cooked custard and peaches for this old-fashioned treat a day ahead.

2¼ cups no-sugar-added
sliced cling peaches, finely
chopped
1½ cups sugar, divided

2 tsp. almond extract
5 large eggs
5 cups milk

1 (14-oz.) can sweetened
condensed milk
1 (12-oz.) can evaporated
milk

1. Combine peaches, ½ cup sugar, and almond extract in a bowl; cover and chill 8 to 24 hours.

2. Combine eggs, whole milk, and remaining 1 cup sugar in a large saucepan; cook over low heat, stirring constantly, 23 minutes or until mixture thickens and coats a spoon. Remove from heat. Whisk in sweetened condensed milk and evaporated milk. Let cool completely (about 1 hour). Cover and chill 8 to 24 hours.

3. Pour custard mixture and peaches into freezer container of a 4-qt. electric freezer; freeze according to manufacturer's instructions. (Instruction times may vary.) Serve immediately as soft-serve ice cream, or store in an airtight container, and freeze 8 hours or until firm. Makes 4 qt.

Note: We tested with Del Monte Orchard Select Sliced Cling Peaches.

BROWNIE BAKED ALASKA

Hands-on Time: 30 min.   Total Time: 2 hr., 5 min.

"Impressive" best describes this dessert! A single cake layer—brownie at that—is topped with a mound of vanilla ice cream and coated in meringue. It's baked in a very hot oven less than 5 minutes, just long enough for the meringue to brown and crisp.

1 qt. vanilla ice cream, softened	2 large eggs	¼ tsp. salt
½ cup butter, softened	1 cup all-purpose flour	1 tsp. vanilla extract
2 cups sugar, divided	½ tsp. baking powder	5 pasteurized egg whites
	2 Tbsp. unsweetened cocoa	

1. Line a 1-qt. bowl (about 7 inches in diameter) with plastic wrap, allowing 2 to 3 inches to extend over sides. Pack ice cream into bowl, and freeze until very firm.

2. Preheat oven to 350°. Beat butter and 1 cup sugar at medium speed with an electric mixer until light and fluffy. Add eggs, 1 at a time, beating well after each addition. Combine flour and next 3 ingredients in a small bowl; add to butter mixture, blending well. Stir in vanilla.

3. Spoon batter into a greased and floured 8-inch round cake pan. Bake at 350° for 25 to 30 minutes or until a wooden pick inserted in center comes out clean. Cool in pan 10 minutes; remove to a wire rack, and cool completely (about 1 hour).

4. Increase oven temperature to 500°. Place brownie layer on an ovenproof serving dish. Invert bowl of ice cream onto brownie layer; remove bowl, leaving plastic wrap on ice cream. Place cake in freezer.

5. Beat egg whites at medium speed with an electric mixer until foamy; gradually beat in remaining 1 cup sugar, 1 Tbsp. at a time, beating until stiff peaks form and sugar dissolves. Remove cake from freezer. Remove and discard plastic wrap. Spread meringue over surface, sealing edges.

6. Bake at 500° for 2 to 3 minutes or until meringue peaks are lightly browned. Serve immediately. Makes 10 to 12 servings.

Note: After meringue is sealed, the dessert can be returned to the freezer for up to 1 week and baked just before serving.

GRAND FLOATING ISLANDS

Hands-on Time: 55 min.   Total Time: 5 hr., 10 min.

This dish of simple poached meringues floating atop chilled custard was one of the original desserts of Louisiana that arrived with the French settlers. All components can be made several hours in advance, so it's perfect for impressing dinner guests.

4½   cups half-and-half, divided

4   egg whites

1½   cups plus ⅔ cup sugar, divided

⅛   tsp. salt

1   vanilla bean

10   egg yolks

¾   cup heavy whipping cream

¼   cup butter

1. Heat 4 cups half-and-half in a large saucepan over medium-low heat 8 minutes or until hot. Beat egg whites in a medium bowl at medium speed with an electric mixer until soft peaks form; gradually add ½ cup sugar and ⅛ tsp. salt, beating until stiff peaks form.

2. Drop egg white mixture by heaping tablespoonfuls into hot half-and-half. Cook, in batches, 2 minutes per side or until slightly firm. Remove "islands" with a slotted spoon; drain on paper towels. Refrigerate in an airtight container until ready to serve.

3. Split vanilla bean lengthwise, and scrape out seeds. Add remaining ½ cup half-and-half and vanilla bean and seeds to hot half-and-half mixture in saucepan; cook until thoroughly heated. Combine egg yolks and ⅔ cup sugar in a medium bowl; whisk until thick and pale. Gradually stir one-fourth of hot half-and-half mixture into yolk mixture; add to remaining hot half-and-half mixture, stirring constantly. Cook, stirring constantly, over medium-low heat 10 minutes or until mixture thickens and coats a spoon and candy thermometer registers 170°. Pour through a fine wire-mesh strainer into a bowl. Cover and chill 4 hours or until cold.

4. Combine remaining 1 cup sugar and ¼ cup water in a heavy saucepan. Cook over low heat 8 to 10 minutes or until sugar caramelizes, tipping pan to incorporate mixture. Add cream and butter carefully, stirring constantly to combine. (Be careful of hot steam; caramel may bubble and spatter when cream and butter are added.) Cook over low heat, stirring constantly, 1 to 2 minutes or until smooth.

5. Spoon chilled custard into a serving bowl. Place "islands" on top of custard; drizzle with caramel sauce. Serve immediately. Makes 8 servings.

PAVLOVA WITH LEMON CREAM AND BERRIES

Hands-on Time: 30 min.   Total Time: 2 hr., plus 12 hr. for standing

This is Marian's twist on her mother's signature dessert. Assemble it just before serving, but you can make the meringue up to two days ahead; store in an airtight container.

1 cup sugar	¼ tsp. cream of tartar	1 (10-oz.) jar lemon curd
1 Tbsp. cornstarch	Pinch of salt	⅓ cup sour cream
4 egg whites, at room temperature	¼ tsp. vanilla extract	Assorted fresh berries
	Parchment paper	Garnish: lemon zest

1. Preheat oven to 225°. Whisk together sugar and cornstarch. Beat egg whites at medium-high speed with a heavy-duty electric stand mixer 1 minute; add cream of tartar and salt, beating until blended. Gradually add sugar mixture, 1 Tbsp. at a time, beating at medium-high speed until mixture is glossy, stiff peaks form, and sugar dissolves. (Do not overbeat.) Beat in vanilla. Gently spread mixture into a 7-inch round on a parchment paper-lined baking sheet, making an indentation in center of meringue to hold filling.

2. Bake at 225° for 1 hour and 30 minutes or until pale golden and outside has formed a crust. Turn oven off; let meringue stand in oven, with door closed and light on, 12 hours.

3. Meanwhile, whisk together lemon curd and sour cream until smooth. Cover and chill.

4. Spoon lemon mixture into center of meringue, and top with berries. (Center of meringue may fall once the lemon mixture and berries have been added.) Garnish, if desired. Makes 8 servings.

RAISING SOUTHERNERS

by Julie Rowell Steed

A map of the world was sprawled across the wall of my daughter's kindergarten classroom. Each child's name was printed on the map, accompanied by arrows pointing to various countries. My mother-in-law seemed surprised to see Mattie's name with an arrow pointing to South America.

I hastily deposited my pecan pie at the refreshment table next to a plate of bratwurst and ran over to look at the map for myself. There was my daughter's name and an arrow pointing to a place I had never even visited. Then it hit me. A few days earlier, Mattie had said, "Mom, where are we from?"

"The South," I responded without hesitation. I should have clarified "the Southeastern United States" so that her kindergarten teacher in Albuquerque would have understood.

I was initially embarrassed to have prepared a Southern treat—pecan pie—for ancestors' day. The other parents had provided exotic international foods: enchiladas, scones, even dolmades. But when I think of my ancestors, I think of the South.

Having been born and bred in Georgia, I have a deep compulsion to raise my children as Southerners, even though they have never lived east of the Mississippi (with the exception of a short stint in Florida). Luckily my husband and I are from the same small town. As we travel the world together, thanks to the Air Force, we strive to teach our children about their heritage.

"Mom, can I have a soda?" Mattie yells from the fridge.

"It's a Coke, not a soda," I holler back, feeling at least one of my grandparents rolling in their graves at her use of the word "soda."

My husband chimes in, "Remember, Asa Chandler was born in Villa Rica, the same town where your granddaddy works. It's a Coke." Denying Mattie's request, I remind her that we are fixin' to eat supper.

"It's not supper, Mom, it's dinner," she replies, totally flustered by my ignorance.

"Where we're from, it's supper," I snap.

Each summer I take the kids to my old stomping grounds for a long visit and plenty of home-cooked suppers, courtesy of doting grandmothers. We attend the church where my husband and I were raised and eventually married. We experience camp meeting, sweat in the humidity, play barefoot in the

creek, and chase lightning bugs. I try desperately to help my girls understand what it means to be from the South.

Is it enough? Are six weeks out of the summer and two desperate parents enough to make our children Southern? Or does a person have to live and breathe the humid Georgia air for years and years before it becomes more than a place on a map? In this case, only time will tell.

The military provides friends who are like family, and for that I am thankful. My children have lived in Japan, climbed a volcano in Hawaii, and hiked in the mountains of northern New Mexico, and for that I am thankful, too. But I am much more appreciative of the generations of Southerners, my ancestors, who laid a firm foundation in a place that will always be home to me.

Pecan pie was perfect for ancestors' day after all!

mama's way or your way

One peach cobbler is a rich summer classic. The other equally delectable version takes a lighter approach.

<u>MAMA'S WAY:</u>
- Double layers of peaches and crust
- Pecan-filled crust
- Family reunion favorite

<u>YOUR WAY:</u>
- Uses less sugar
- Fast prep time
- Individual party servings

mama's way

PECAN-PEACH COBBLER

Hands-on Time: 45 min. Total Time: 1 hr., 41 min.

½ cup chopped pecans
12 to 15 fresh peaches, peeled and sliced (about 16 cups)
⅓ cup all-purpose flour
½ tsp. ground nutmeg
3 cups sugar

⅔ cup butter
1½ tsp. vanilla extract
2 (14.1-oz.) packages refrigerated piecrusts
5 Tbsp. sugar, divided
Sweetened whipped cream

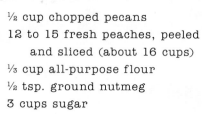

1. PREHEAT oven to 350°. Bake pecans in a single layer in a shallow pan 8 to 10 minutes or until lightly toasted, stirring halfway through.
2. STIR together peaches, flour, nutmeg, and 3 cups sugar in a Dutch oven. Bring to a boil over medium heat; reduce heat to low, and simmer 10 minutes. Remove from heat; stir in butter and vanilla. Spoon half of mixture into a lightly greased 13- x 9-inch baking dish. Increase oven temperature to 475°.
3. Unroll 2 piecrusts. Sprinkle ¼ cup pecans and 2 Tbsp. sugar over 1 piecrust; top with other piecrust. Roll to a 14- x 10-inch rectangle. Trim sides to fit baking dish. Place pastry over peach mixture in dish.
4. BAKE at 475° for 20 to 25 minutes or until lightly browned. Unroll remaining 2 piecrusts. Sprinkle 2 Tbsp. sugar and remaining ¼ cup pecans over 1 piecrust; top with remaining piecrust. Roll into a 12-inch circle. Cut into 1-inch strips, using a fluted pastry wheel.
5. SPOON remaining peach mixture over baked pastry. Arrange pastry strips over peach mixture; sprinkle with remaining 1 Tbsp. sugar. Bake 15 to 18 minutes or until lightly browned. Serve with whipped cream. Makes 10 to 12 servings.

SO-EASY PEACH COBBLER

Hands-on Time: 30 min.   Total Time: 30 min.

¼ cup butter

7 fresh peaches, peeled and sliced (about 7 cups, 3 lb.)

1 cup sugar

2 Tbsp. all-purpose flour

2 Tbsp. fresh lemon juice

¼ tsp. ground cinnamon

½ (14.1-oz.) package refrigerated piecrusts

Parchment paper

1 egg white, lightly beaten

1 Tbsp. sugar

1. Preheat oven to 450°. Melt butter in a Dutch oven over medium heat. Add peaches, 1 cup sugar, and next 3 ingredients; bring to a boil over medium heat, stirring occasionally. Reduce heat to medium-low; simmer 7 to 8 minutes or until tender.

2. Meanwhile, unroll piecrust on a flat surface. Cut into 12 circles, using a 3½-inch round cutter with fluted edges. Make 4 small holes in center of each circle, using a plastic straw. Place circles on a parchment paper-lined baking sheet. Whisk together egg white and 1 Tbsp. water. Brush circles with egg mixture; sprinkle with 1 Tbsp. sugar.

3. Bake at 450° for 8 to 10 minutes or until lightly browned.

4. Place 1 pastry circle in each of 6 (7-oz.) ramekins. Spoon peach mixture over pastry circles; top with remaining pastry circles. Makes 6 servings.

your way

HOLIDAY TRADITIONS

recipes that become the food memories of family celebrations

Holiday meals at our house were grand affairs. It was the time when Mom brought out the crystal and polished the silver and set the table easily a week in advance. The setting was always very formal and the food fancy and exotic or unexpected.

a note from
Marian

That was our tradition...the same old standards were not. You could count on something entirely new and different from year to year and occasion to occasion—beef tenderloin, rack of lamb, crown roast of pork, finger bowls on the table,

and caviar or truffles making an appearance, perhaps. These milestones throughout each year demanded five-star fare in Mom's opinion. She really had fun with it and always went over the top during family holiday gatherings. I suppose, in a way, it was great expectations of what the meal might be that were part of both the thrill and tradition of our family holidays.

ROAST TURKEY WITH CHESTNUT STUFFING

Hands-on Time: 40 min.   Total Time: 5 hr., 5 min., including Chestnut Stuffing and Giblet Gravy

For a festive and colorful presentation, decorate the serving platter with fresh herbs that echo the ones in the stuffing along with seasonal fruit such as kumquats and Concord grapes.

1 (14-lb.) whole turkey	1 tsp. kosher salt	Garnishes: fresh oregano,
Chestnut Stuffing	1 tsp. pepper	fresh thyme, red grapes,
Kitchen string	1 cup chicken broth	kumquats
½ cup butter, melted	Giblet Gravy	

1. Preheat oven to 325°. Remove giblets and neck from turkey; reserve for Giblet Gravy. Rinse turkey thoroughly with cold water. Drain cavity well; pat dry.

2. Place turkey on a work surface, and spoon Chestnut Stuffing into turkey. Tie ends of legs together with string. Tuck wingtips securely under bird.

3. Brush turkey with melted butter, and sprinkle with salt and pepper; place, breast side up, on a roasting rack in a roasting pan. Add broth to pan.

4. Bake at 325° for 3 hours and 30 minutes, basting every 45 minutes with drippings. Bake an additional 30 minutes to 1 hour or until a meat thermometer inserted into thickest portion of thigh registers 180° and center of stuffing registers 165°. (Cover with aluminum foil during last hour of cooking to prevent excessive browning, if necessary.)

5. Transfer turkey to a serving platter, reserving drippings in roasting pan for Giblet Gravy. Skim fat from pan drippings, being careful not to loosen browned particles in pan; discard fat. Let turkey stand 15 minutes before carving. Serve with warm Giblet Gravy. Makes 10 to 12 servings.

CHESTNUT STUFFING

Hands-on Time: 20 min.   Total Time: 20 min.

1 cup butter	1 Tbsp. chopped fresh	1 (14.8-oz.) jar whole
1½ cups chopped celery	oregano	chestnuts
1 medium onion, chopped	½ tsp. pepper	1 cup chicken broth
2 tsp. salt	8 cups soft, fresh	
1 Tbsp. chopped fresh	breadcrumbs	
thyme		

Melt butter in a large Dutch oven over low heat. Add celery and next 5 ingredients, stirring well. Sauté over medium heat 12 minutes or until celery and onion are tender. Remove from heat; gradually add breadcrumbs and chestnuts, stirring until combined. Add chicken broth, and stir to moisten. Makes about 9 cups.

GIBLET GRAVY

Hands-on Time: 25 min.   Total Time: 1 hr., 45 min.

Reserved giblets and neck
from turkey

1   small onion, quartered

2   celery ribs, halved

½   tsp. salt

Reserved pan drippings from
turkey

3   Tbsp. all-purpose flour

1. Reserve turkey liver. Bring remaining giblets, neck, onion, celery, salt, and water to cover to a boil in a medium saucepan over medium heat. Cover, reduce heat to low, and simmer 45 minutes or until giblets are tender. Add liver, and simmer 10 minutes. Drain, reserving broth; discard onion and celery. When cool enough to handle, remove meat from neck; coarsely chop neck meat and giblets.

2. Add reserved broth to roasting pan; bring to a boil over medium-high heat, stirring to loosen browned particles from bottom of pan. Combine broth mixture and enough water to equal 1½ cups, if necessary. Pour mixture into a medium saucepan.

3. Whisk in flour, and cook, whisking constantly, over medium-high heat, 5 minutes or until thickened. Stir in neck meat and giblets. Season with salt and pepper to taste. Makes about 2 cups.

CITY GIRLS, COUNTRY TABLE

by Rick Bragg

For a long time, I lived in fear of a Butterball turkey.

I dreaded pecan pie and anything to do with a giblet. Green bean casserole, even now, makes me uneasy. I glimpse a can of French's French Fried Onions, and it all comes rushing back.

I had not always been frightened of Thanksgiving, of the holidays. I even loved it all as a boy. It meant hot biscuits and cornbread dressing and pools of butter melting into mashed potatoes, and...and then I started keeping company with city girls and started bringing them home to meet my people.

Only then did I begin to regard the season much the same, I believe, as a gobbler does. Maybe this needs some explaining.

I am not a backward hillbilly, though I might appear one from the distance of, say, a nine iron. Up close, I am obviously refined. I have read Sun Tzu. I have seen London, walked the wastes of Ethiopia, and know Kashmir is not the name of a hairdresser in Mountain Brook.

But I am also a boy of the highlands of Alabama, who would rather catch a fish than a foreign film. I know a Georgia Sweet is an onion, and Silver Queen is an ear of corn. I can smell a water moccasin and run a chain saw. I love my people and have honored them in books.

That said, my folks ran off a lot of good women. It usually happened at Thanksgiving, though they lit a match under a few at Christmas, too.

Our little holiday tradition goes back to '77. The lady in question was from the suburbs of Anniston, Alabama, and so a woman of the world. She bought her clothes at Parisian and had been to Six Flags, like, 13 times. We walked into my mother's house to the rich smells of the season.

"What is that?" she asked, sweetly, pointing to a roasted haunch of meat.

"Possum," one of my uncles said.

It was venison, but what fun is that?

She did not make it to the yuletide.

Years later, one young woman from Florida worked up the nerve to spend the night and awoke to gunfire from pretty much every yard for 15 miles.

I tried to explain it was tradition, that everyone was trying out the new guns that Santa Claus brought early, to get ready for deer season.

Another—and I am not making this up—awoke to find me burying a dog. I told her we did not bury a dog every Thanksgiving. She told me, later, she was relieved it was just a dog.

At dinner, my uncles regaled my women with stories of our culture, like the time Uncle Jimbo won a bet by eating a bologna sandwich while sitting on a dead mule. My aunts told stories of the time I sucked a poinsettia berry up my nose. It went that way for years.

Six years ago, a lovely woman from Memphis, who taught college kids and Sunday school, came to meet my people. She brought muffins. I sat in the corner, waiting. She bragged on the green beans.

"They was raised in donkey manure," my little brother said, proudly.

She heard a hundred stories about snake killings and how I had shingles in first grade and cried like a little girl. Cigarette smoke roiled. Snuff drifted in the air.

She was unfazed.

"I raised three boys," is all she said.

We were married in the Peabody hotel.

PERFECT PRIME RIB

Hands-on Time: 10 min.   Total Time: 1 hr., 32 min.

Although it is covered in salt, this prime rib comes out perfectly seasoned; the salt crust locks in all the moisture and flavor, resulting in a perfectly cooked prime rib.

1   (6-lb.) boneless prime rib roast
1   Tbsp. Worcestershire sauce
1   tsp. garlic powder
3   Tbsp. cracked pepper
2   (4-lb.) boxes rock salt

1. Preheat oven to 500°. Brush roast with Worcestershire sauce; sprinkle with garlic powder. Rub pepper on all sides of roast.

2. Pour salt to a depth of ½ inch into a disposable aluminum roasting pan; place roast in center of pan. Pat remaining salt onto roast; sprinkle with ½ cup water.

3. Bake at 500° for 12 minutes per pound or until a meat thermometer inserted in thickest portion registers 145° (medium-rare) or to desired degree of doneness. (Be sure to use a meat thermometer for best results.) Crack salt with a hammer; remove roast, and brush away rock salt. Let stand at least 15 minutes before serving. Makes 12 to 15 servings.

"I love barbecue. Always have. From the first time that I had it with a sticky sweet sauce as a kid living in Kentucky and Tennessee, to beef when I lived in Oklahoma, to the ultimate barbecue dream of participating in the Memphis in May barbecue cook-off, I've always enjoyed the combination of meat and smoke and vinegar. I felt enlightened the first time I tried barbecue in North Carolina. It may be the most perfect combination of meat and garnish ever. In fine-dining kitchens, you are always trying to convey the idea of balance in a dish to new cooks, and it is my go-to example of what that means. It is familiar to everyone. Delicious smoked pork is the base and fat, with the vinegar sauce to cut it, and just a bit of coleslaw for crunch and sweetness. You can actually taste the time dedicated to bringing that dish to the plate. It makes me hungry just thinking about it."

—Chef Stephen Stryjewski
Cochon Restaurant

ROAST LEG OF LAMB

Hands-on Time: 15 min.   Total Time: 4 hr.,
including Mint Sauce

*Succulent roast lamb is the centerpiece of the Easter celebration.
It's a sure sign of spring.*

1   (5- to 6-lb.) leg of lamb
¼   cup butter, melted
2   tsp. salt
1   tsp. freshly ground pepper
1   tsp. dried rosemary
Mint Sauce or mint jelly

1. Pat lamb dry, and place, fat side up, on a rack in a shallow
roasting pan. Combine butter and next 3 ingredients; rub
butter mixture over lamb. Cover loosely with aluminum foil,
and let stand at room temperature 30 minutes.
2. Meanwhile, preheat oven to 400°. Uncover lamb, and
bake at 400° for 2 hours and 30 minutes or until a meat
thermometer inserted into thickest portion registers 145°
(medium-rare). Let stand 30 minutes before slicing. Serve
with Mint Sauce. Makes 8 servings.

MINT SAUCE

Hands-on Time: 15 min.   Total Time: 15 min.

¼   cup chopped fresh mint leaves
¼   cup light corn syrup
1½   Tbsp. white vinegar
1½   tsp. cornstarch

Combine mint leaves, corn syrup, and vinegar in a small
saucepan. Whisk together cornstarch and ¼ cup water,
whisking until blended. Add to mint mixture. Cook over
medium heat, whisking constantly, 3 minutes or until
thickened and bubbly. If desired, pour sauce through a fine
wire-mesh strainer into a serving bowl, discarding solids.
Makes ½ cup.

TASTY TRIVIA

Lamb sent to market is
divided into large whole-
sale cuts that butchers
later divide into smaller
cuts. It's important to
have an idea where each
cut comes from because
this will tell you how
tender it will probably
be. Keep in mind that all
lamb tends to be tender
because it comes from
such a young animal.
However, the tenderest
cuts come from the lightly
used muscles along the
upper back (rib and loin
sections), and the less
tender cuts come from the
more heavily used muscles
(shoulder, leg, foreshank,
and breast). Except for
the shank cuts, you can
use dry-heat cooking methods. Roast, grill, broil, or
panbroil the rack, loin,
shoulder, and leg cuts.
Braising and cooking in
liquid, which are moist-
heat methods, are better
when preparing the
less-tender shank cuts.

SAUSAGE-CORNBREAD DRESSING

Hands-on Time: 30 min.   Total Time: 1 hr., 40 min.

You can make your own cornbread muffins, but to save time, pick up some from the supermarket deli or from the freezer section.

10 (2-inch) cornbread muffins, crumbled (about 5⅓ cups)

6 white sandwich bread slices, torn into small pieces

2 (14-oz.) cans chicken broth

3 Tbsp. butter

2 medium onions, chopped

4 celery ribs, chopped

½ (1-lb.) package mild ground pork sausage

2 large eggs, lightly beaten

¼ tsp. pepper

1. Preheat oven to 350°. Lightly grease a 13- x 9-inch baking dish. Soak cornbread and sandwich bread in chicken broth in a large bowl 10 minutes; stir until liquid is absorbed.

2. Melt butter in a large skillet over medium heat; add onions and celery, and sauté 10 to 12 minutes or until tender. Add sausage, and cook, stirring often, over low heat 8 minutes or until sausage crumbles and is no longer pink; drain. Add sausage mixture, eggs, and pepper to bread mixture; stir well. Spoon dressing into prepared dish.

3. Bake at 350° for 1 hour or until lightly browned. Makes 8 servings.

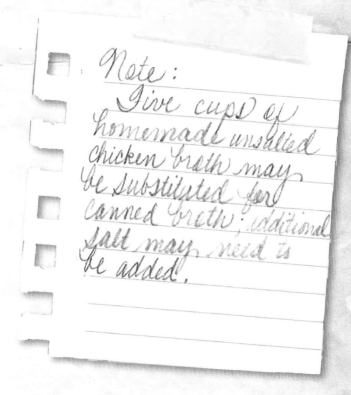

Note:
Five cups of homemade unsalted chicken broth may be substituted for canned broth; additional salt may need to be added.

TART CRANBERRY SAUCE

Hands-on Time: 13 min.   Total Time: 30 min.

When fresh cranberries are in season, stock up and freeze. No need to remove them from the bag. They freeze beautifully.

2   cups fresh cranberries
½   cup honey
2   Tbsp. orange zest

½   tsp. ground cinnamon
¼   tsp. ground cloves
¼   tsp. ground ginger

COMBINE cranberries and ½ cup water in a medium-size heavy saucepan; bring to a boil over medium-high heat. Cook, stirring often, 8 to 10 minutes or until cranberry skins begin to pop. Remove from heat, and cool 15 minutes. (Mixture will thicken as it cools.) Stir in honey and remaining ingredients. Serve warm or cold with turkey or ham. Makes about 1½ cups.

MICROWAVE DIRECTIONS:
COMBINE cranberries and ½ cup water in a microwave-safe 2-qt. baking dish. Microwave, covered, at HIGH 5 minutes or until cranberry skins begin to pop. Stir in honey and remaining ingredients.

HOLIDAY CRANBERRY SALAD

Hands-on Time: 5 min.   Total Time: 1 hr., 38 min., plus 8 hr. for chilling

Remember the first time you tasted a gelatin salad? The squiggly mixture was magic in your mouth! Continue the fun and make this colorful, festive salad a part of your holiday menu.

1 cup chopped walnuts	1 cup sugar	1 cup boiling water
2 cups fresh or frozen cranberries, thawed	1 (3-oz.) package lemon-flavored gelatin	1 cup chopped celery Lettuce leaves

1. Preheat oven to 350°. Bake walnuts in a single layer in a shallow pan 8 to 10 minutes or until toasted, stirring halfway through.
2. Process cranberries in a food processor 30 seconds or until chopped, stopping to scrape down sides as needed.
3. Combine cranberries and sugar in a large bowl; let stand 1 hour or until sugar dissolves.
4. Combine gelatin and 1 cup boiling water in a large bowl; stir 2 minutes or until gelatin dissolves. Chill until the consistency of unbeaten egg white.
5. Stir cranberry mixture, celery, and walnuts into gelatin mixture. Pour into a lightly greased 4-cup mold. Cover and chill 8 hours or until firm.
6. Unmold salad onto a lettuce-lined plate. Makes 6 to 8 servings.

POPOVERS

Hands-on Time: 10 min.   Total Time: 50 min.

Popovers rise and bake into crusty, golden shells that you can serve alone or filled with chicken salad or ice cream. Eggs and high heat give this specialty quick bread its lift and lightness.

1 cup all-purpose flour	2 large eggs, lightly beaten	2 Tbsp. butter, melted
½ tsp. salt	1 cup milk	

1. Preheat oven to 450°. Heat a popover pan in oven while oven preheats.
2. Sift together flour and salt. Combine eggs and milk. Add milk mixture to dry ingredients, stirring just until blended.
3. Remove pan from oven; brush pan with melted butter. Pour batter into pan, filling each cup half full.
4. Bake at 450° for 15 minutes; reduce oven temperature to 350°, and bake 25 more minutes or until golden brown and crusty. Remove pan to a wire rack; pierce sides of popovers with the tip of a knife to release steam. Serve hot. Makes 6 servings.

GREEN BEAN CASSEROLE

Hands-on Time: 20 min.   Total Time: 1 hr., 10 min.

A holiday mainstay, this classic casserole gets an update using frozen green beans instead of canned. The end result is still the same great dish.

1 (2-oz.) package slivered almonds

2 (16-oz.) packages frozen French-style green beans

1 cup warm water

1 (10¾-oz.) can cream of mushroom soup

1 cup milk

4 oz. cream cheese, softened

1 (8-oz.) can sliced water chestnuts, drained

1½ cups (6 oz.) shredded Cheddar cheese

1 (2.8-oz.) can French fried onions, divided

¼ cup sour cream

2 Tbsp. finely chopped onion

1 garlic clove, minced

½ tsp. salt

½ tsp. pepper

1. Preheat oven to 350 °. Bake almonds in a single layer in a shallow pan 5 to 7 minutes or until toasted, stirring halfway through.

2. Lightly grease a 2-qt. baking dish.

3. Place beans and 1 cup warm water in a large microwave-safe bowl. Cover with plastic wrap, and microwave at HIGH 15 minutes or until tender, stirring halfway through cooking time; drain.

4. Combine soup, milk, and cream cheese in a large saucepan. Cook over medium heat, stirring constantly, 5 minutes or until cream cheese melts. Remove from heat; stir in green beans, water chestnuts, cheese, ⅔ cup fried onions, and next 5 ingredients. Spoon mixture into prepared baking dish.

5. Bake at 350° for 30 minutes. Top with almonds and remaining fried onions. Makes 8 servings.

CLASSIC CHEESE SOUFFLÉ

Hands-on Time: 45 min.   Total Time: 1 hr., 10 min.

This sunny soufflé has a certain "wow" factor. Substitute mild Cheddar cheese for high-voltage sharp Cheddar, if you'd like.

2 Tbsp. butter	¼ tsp. dry mustard	1½ cups (6 oz.) shredded
¼ cup all-purpose flour	⅛ tsp. hot sauce	sharp Cheddar cheese
½ tsp. salt	1 cup milk	6 large eggs, separated
¼ tsp. pepper		

1. Preheat oven to 475°. Lightly butter a 2-qt. soufflé dish. Cut a piece of aluminum foil long enough to fit around dish, allowing a 1-inch overlap; fold foil lengthwise into thirds. Lightly butter 1 side of foil and bottom of dish. Wrap foil around outside of dish, buttered side against dish, allowing it to extend 3 inches above the rim to form a collar; secure with string.

2. Melt 2 Tbsp. butter in a heavy saucepan over low heat; whisk in flour and next 4 ingredients, whisking until smooth. Cook over low heat, stirring constantly, 1 minute. Gradually add milk; cook over medium heat, stirring constantly, until thickened and bubbly. Add cheese, stirring until melted; remove from heat.

3. Whisk egg yolks until thick and pale. Gradually stir about one-fourth of hot cheese mixture into yolks; add yolk mixture to remaining hot cheese mixture, stirring constantly.

4. Beat egg whites at high speed with an electric mixer until stiff peaks form; fold into cheese mixture. Pour into prepared soufflé dish.

5. Bake at 475° for 10 minutes. Reduce oven temperature to 400°, and bake 15 more minutes or until puffed and golden brown. Remove collar, and serve immediately. Makes 6 servings.

Individual Cheese Soufflés: Spoon cheese mixture into 6 (10-oz.) buttered soufflé dishes or custard cups. Bake at 350° for 15 to 20 minutes or until puffed and golden brown.

Note: Individual Cheese Soufflés may be frozen before baking; cover with plastic wrap, and freeze. To bake, place frozen soufflés on baking sheet; bake at 350° for 40 minutes or until golden brown. Use only freezer-to-oven dishes.

DRESSED-UP POTATOES

Hands-on Time: 10 min.   Total Time: 1 hr.

When using a mixer with potatoes, beat just until whipped. Overbeating them leads to gluey, gummy spuds. A potato masher gives you more control of the outcome—creamy or chunky.

12 medium potatoes (about 5¾ lb.), peeled and quartered
1 (8-oz.) container sour cream
½ cup milk
2 Tbsp. chopped fresh chives
3 tsp. salt
¼ tsp. ground white pepper
⅛ tsp. onion powder
⅛ tsp. garlic powder
¼ cup butter, melted
⅓ cup sliced almonds

1. Preheat oven to 400°. Grease a 13- x 9-inch baking dish. Bring potatoes and water to cover to a boil in a large Dutch oven over medium-high heat, and cook 20 minutes or until tender; drain and mash.
2. Add sour cream and next 6 ingredients to potatoes; beat at low speed with an electric mixer just until blended. (Do not overbeat.) Spoon potato mixture into prepared dish.
3. Drizzle butter lightly over top; sprinkle with almonds.
4. Bake at 400° for 15 minutes or until golden brown. Increase oven temperature to broil, and broil just until browned. Makes 10 to 12 servings.

"My best food memory is enjoying Thanksgiving dinner with my family. I start off with some white meat turkey, then mashed potatoes with a generous serving of corn on the top, a little dressing, and a spoonful of my mom's spinach soufflé. Lastly, everything except the soufflé gets smothered with gravy. Dessert is normally a second helping of the above before rolling off my chair for a long nap."

—Mark Richt
UGA Football Coach

PARTY'S OVER NOBODY'S HOME

by Ann Patchett

When I was a child, Thanksgiving and Christmas were two separate holidays, and the month I had to wait in between them was a tortuous eternity. Now, it seems as if Thanksgiving and Christmas arrive in the same week. I'm finishing off the turkey soup while baking the first batch of tree-shaped cookies. I barely get fresh sheets tucked in the beds of the departing Thanksgiving guests before the Christmas guests start ringing the doorbell. So forgive me if it feels like I'm rushing things here, talking about December in November, but really, I have to figure out what I'm going to do about our great big holiday party.

My husband (who's from Mississippi) and I were both born under the sign of The More The Merrier. Five years ago we decided to invite friends over for a little Christmas Eve party. Our friends invited various strays who had no place to go. Bring them along! I'm a great believer in showing love to holiday strays. And, why yes, the strays can bring their in-laws who are driving them crazy. After all, sit-down holiday dinners with mismatched families, various exes, and exes of exes can be awkward for everyone, but if you fill up the entire house, it's easy for certain key family members to avoid one another. I hired a piano player. My sister had books of carols printed up. We told folks to bring ornaments for a swap. Our house was bursting with people I'd never seen before in my life—and they were all having a fabulous time. It was a huge success. Huge.

And the next year? They all came back.

Apparently, my husband and I throw a fantastic Christmas Eve party, but it's starting to feel like the monster I can't cram back into the box. We're fast on our way to becoming a can't-miss holiday tradition for people whose names I've yet to catch. There are children—loads of them—who are growing up believing that Santa gets his work done when they're at our house. How do you pull the plug on that? Seeing as I've never sent out invitations before, I hardly think that skipping that step this year will be a deterrent to these people.

All this party business reminds me of when I was a child and my family drove to Rome, Georgia, every year to visit friends who had a spectacular New Year's Day party. They filled up a big bathtub with ice and

bottles of Champagne, and my sister and I were entrusted to pour the bubbly and Bloody Marys. We loved our role as tiny cocktail waitresses, we loved the party, but I wonder now if those Georgian friends might have enjoyed the occasional quiet and sober January first. I wonder if the hosts ever felt there was no way out.

I guess we could always go to Barbados for Christmas. Although I can see it now: partygoers standing on our dark front porch, peering in the windows. I mean, who's to say they wouldn't carry on without us? Many of them never knew whose house it was anyway. I could just leave the front door open and the twinkle lights on. Hire a caterer and send the piano player a check.

Merry Christmas to all.

CHRISTMAS MORNING STRATA

Hands-on Time: 18 min.   Total Time: 58 min., plus 8 hr. for chilling

Get a jump start on your day by preparing this make-ahead casserole. Assemble it the night before, and refrigerate it. Forget alarm clocks—the aroma of baking strata will bring them to the table the next morning.

1 (1-lb.) package ground pork sausage	1 cup (4 oz.) shredded sharp Cheddar cheese	¼ tsp. salt
6 white sandwich bread slices, torn into pieces	1½ cups milk	¼ tsp. pepper
1 cup (4 oz.) shredded Swiss cheese	1 tsp. Dijon mustard	
	3 large eggs, lightly beaten	
	½ tsp. Worcestershire sauce	

1. Grease an 11- x 7-inch baking dish.
2. Cook sausage in a large skillet over medium heat, stirring often, 8 minutes or until sausage crumbles and is no longer pink; drain well.
3. Arrange bread in a single layer in prepared baking dish; top with sausage and cheeses.
4. Combine milk and remaining ingredients; pour over bread mixture. Cover and chill 8 to 24 hours.
5. Preheat oven to 350°. Bake at 350° for 40 minutes or until set. Makes 6 servings.

COUNTRY HAM WITH REDEYE GRAVY

Hands-on Time: 30 min.   Total Time: 30 min.

Served with creamy grits and biscuits to sop the gravy, this traditional Southern favorite is a grand morning eye-opener.

½ cup strong brewed coffee	6 (¼-inch-thick) slices country ham	2 Tbsp. butter, melted
2 Tbsp. firmly packed light brown sugar		

1. Stir together coffee and sugar. Cook ham in butter in a large cast-iron skillet over medium heat 2 minutes on each side or until lightly browned. Remove ham from skillet, reserving drippings in skillet. Keep ham warm.
2. Add coffee mixture to reserved drippings in skillet, stirring to loosen particles from bottom of skillet; bring to a boil. Boil, stirring occasionally, 5 minutes or until reduced by half. Serve with ham. Makes 6 servings.

Christmas Morning Strata

FAVORITE PECAN PIE

Hands-on Time: 18 min.   Total Time: 1 hr., 53 min.

In the South, we prize our pecans and showcase them in this classic dessert. It's this regional favorite that made Southern pies famous.

½	(14.1-oz.) package refrigerated piecrusts	1 cup sugar
½	cup butter, melted	1 cup light corn syrup
		4 large eggs, lightly beaten

1 tsp. vanilla extract
¼ tsp. salt
1 to 1¼ cups pecan halves

1. Preheat oven to 325°. Fit piecrust into a 9-inch pie plate according to package directions; fold edges under, and crimp.

2. Stir together butter, sugar, and corn syrup in a medium saucepan; bring to a boil over medium heat, stirring constantly. Cook, stirring constantly, 3 minutes or until sugar dissolves. Remove from heat. Cool slightly (about 5 minutes). Whisk together eggs, vanilla, and salt, whisking until well blended. Stir into sugar mixture.

3. Pour filling into prepared piecrust, and top with pecan halves.

4. Bake at 325° for 50 to 55 minutes or until filling is set. Cool completely in pan on a wire rack (about 30 minutes). Makes 8 servings.

Rum Pecan Pie: Prepare recipe as directed, adding 3 Tbsp. rum with the egg mixture; mix well.

COCONUT CAKE

Hands-on Time: 1 hr., 2 min.   Total Time: 3 hr., 10 min., including Coconut
Filling and Whipped Cream Frosting

Large flakes of toasted coconut make a beautiful garnish for this cream-filled cake. Look for organic unsweetened coconut flakes at health and specialty grocery stores. You may substitute regular sweetened flaked coconut, if you'd prefer.

3 cups all-purpose flour	1 cup milk	Coconut Filling
1 tsp. baking powder	2 tsp. coconut extract	Whipped Cream Frosting
½ tsp. salt	5 large eggs	
2⅔ cups sugar	1 (6-oz.) package frozen	
1 cup shortening	flaked coconut, thawed	
½ cup butter, softened	Coconut shavings	

1. Preheat oven to 400°. Grease and flour 4 (9-inch) round cake pans.

2. Beat first 7 ingredients at medium speed with an electric mixer until well blended. Add extract, beating well. Add eggs, 1 at a time, beating until blended after each addition. Stir in flaked coconut. Pour batter into prepared pans.

3. Bake at 400° for 20 minutes or until a wooden pick inserted in center comes out clean. Let cool in pans on wire racks 10 minutes. Remove from pans to wire racks, and cool completely (about 1 hour).

4. Meanwhile, reduce oven temperature to 350°. Arrange coconut shavings in a single layer in a shallow pan. Bake, stirring occasionally, 8 to 10 minutes or until toasted.

5. Spread Coconut Filling between layers of cake, leaving a 1-inch border. Spread Whipped Cream Frosting on top and sides of cake. Sprinkle toasted coconut on top of cake, pressing gently to adhere. Makes 12 servings.

COCONUT FILLING

Hands-on Time: 22 min.   Total Time: 52 min.

1 cup sugar	2 large eggs, lightly beaten	½ tsp. vanilla extract
2 Tbsp. all-purpose flour	1 (6-oz.) package frozen	½ tsp. coconut extract
1 cup milk	flaked coconut, thawed	

Cook first 4 ingredients in a large saucepan over medium-low heat, whisking constantly, 12 to 15 minutes or until thickened and bubbly. Remove from heat, and stir in coconut and extracts. Let cool completely (about 30 minutes). Makes about 3 cups.

WHIPPED CREAM FROSTING

Hands-on Time: 10 min.   Total Time: 10 min.

1½ cups heavy cream	3 Tbsp. powdered sugar	1½ tsp. coconut extract

Beat all ingredients at high speed with an electric mixer until stiff peaks form. Makes about 3 cups.

CHOCOLATE YULE LOG

Hands-on Time: 44 min.   Total Time: 2 hr., 9 min.,
including Creamy Mocha Frosting

Vegetable oil
Wax paper
¾ cup cake flour
¼ cup unsweetened cocoa
¼ tsp. salt
5 eggs, separated

1 cup granulated sugar, divided
1 Tbsp. lemon juice
2 to 3 Tbsp. powdered sugar

1 cup whipping cream, whipped
Creamy Mocha Frosting
Candied cherries

1. Preheat oven to 350°. Grease bottom and sides of a 15- x 10-inch jelly-roll pan with vegetable oil; line with wax paper, and grease lightly.

2. Sift together flour, cocoa, and salt. Beat egg yolks at high speed with an electric mixer 5 minutes or until thick and pale. Gradually add ½ cup granulated sugar, beating well. Stir in lemon juice.

3. Beat egg whites (at room temperature) at medium speed until foamy. Gradually add remaining ½ c. granulated sugar, beating until stiff. Gently fold egg yolk mixture into whites. Gradually fold flour mixture into egg mixture. Spread batter evenly in prepared pan. Bake at 350° for 15 to 20 minutes or until top springs back when lightly touched.

4. Sift powdered sugar in a 15- x 10-inch rectangle on a linen towel. When cake is done, immediately loosen from sides of pan, and turn out onto sugar. Peel off wax paper. Starting at narrow end, roll up cake and towel together; cool on a wire rack, seam side down. Unroll cake, and remove towel. Spread cake with whipped cream. Carefully reroll cake, without towel, and place on serving plate, seam side down; chill at least 1 hour.

5. Spread Creamy Mocha Frosting over cake roll. Garnish with candied cherries. Makes 10 to 12 servings.

CREAMY MOCHA FROSTING

Hands-on Time: 11 min.   Total Time: 21 min.

1 Tbsp. instant coffee granules
⅓ cup boiling water

3 (1-oz.) unsweetened chocolate baking squares
¼ cup butter

Dash of salt
2½ cups sifted powdered sugar

1. Combine coffee granules and boiling water, stirring until coffee is dissolved.

2. Combine chocolate, butter, and salt in top of a double boiler. Cook over medium heat, stirring until smooth. Remove from heat; cool.

3. Stir chocolate mixture into coffee. Gradually add powdered sugar, beating at medium speed with an electric mixer until smooth and creamy (about 1 minute). Frosting will thicken while spreading. Makes 1⅔ cups.

Note: Yule log will slice neatly if stored in refrigerator until serving time.

WASSAIL

Hands-on Time: 10 min.   Total Time: 2 hr., 20 min.

Welcome guests with this warming beverage at your next holiday party. Depending on the guests, you can increase or decrease the amount of bourbon.

¾   cup sugar
6   whole cloves
1   (3-inch) cinnamon stick
½   tsp. whole allspice
1   Tbsp. chopped
     crystallized ginger

1   Tbsp. lemon zest
1   Tbsp. orange zest
Kitchen string
Cheesecloth
2   cups unsweetened apple
     cider

1½ cups fresh orange juice
¾   cup fresh lemon juice
½   cup bourbon (optional)

1. Combine sugar and 1 cup water in a medium saucepan; bring to a boil. Boil, stirring often, 5 minutes or until sugar dissolves.
2. Place cloves and next 5 ingredients on a 5-inch square of cheesecloth. Gather edges of cheesecloth, and tie securely with kitchen string. Place spice bag in hot mixture. Remove from heat. Cover and let stand 2 hours; discard spice bag.
3. Stir in apple cider, orange juice, and lemon juice; bring to a boil. Remove from heat; add bourbon, if desired. Serve hot. Makes 5½ cups.

CLASSIC EGGNOG

Hands-on Time: 45 min.   Total Time: 5 hr., 45 min.

A cup of this Christmas cheer is sheer decadence. Don't forget to keep eggnog cool when it's in a punch bowl; even after cooking, eggs and milk remain perishable.

1½ cups sugar
12 large eggs
4   cups half-and-half
4   cups milk

¼   tsp. salt
½   to ¾ cup bourbon
½   to ¾ cup brandy

2   tsp. vanilla extract
2   cups whipping cream
2   tsp. ground nutmeg

1. Beat sugar and eggs in a large mixing bowl at high speed with an electric mixer until blended.
2. Stir together half-and-half, milk, and salt in a Dutch oven over medium-low heat. Cook, stirring occasionally, 12 minutes or just until mixture begins to bubble around edges of pan. (Do not boil).
3. Gradually add half of hot milk mixture to egg mixture using a hand-held blender. Stir egg mixture into remaining hot milk mixture in Dutch oven.
4. Cook over medium-low heat, stirring constantly, 10 minutes or until mixture thickens slightly and a thermometer registers 160°. Remove from heat, and stir 1 minute. Stir in bourbon, brandy, and vanilla. Chill, uncovered, 1 hour. Cover and chill 4 to 48 hours or until very cold.
5. Beat whipping cream at high speed until soft peaks form. Fold whipped cream into chilled eggnog, and sprinkle with nutmeg. Makes 15½ cups.

CANDIED CITRUS PEEL

Hands-on Time: 10 min.   Total Time: 2 hr., 30 min.

Good cooks never let anything go to waste. And this recipe is no exception. The citrus peel is turned into a holiday dessert nibble. When removing the peel, be careful not to include the bitter white pith. Save the juice of the peeled lemons to make lemonade or curd.

3   navel oranges or
     4 lemons

1   cup sugar plus ½ cup for
     rolling

1. Remove peel from citrus, using a vegetable peeler or sharp knife. Cut peel into ¼-inch-wide strips.
2. Place peel and 1 cup water in a medium saucepan. Bring to a boil over medium-high heat. Boil, covered, 30 minutes; drain. Repeat procedure twice. (Repeat procedure 3 times if using lemon. Lemon peel may need longer boiling.) Bring 1 cup sugar and ¼ cup water to a boil over medium-high heat, stirring until sugar dissolves; add peel, reduce heat to low, and simmer until syrup is almost absorbed and peel is translucent (about 40 minutes). Drain and roll peel in ½ cup sugar. Let dry on a wire rack. Makes about 2 cups.

PEANUT BRITTLE

Hands-on Time: 45 min.   Total Time: 1 hr., 15 min.

Georgia is known for its peanut crop. The locals like to use raw peanuts for roasted, salted nuts in the fall and for peanut brittle during the holidays.

Butter
2   cups sugar
1   cup light corn syrup

2½   cups raw peanuts
½   tsp. baking soda

1   Tbsp. butter
1   tsp. vanilla extract

1. Preheat oven to 250°. Lightly butter a 15- x 10-inch jelly-roll pan. Heat pan in oven 5 minutes.
2. Stir together sugar and syrup in a large heavy saucepan; cook over medium-low heat, stirring occasionally, 25 minutes or until sugar mixture starts to bubble and a candy thermometer registers 240° (soft ball stage). Cover pan, and cook 2 to 3 minutes to wash down sugar crystals from sides of pan.
3. Add peanuts; cook over medium-low heat, without stirring, until candy thermometer registers 300° (hard crack stage), about 25 minutes. Remove from heat; stir in baking soda, 1 Tbsp. butter, and vanilla. Spread mixture onto warm pan. Cool completely (about 1 hour); break into pieces. Makes about 2 lb.

PULLED CANDY

Hands-on Time: 50 min.   Total Time: 1 hr., 30 min.

Years past, in the snowy winters of the Blue Ridge Mountains, women and girls busied themselves with handwork while the men whittled by the fire. The teenagers? They pulled taffy for fun!

Butter
3   cups sugar
½   cup light corn syrup
¼   cup white vinegar
¼   tsp. orange or peppermint extract
Desired food coloring
Wax paper

1. Lightly butter a 15- x 10-inch jelly-roll pan.
2. Combine sugar, corn syrup, vinegar, and ½ cup water in a large saucepan. Cook over medium-low heat, stirring occasionally, 5 to 10 minutes or until sugar dissolves. (Do not stir after sugar is dissolved.) Cover and cook over medium heat 2 to 3 minutes to wash down sugar crystals from sides of pan. Uncover and cook, without stirring, until a candy thermometer registers 270° (soft crack stage), about 25 minutes. Remove from heat. Add ¼ tsp. orange or peppermint extract and desired food coloring. Pour into prepared pan. Let cool 10 minutes.
3. With buttered hands, pull candy until porous and light colored (about 30 minutes). Cut into small pieces, using buttered kitchen shears. Wrap in wax paper. Makes about 100 (1-inch) pieces.

TASTY TRIVIA

This soft, chewy candy is made with cooked sugar, butter, and flavoring; the mixture is pulled repeatedly into long ropes and twisted as it cools, giving it a shiny opaque color. Saltwater taffy, made popular in the late 1800s in Atlantic City, was given its name because a small amount of saltwater was added to the mixture.

Tips for pulling taffy:

• When taffy is cool enough to handle, pull it with buttered hands until it lightens in color, becomes more elastic and springs back. (Look for parallel ridges that will form on the surface.)
• When the taffy is ready for cutting, pull it into a rope about ½ to ¾ inch in diameter, and cut with buttered shears or a knife.

SOUTHERN PRALINES

Hands-on Time: 30 min.   Total Time: 40 min.

Pralines are the South's iconic candy. These irresistible nuggets of caramel and pecans aren't difficult to make, and the requirements are few: plenty of stirring, patience, and careful attention. A candy thermometer is a surefire key to success.

2   cups sugar
2   cups pecan halves
¾   cup buttermilk
2   Tbsp. butter
⅛   tsp. salt
¾   tsp. baking soda
Parchment paper

1. Combine first 5 ingredients in a large heavy saucepan. Cook over low heat, stirring gently, 10 minutes or until sugar dissolves. Cover and cook over medium heat 2 to 3 minutes to wash down sugar crystals from sides of pan. Uncover and cook, stirring constantly, until a candy thermometer registers 235° (soft ball stage).

2. Remove from heat, and stir in baking soda. Beat with a wooden spoon just until mixture begins to thicken. Working rapidly, drop by tablespoonfuls onto parchment paper; let stand 30 minutes or until firm. Makes 1½ to 2 dozen.

TASTY TRIVIA

This delectable Louisiana brittle candy dates back to 1750. Originally the patty-shaped, fudge-like delicacy was made with almonds—the preferred nut of the French—and was considered an aid to digestion at the end of a meal. However, the Creoles quickly found a better alternative in the abundant pecan and replaced the white sugar with brown. Today it's considered one of the paramount sweets in the South, particularly in Texas and Louisiana.

DIVINITY

Hands-on Time: 50 min.   Total Time: 1 hr., 30 min.

Don't leave anything to chance when making candy. Choose a sunny day with low humidity, gather your equipment before you begin, and measure ingredients precisely. This will help ensure your divinity is feather-light and tender.

1 cup chopped pecans	½ cup light corn syrup	1 tsp. vanilla extract
Wax paper	¼ tsp. salt	
2½ cups sugar	2 egg whites	

1. Preheat oven to 350°. Bake pecans in a single layer in a shallow pan 8 to 10 minutes or until lightly toasted, stirring halfway through. Lightly grease wax paper.

2. Combine sugar, corn syrup, salt, and ½ cup water in a heavy 2-qt. saucepan, and cook over low heat, stirring until sugar dissolves and a candy thermometer registers 248° (firm ball stage). Remove from heat.

3. Beat egg whites at high speed with an electric mixer until stiff peaks form. Gradually add half of hot syrup to egg whites in a slow, steady stream, beating constantly at high speed 5 minutes. Cook remaining syrup over medium heat, stirring occasionally, 4 to 5 minutes or until a candy thermometer registers 272° (soft crack stage). Gradually add hot syrup and vanilla to egg white mixture in a slow, steady stream, beating constantly at high speed until mixture holds its shape (6 to 8 minutes). Stir in chopped pecans.

4. Drop mixture quickly by rounded teaspoonfuls onto greased wax paper. Cool 30 minutes. Makes about 1¾ lb.

Cherry Divinity: Substitute 1 cup chopped red candied cherries for pecans.

Peanut Ripple Divinity: Omit pecans, and stir in ½ cup peanut butter morsels and ½ cup chopped roasted peanuts.

DECEMBER 1966 35¢

Southern Living®

BOURBON BONBONS

Hands-on Time: 30 min.   Total Time: 2 hr.

Keep these bonbons in the refrigerator until ready to serve so they stay firm. They soften once they stand at room temperature.

1½ cups finely chopped pecans	1½ Tbsp. milk	2 Tbsp. shortening
½ cup butter, softened	5½ cups powdered sugar	Wax paper
⅓ cup bourbon	2½ cups semisweet chocolate morsels	

1. Preheat oven to 350°. Bake pecans in a single layer in a shallow pan 8 to 10 minutes or until lightly toasted, stirring halfway through.

2. Beat butter at medium speed with an electric mixer until creamy. Add bourbon and milk; beat until blended. Gradually add sugar, 1 cup at a time, beating until well blended after each addition. Stir in pecans. Chill 1 hour. Shape into ¾-inch balls; freeze 20 minutes or until firm.

3. Microwave chocolate morsels and shortening in a medium-size microwave-safe bowl at HIGH 1 to 2 minutes or until melted, stirring every 30 seconds. Dip each ball of candy into chocolate mixture. Place on wax paper to cool. Store in refrigerator. Makes about 4 dozen.

GINGERBREAD MEN COOKIES

Hands-on Time: 30 min.   Total Time: 1 hr., plus 8 hr. for chilling

You can make these cookies ahead and freeze them for several months in airtight containers. When Santa's fans drop in, you're ready with treats.

1 cup butter, softened	2 Tbsp. white vinegar	1 Tbsp. ground ginger
1 cup sugar	1 large egg	1 tsp. ground cinnamon
½ tsp. salt	5 cups all-purpose flour	1 tsp. ground cloves
1 cup molasses	1½ tsp. baking soda	Currants

1. Beat butter at medium speed with an electric mixer until creamy; gradually add next 2 ingredients, beating well. Add molasses and next 2 ingredients, beating at low speed just until blended.

2. Combine flour and next 4 ingredients; add to butter mixture, beating at low speed until blended. Cover and chill 8 hours.

3. Preheat oven to 375°. Lightly grease baking sheets or line with parchment paper. Divide dough into fourths. Place dough portions on a lightly floured surface, and roll each portion to ⅛-inch thickness. Cut with a 3-inch gingerbread man cookie cutter; place 2 inches apart on prepared baking sheets. Press currants into dough for eyes, nose, and mouth.

4. Bake at 375° for 8 minutes. Cool on baking sheets 1 minute; remove to wire racks to cool completely (about 20 minutes). Store in airtight containers. Makes about 4 dozen.

Gingerbread Men Cookies

PECAN TASSIES

Hands-on Time: 15 min.   Total Time: 1 hr., including Tart Shells

A tender, flaky crust cradles a gooey pecan filling. You can bake these delicious delights in batches if you don't have enough mini muffin pans on hand. Just keep the dough chilled until ready to roll.

¾ cup firmly packed light brown sugar	1 large egg	⅛ tsp. salt
¾ cup chopped pecans	1 Tbsp. butter, softened	Tart Shells
	1 tsp. vanilla extract	

1. Preheat oven to 350°. Whisk together brown sugar and next 5 ingredients; spoon into Tart Shells, filling three-fourths full.

2. Bake at 350° for 20 minutes or until filling is set. Cool in pans on a wire racks 10 minutes. Remove from pans; cool on wire racks 20 minutes or until completely cool. Makes 2 dozen.

TART SHELLS

Hands-on Time: 15 min.   Total Time: 15 min.

¼ cup plus 3 Tbsp. butter, softened	1 (3-oz.) package cream cheese, softened	1 cup all-purpose flour

Beat butter and cream cheese at medium speed with an electric mixer until creamy. Gradually add flour, beating at low speed until blended after each addition. Shape into 24 balls. Place 1 ball into each muffin cup of a greased (24-cup) miniature muffin pan, shaping into a shell. Makes 2 dozen.

"The turnovers were there. She'd eaten all her shrimp. None left over for him. . . .

'Let's eat this before the cheese sauce gets cold,' Jonathan said. He loved the sugary graininess of the sweet melted cheese, and the cherries were allowed to be authentically cherries, not mired in overly sweet goo. The pastry was flaky and flavorful—probably made with pure lard. 'My Jewish mother would be ashamed of the way I've eaten this evening,' he said soberly. 'No, she wouldn't,' Stella said. 'She'd be glad you were having a good time. So would mine.'"

—from *Four Spirits* by Sena Jeter Naslund

FRUITCAKE COOKIES

Hands-on Time: 30 min.   Total Time: 1 hr., 8 min.

These moist, chewy holiday cookies boast the same colorful, flavorful assortment of candied fruit, nuts, and spices as traditional fruitcake. You can make these cookies ahead and store them in airtight containers for one week, or freeze up to three months.

2 (8-oz.) packages yellow candied pineapple, chopped	4 cups chopped pecans or walnuts	3 Tbsp. milk
1 (8-oz.) package red candied cherries, chopped	3½ cups all-purpose flour, divided	1 Tbsp. baking soda
1 (8-oz.) package green candied cherries, chopped	½ cup butter, softened	¼ cup brandy
2 cups golden raisins	1 cup firmly packed light brown sugar	1 tsp. ground cinnamon
	4 large eggs, separated	1 tsp. ground nutmeg

1. Preheat oven to 325°. Combine first 5 ingredients in a large bowl; add 1 cup flour, and toss gently to coat.

2. Beat butter at medium speed with an electric mixer until creamy; gradually add sugar, beating well after each addition. Add egg yolks, beating well.

3. Combine milk and baking soda, stirring until baking soda is dissolved; add to butter mixture. Add brandy, spices, and remaining 2½ cups flour, beating until blended.

4. Beat egg whites at medium speed until stiff peaks form; fold into batter. Fold fruit mixture into batter.

5. Drop dough by level tablespoonfuls onto lightly greased baking sheets.

6. Bake at 325° for 12 to 15 minutes or until lightly browned. Let cool 2 to 3 minutes on baking sheets. Remove to wire racks to cool. Store in airtight containers. Makes about 10 dozen.

DATE-NUT PINWHEEL COOKIES

Hands-on Time: 30 min.   Total Time: 4 hr.

A handy way to slice these cookies cleanly is to use dental floss. Place a piece of floss under a cookie dough log, bring up ends of floss, and then crisscross them through dough to make clean, even cuts.

1   (10-oz.) package chopped dried dates
1   cup granulated sugar
1   cup hot water
1   cup very finely chopped walnuts

2   cups firmly packed light brown sugar
1   cup butter, softened
2   large eggs
3½ cups all-purpose flour

½   tsp. baking soda
½   tsp. cream of tartar
½   tsp. salt
1   tsp. vanilla extract
Parchment paper

1. Stir together first 3 ingredients in a medium saucepan; cook over medium heat, stirring often, until thickened (about 12 minutes). Remove from heat, and stir in walnuts.

2. Beat brown sugar and butter at medium speed with a hand-held blender until light and fluffy; add eggs, 1 at a time, beating until blended after each addition. Combine flour and next 3 ingredients; gradually add to butter mixture, beating until blended. Add vanilla; mix well. Chill 1 hour.

3. Divide dough into thirds. Roll each dough portion into a 12-inch square on lightly floured plastic wrap. (Dough will be soft.) Spread each portion with ⅔ cup date mixture, leaving a ½-inch border. Roll up dough, jelly-roll fashion. Wrap dough in plastic wrap; chill 1 hour.

4. Preheat oven to 375°. Cut dough into ¼-inch-thick slices; place 2 inches apart on parchment paper-lined baking sheets.

5. Bake at 375° for 15 minutes or until lightly browned. Let cool 2 to 3 minutes on baking sheet. Remove cookies to wire racks to cool completely. Makes about 6 dozen.

NEW YEAR'S IRRESOLUTIONS

by Rick Bragg

The best resolution I ever heard was my Uncle Jimbo's.

"Son," he told me, "I have given up lying."

"How's that working out for you, Jim?" I asked.

"It's hard, son," Jimbo said, woeful.

"How long you been quit?"

He looked at his watch.

" 'Bout 15 minutes."

By the standards of the average Southern male, he was actually doing quite well.

Resolutions start out noble and fine. After a solid year of beer joints and buttered biscuits, backsliding six ways to Sunday, we stand on the threshold of a new year and swear that this year, it'll be different. We will do right, do good, for 365 long, long days.

Some of us—deacons, Sisters of Mercy, and my mother—make it, with prayer, almost to Valentine's Day. The rest of us are on Jimbo time.

I do not believe Southern men should be asked to make a resolution to start with. It's not that we don't have the will. It has to do with what we have to give up. We promise to forfeit liquor, bad language, loafering, sloth, poker, and sausage gravy.

We resolve to go to church for more than just weddings, funerals, and dinner on the grounds when they are said to have homemade ice cream. We say we will take out the trash, even if it is not full. We swear off eating barbecue after 1 a.m., in our jammies, in the glow of a Frigidaire.

We promise to say "I love you" and mean it, and not just because the object of our devotion found in our pants a receipt for an eight-piece bucket and extra-large Pepsi. We promise not to cheat at cards, especially while playing with children. We promise not to look at majorettes.

That is a lot to give up.

Still, after a healthy New Year's Day meal of Hoppin' John, it's easy to be optimistic. With your belly full of collards, which our society equates with financial prosperity, and black-eyed peas for luck, it's easy to go to bed with good intentions.

But with the dawn comes bacon. And then we drive by a sausage and biscuit, and it all goes straight to Hardee's.

I think it would not be so hard if I lived in the frozen wastes of the Far North. What do you have to give up in Rhode Island? Halibut? I could swear off halibut for the rest of my natural life.

Every year, because she loves me, my wife makes me promise to exercise more, to walk outside in good

weather, even if that occasionally means it's uphill, and to walk in bad weather in the gigantic recreation center, which is—thank you, Lord— quite flat.

And I do walk, at least until I am lapped by the first septuagenarian. "It's hard to get around this thing when you're 86," one woman told me, after lapping me for spite, then sitting down to breathe.

"You should try it," I said, patting my belly, "at 286."

And so my resolve dwindles with every mile and every speed demon who was alive when Teddy stormed up San Juan Hill. But still, I resolve.

One year, I resolved not to get any speeding tickets.

The Alabama state troopers resolved to break my resolve and charge me $300 in state court north of McIntosh.

Another year, I resolved not to get upset about something as piddling as football. That was the year we got beat by Utah.

Last year, I resolved to diet, drive slowly, exercise four days a week, and, sometimes on Sunday, be affectionate even when mostly innocent of wrongdoing, and not eat Buffalo wings in any Marriott, any-where, unless it was the only thing on the menu (and sometimes that happens).

This year, I resolve not to look at majorettes. Again.

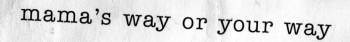

mama's way or your way

One is a showstopping Southern classic; the other cooks in half the time. Both get rave reviews.

<u>MAMA'S WAY:</u>
- Delicious hot or cold
- Bone-in delivers exceptional flavor
- Beautiful on holiday buffet

<u>YOUR WAY:</u>
- Faster cook time
- Perfect size for small families
- Easy to carve

HONEY-BOURBON GLAZED HAM

Hands-on Time: 20 min.   Total Time: 3 hr., 20 min.

1 (9¼-lb.) fully cooked, bone-in ham
40 whole cloves
½ cup firmly packed light brown sugar

½ cup honey
½ cup bourbon
⅓ cup Creole mustard
⅓ cup molasses

1. PREHEAT oven to 350°. Remove skin from ham, and trim fat to ¼-inch thickness. Make shallow cuts in fat 1 inch apart in a diamond pattern; insert cloves in centers of diamonds. Place ham in an aluminum foil-lined 13- x 9-inch pan.

2. STIR together brown sugar and next 4 ingredients; spoon over ham.

3. BAKE at 350° on lowest oven rack 2 hours and 30 minutes, basting with pan juices every 30 minutes. Shield ham with foil after 1 hour to prevent excessive browning. Remove ham from oven, and let stand 30 minutes. Makes 15 servings.

mama's way

ORANGE GLAZED HAM

Hands-on Time: 10 min.   Total Time: 1 hr., 50 min.

1   (4-lb.) smoked, fully
     cooked boneless ham

1   cup orange marmalade

1   cup fresh orange juice

¼   cup firmly packed brown
     sugar

2   Tbsp. creamy Dijon
     mustard

1   tsp. ground ginger

1. Preheat oven to 350°. Place ham in an aluminum foil-lined 13- x 9-inch pan.

2. Stir together marmalade and next 4 ingredients; spoon mixture over ham.

3. Bake at 350° on lowest oven rack 1 hour and 30 minutes, basting with pan juices every 30 minutes. Remove ham from oven, and let stand 10 minutes before slicing. Makes 10 servings.

your way

Ham 101

• Cooked ham can be served directly from the refrigerator. If you'd like to serve it hot, heat in a 350° oven to an internal temperature of 140°.

• Uncooked ham should be heated to an internal temperature of 160° in a 350° oven. Plan to cook it 18 to 20 minutes per pound.

• Dry-cured ham is rubbed with salt and seasonings and then stored until the salt fully penetrates the meat.

• Wet-cured ham is seasoned with a brine solution, which keeps the meat moist and the texture tender.

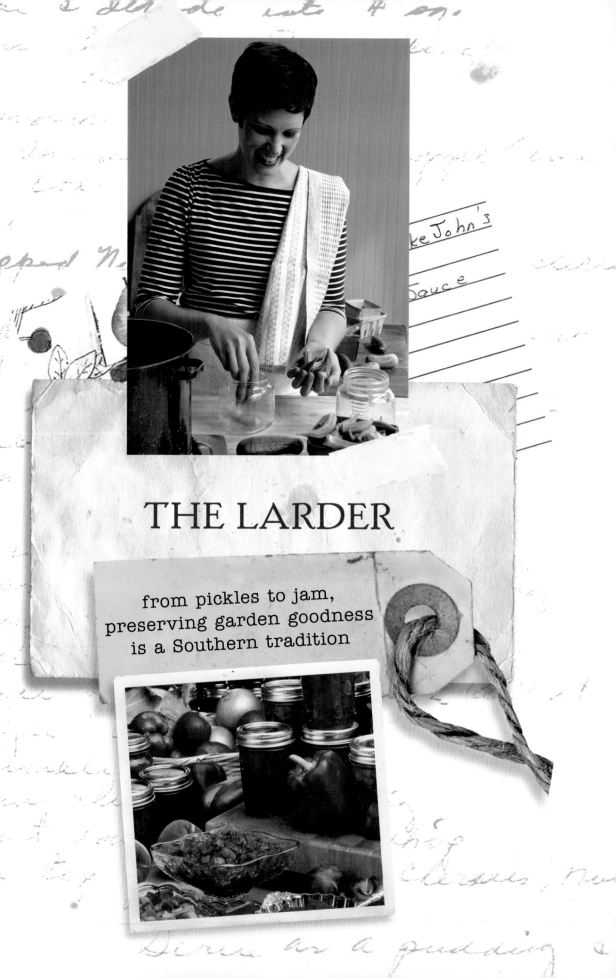

THE LARDER

from pickles to jam,
preserving garden goodness
is a Southern tradition

Every year we came up with some large-batch recipes for giving as hostess gifts, to houseguests, to the mailman, or to coworkers during the holidays. One year Mom made fire-and-ice pickles. It was really easy...more or less a pickle "dress-up."

a note from
Marian

While it's true that she most often went the whole nine yards when it came to cooking, she also knew when it was worth taking shortcuts. And these pickles were really, really good and required only a little effort. Dad would get a big 5-gallon jar of pickles from his Dairy Queen and she would transfer them to individual Mason jars and gussy them up with herbs and spices and labels for giving. Rows of canning jars were not uncommon at our house, either. It wasn't unusual for farmers to come into the Dairy Queen and trade for food. Dad would give them a family meal of chili dogs in exchange for some jars of jam or dilly beans. It was a win-win. We got some great fresh-from-the-farm goodies, and the farmer treated his family to a meal in town. It seems old-fashioned, but it's the way of life in small Southern towns where everybody knows everybody.

BREAD-AND-BUTTER PICKLES

Hands-on Time: 55 min.   Total Time: 4 hr., 25 min.

Turn summer's bounty of cool, crisp cucumbers into bread-and-butter pickles, the perfect sandwich companion.

6½ lb. small pickling cucumbers, cut into ¼-inch slices (about 33 cucumbers)
4 large sweet onions, thinly sliced
½ cup pickling salt
5 cups white vinegar (5% acidity)
4 cups sugar
2 Tbsp. mustard seeds
½ Tbsp. ground turmeric
1 tsp. ground cloves

1. Combine cucumbers and onions in a very large Dutch oven; sprinkle with salt, and add water to cover (about 18 cups). Cover and let stand 3 hours. Drain well. Rinse with cold water.

2. Combine vinegar, sugar, mustard seeds, turmeric, and cloves in Dutch oven; cook over medium heat 5 minutes. Add cucumbers and onion; bring to a boil. Remove from heat.

3. Pack hot cucumber mixture into hot jars, filling to ½ inch from top. Remove air bubbles; wipe jar rims. Cover at once with metal lids, and screw on bands. Process, in 2 batches, in boiling-water bath 12 minutes; cool. Chill pickles before serving. Makes 10 (1-pt.) jars.

Canning Storage 101

- Foods properly processed in a water-bath canner need no refrigeration until you open them.
- Store unopened canned foods in a cool, dark, dry place up to one year.
- Store in refrigerator once opened and use within one month.

TASTY TRIVIA

The "official" Vidalia onion (sanctioned by the Vidalia, Georgia Chamber of Commerce) is grown only within a 30-mile radius of the town. Similar onions are grown in other areas but without the stamp of approval of the place of origin. Sweet as an orange with natural sugar, the Vidalia is quite perishable. Vidalias cannot be shipped very long distances and are best stored in a cool, dry place, not touching one another.

KOSHER DILLS

Hands-on Time: 30 min.   Total Time: 50 min.

Pickling cucumbers are the variety used for pickles. They're small, about 3 to 4 inches long, with a thin green skin and a mild, crisp flesh.

4 lb. (4-inch) pickling cucumbers	¼ cup pickling salt	14 fresh dill sprigs
14 garlic cloves, peeled and halved	2¾ cups white vinegar (5% acidity)	28 peppercorns

1. Wash cucumbers, and cut in half lengthwise.

2. Combine garlic, salt, 3 cups water, and vinegar; bring to a boil over medium-high heat, and boil 1 minute. Remove garlic, and place 4 halves into each hot jar. Pack cucumbers into jars. Add 2 dill sprigs and 4 peppercorns to each jar. Carefully pour vinegar mixture into jars, filling to ½ inch from top. Remove air bubbles; wipe jar rims. Cover at once with metal lids, and screw on bands. Process jars in boiling-water bath 10 minutes; cool. Makes 7 (1-pt.) jars.

WATERMELON RIND PICKLES

Hands-on Time: 1 hr., 5 min.   Total Time: 1 hr., 35 min., plus 8 hr. for chilling

1   large watermelon (about 21 lb.), quartered
¾   cup pickling salt
2   Tbsp. plus 2 tsp. whole cloves

½   tsp. mustard seeds
16   (1½-inch) cinnamon sticks
    Cheesecloth
    Kitchen string

8   cups sugar
1   qt. white vinegar (5% acidity)

1. Remove pulp from watermelon, and reserve for another use. Peel watermelon, and cut rind into 1-inch cubes; reserve 12 cups rind cubes in a large plastic container.

2. Stir together salt and 3 qt. water; pour over rind. Cover and refrigerate 8 to 24 hours. Drain well. Rinse with cold water.

3. Cook rind and water to cover in a large Dutch oven over high heat 10 minutes or until almost tender; drain.

4. Place cloves, mustard seeds, and cinnamon sticks on a 5-inch square of cheesecloth; tie with kitchen string. Stir together sugar and vinegar; add spice bag, and bring to a boil. Boil 5 minutes; remove from heat, and let stand 15 minutes.

5. Add rind to syrup mixture; bring to a boil over medium-high heat. Reduce heat to low, and simmer, stirring occasionally, 25 to 30 minutes or until rind is transparent. Discard spice bag.

6. Pack hot rind mixture into hot jars, filling to ½ inch from top. Remove air bubbles; wipe jar rims. Cover at once with metal lids, and screw on bands. Process in boiling-water bath 10 minutes; cool. Makes 5 (1-pt.) jars.

THE GIFT OF HOSPITALITY

by Tanner Latham

It's a long way from Birmingham to Jerusalem. Even though four out of five Israelis quoted "that Skynyrd chorus" when I told them I was from Alabama, I was still a total foreigner. But that's exactly why I had come—to immerse myself in a culture so unlike my own.

The minute I arrived, I found myself sharing hand-gestured connections with hospitable strangers who knew only clips of English. One day, a man from Sajur named Galeb led me through his garden, pinching the ingredients he used to make za'atar (a spice rub), which I later sprinkled on my pita in his courtyard.

As I traveled the country, I nearly bent beneath the gravity of the settings from all those Sunday School stories I knew by heart. From a ridge, I watched the sun rise over the Dead Sea. I bowed my head when a man prayed for me at the Wailing Wall.

One afternoon, I stepped into the pulsing stream of shoppers on David Street, a narrow road that scores Jerusalem's Old City. It's paved with stones polished smooth by the steps of millions of people over thousands of years. The street is actually one long market, crammed with stalls peddling souvenirs—from hookahs to knockoff Hard Rock T-shirts.

Think Gatlinburg Parkway minus the taffy pulls.

Then, suddenly, above a shop near the intersection of David Street and Muristan Road, I spied a sign that read, "Alabama The Heart of Dixie." Crimson Tide stickers were tacked everywhere: on shelves full of pottery, above drawers filled with Roman glass, and beside stands gridded with Star of David pendants.

I got the shop's story from a proud Bama grad named Hani Imam, whose father began selling menorahs, silver jewelry, and other gifts on David Street in 1970. Very little distinguished the shop from its neighbors. But then Hani entered The University of Alabama in 1984. He earned his degree and picked up a deep loyalty to his school along the way. After working six years in Alabama, he returned to Jerusalem to take over the family business. He reinvented the shop, and the tourist traffic increased.

I told Hani we had a Roll Tide bond, and I commended him on the marketing strategy to attract map-toting Americans—especially Southerners—with shekels burning holes in their pockets.

"It wasn't a strategy at all," he corrected me. "When I came back from the States, I missed Alabama a lot. I just felt that Alabama was part of me. I felt homesick for it, so I decided to name my store after it." I now understand how transported Hani must feel when he sees Big Al stickers stuck to his display cases. It's the same way I feel when I spot a bag of za'atar on aisle three at my local Piggly Wiggly.

It makes me remember who I met and what I touched and the things I smelled, tasted, and experienced in Israel. And it makes me believe that it's okay to be homesick for a place—even if it's not your "sweet home."

BEET PICKLES

Hands-on Time: 1 hr. Total Time: 1 hr., 25 min.

Jewel-tone beets are beautiful, but they come with a price. To avoid staining your hands when handling beets, wear rubber gloves.

4   lb. trimmed small fresh beets, halved

2   cups sugar

1   Tbsp. whole allspice

1½ tsp. salt

2   (3-inch) cinnamon sticks

3½ cups white vinegar (5% acidity)

1. Cook beets in boiling water to cover in a Dutch oven 10 to 15 minutes or until tender; drain, discarding liquid. Let cool 15 minutes; peel beets. Pack beets into hot sterilized jars.

2. Bring sugar, next 4 ingredients, and 1½ cups water to a boil in Dutch oven. Remove cinnamon sticks. Pour hot mixture into jars, filling to ½ inch from top. Remove air bubbles; wipe jar rims. Cover at once with metal lids, and screw on bands. Process in boiling-water bath 30 minutes; cool. Makes 5 (1-pt.) jars.

Makeover in Minutes: For a dose of Asian flavor, substitute broken star anise for cinnamon sticks and 1 (1-inch) piece fresh ginger, peeled, for allspice.

OKRA PICKLES

Hands-on Time: 15 min.   Total Time: 36 min.

Pickling fresh garden or farmers' market produce is a great way to enjoy summer's bounty all year long. Vinegar is essential for pickling; make sure it's 5% acidity. In this recipe dill seeds and garlic give the pickles a distinctive flavor.

3½ lb. small okra pods
7   garlic cloves
7   small fresh hot peppers
2   cups white vinegar (5% acidity)
⅓   cup pickling salt
2   tsp. dill seeds

1. Pack okra tightly into hot jars, filling to ½ inch from top; place a garlic clove and hot pepper into each jar.
2. Combine vinegar, pickling salt, dill seeds, and 4 cups water in a saucepan; bring to a boil, and boil 1 minute. Carefully pour vinegar mixture into jars, filling to ½ inch from top. Remove air bubbles; wipe jar rims. Cover at once with metal lids, and screw on bands. Process in boiling-water bath 10 minutes; cool. Makes 7 (1-pt.) jars.

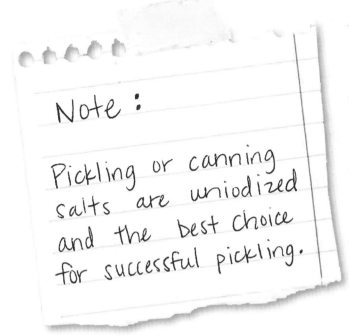

Note:

Pickling or canning salts are uniodized and the best choice for successful pickling.

Pickle recipes often call for pickling spice in addition to pickling salt. This blend of whole spices lends a signature flavor to a pickle recipe and is what sets Aunt Edna's apart from Grandma's. The pungent blend of herbs, spices, and seeds is used to flavor the brine or vinegar solution used in making pickles, relishes, and even preserved meats. Spice blends vary, but often include whole or broken allspice, bay leaves, cardamom, coriander, cinnamon, cloves, ginger, mustard seeds, and peppercorns. Ground spices are never used. Packaged pickling spice mix is sold in most supermarkets.

BRANDY-SPICED PEACHES

Hands-on Time: 30 min.   Total Time: 4 hr., 5 min., plus 1 day for chilling

These are delicious served with turkey or pork. Be sure to choose small peaches that will fit through the mouths of the jars.

1	(1-inch) piece fresh ginger, peeled and sliced	Cheesecloth		5	cups sugar, divided
3	(3-inch) cinnamon sticks	Kitchen string		24	small, firm, ripe peaches, peeled (about 6 lb.)
1	Tbsp. whole allspice	3	cups white vinegar (5% acidity)		
1	Tbsp. whole cloves	1¼	cups brandy		

1. Place first 4 ingredients on a piece of cheesecloth; tie with kitchen string. Combine spice bag, vinegar, brandy, 2 cups sugar, and ¾ cup water in a large Dutch oven; bring to a boil over medium-high heat. Reduce heat to medium-low, and add peaches; simmer 2 minutes or until thoroughly heated. Remove from heat; let peaches stand 3 hours.

2. Carefully transfer peaches from syrup to a bowl. Add remaining 3 cups sugar to syrup, and bring to a boil. Remove mixture from heat, and add peaches; cover and chill 24 hours.

3. Heat peaches in syrup over low heat to a low boil. Pack hot peaches into hot jars, filling to ½ inch from top. Remove air bubbles; wipe jar rims. Cover at once with metal lids, and screw on bands. Process in boiling-water bath 15 minutes; cool. Makes 3 (1-qt.) jars.

NANNIE'S CHOWCHOW

Hands-on Time: 40 min.   Total Time: 1 hr., 10 min., plus 8 hr. for chilling

This vegetable relish has appeared in many early Southern cookbooks as "piccalilli" and "Indian pickle." The vegetables were chopped, cooked, seasoned, and put up in jars to be enjoyed year-round as a condiment with meats and vegetables. For a fiery touch, add chopped jalapeños to the vegetables.

2½	lb. green tomatoes, chopped (4 cups)	2	red bell peppers, chopped (2¼ cups)	1½	qt. white vinegar (5% acidity)
2	large yellow onions, chopped (4 cups)	1	(2½-lb.) cabbage, shredded (8 cups)	1½	cups sugar
3	large green bell peppers, chopped (4 cups)	½	cup pickling salt	½	cup mustard seeds
				2	Tbsp. celery seeds
				1	Tbsp. whole allspice

1. Combine first 5 ingredients in a large Dutch oven. Combine salt and 4 cups water; stir until salt dissolves. Pour over vegetables in Dutch oven. Chill 8 hours. Drain vegetables; discard liquid.

2. Combine vinegar and next 4 ingredients in Dutch oven; add vegetables. Bring to a boil over medium heat; reduce heat to medium-low, and simmer, covered, 10 minutes.

3. Pack hot mixture into hot jars, filling to ½ inch from top. Remove air bubbles; wipe jar rims. Cover at once with metal lids, and screw on bands. Process in boiling-water bath 10 minutes; cool. Makes 12 (1-pt.) jars.

Nannie's Chowchow

BLUE-RIBBON MANGO CHUTNEY

Hands-on Time: 35 min.   Total Time: 2 hr., 8 min., plus 8 hr. for chilling

Try this delicious condiment over grilled fish or chicken.

3 large mangoes, peeled and chopped (about 2½ lb.)*	1 cup cider vinegar	2 Tbsp. fresh lime juice
1½ cups chopped onion	1¼ cups firmly packed light brown sugar	1 Tbsp. mustard seeds
½ cup peeled, chopped cooking apple	½ cup sugar	1½ tsp. celery seeds
½ cup raisins	¼ cup minced fresh ginger	¾ tsp. salt
	½ tsp. lime zest	¼ tsp. ground cinnamon
		¼ tsp. ground cloves

1. Combine all ingredients in a glass bowl; cover and chill 8 hours.

2. Transfer to a Dutch oven; bring to a boil over medium heat. Reduce heat to medium-low; cook, stirring occasionally, 1 hour and 10 minutes.

3. Divide mango mixture into hot, sterilized jars; filling to ½ inch from top. Remove air bubbles; wipe jar rims. Cover at once with metal lids, and screw on bands; cool. Chill up to 1 week, or freeze up to 6 months. Makes 4 (½-pt.) jars.

* 1 (26-oz.) jar refrigerated mango slices drained and chopped may be substituted.

TASTY TRIVIA

Ever wonder what the difference is between jelly, jam, and preserves? A jelly is made from fruit juice and is translucent. Jams and preserves are similar except preserves contain larger pieces of fruit than jams. Preserves are sometimes made from whole fruits, such as strawberries and other berries; hence the term "preserves," because the shape of the whole fruit is "preserved."

FREEZER STRAWBERRY JAM

Hands-on Time: 10 min.   Total Time: 30 min., plus 1 hr. for freezing

If you've always wanted to try your hand at jam, here's your chance. Pair it with peanut butter for some good eats.

3   cups crushed strawberries
5   cups sugar
1   (1.59-oz.) envelope freezer jam pectin

1. Combine strawberries and sugar; let stand 15 minutes, stirring occasionally. Gradually stir in pectin. Stir 3 minutes; let stand 5 minutes.
2. Spoon fruit mixture into plastic freezer jars. Remove air bubbles. Cover and freeze until thickened. Makes 7 (½-pt.) jars.

Note: Jam may be stored in refrigerator 3 weeks.

BLACKBERRY JELLY

Hands-on Time: 15 min. Total Time: 40 min.

3   to 4 qt. fresh blackberries, stems and caps removed
7½ cups sugar
2 (3-oz.) packages liquid pectin

1. SORT and rinse blackberries. Pulse blackberries in a blender or food processor until finely chopped. Press through a fine wire-mesh strainer or cheesecloth
to remove seeds. Cook blackberries and sugar in a heavy medium saucepan over
medium-high heat, stirring constantly, until sugar dissolves. Stir in pectin, and
return to a boil; boil, stirring constantly, 5 minutes or until mixture thickens.
Remove from heat, and skim off foam with a metal spoon.
2. QUICKLY pour hot jelly into hot, sterilized jars, filling to ¼ inch from top;
wipe jar rims. Cover at once with metal lids, and screw on bands. Process in
boiling-water bath 5 minutes. Makes 8 (½-pt.) jars.

JALAPEÑO JELLY

Hands-on Time: 15 min.   Total Time: 50 min.

The seeds of a pepper contain the fire, so if you want to tame the heat in this jelly, remove them.

7   jalapeño peppers, stems and seeds removed

1   small green bell pepper, stem, seeds, and membranes removed

1¼   cups white vinegar (5% acidity)

6½   cups sugar

2   (3-oz.) packages liquid fruit pectin

1. Process peppers in a food processor 10 to 20 seconds, stopping once to scrape down sides. Combine peppers, vinegar, and sugar in a large Dutch oven. Bring to a boil over medium-high heat; boil 9 minutes. Reduce heat to low; simmer, uncovered, 5 minutes. Add liquid pectin to pepper mixture; return to a boil, and boil 1 minute. Reduce heat to low, and simmer 4 minutes. Remove from heat, and skim off foam with a metal spoon.

2. Pour hot jelly into hot, sterilized jars, filling to ¼ inch from top; wipe jar rims. Cover at once with metal lids, and screw on bands. Process in boiling-water bath 5 minutes; cool. Serve jelly with beef, veal, or lamb. Makes 7 (½-pt.) jars.

MUSCADINE JAM

Hands-on Time: 45 min. Total Time: 2 hr., 55 min.

This jam is great made with Scuppernongs, too.

7   lb. Muscadine grapes, divided
Cheesecloth
2   (1¾-oz.) packages powdered fruit pectin
14   cups sugar

1. Remove skins from 3 lb. Muscadines; reserve pulp. Pulse skins in a food processor 5 times or until chopped. Cover and chill.

2. Bring pulp, remaining 4 lb. Muscadines, and 4 cups water to a boil in a large Dutch oven over medium-high heat. Reduce heat to medium-low; simmer, stirring occasionally, 1 hour. (Skins should be tender, and liquid should be plum colored.) Remove to a bowl; cool 30 minutes.

3. Pour cooled Muscadine mixture through a triple thickness of damp cheesecloth into Dutch oven, and discard solids. Stir in powdered fruit pectin until blended. Bring mixture to a boil, stirring constantly.

4. Stir in sugar; return to a boil, and boil, stirring constantly, 1 minute. Remove from heat, and skim off foam with a metal spoon.

5. Add ½ cup chopped skins to each hot, sterilized jar, and immediately pour hot jam into jars, filling to ¼ inch from top; wipe jar rims. Cover at once with metal lids, and screw on bands. Process in boiling-water bath 10 minutes; cool. Makes 8 (1-pt.) jars.

TASTY TRIVIA

Muscadine grapes and one of its varieties, called Scuppernongs, are found in the Southern states. They have thick skins, are greenish-purple, and have a strong, musky flavor. They can still be found growing wild in parts of the South and are most often eaten as a snack or used to make jam or jelly, though the grapes are also used to make a sweet wine.

OVEN APPLE BUTTER

Hands-on Time: 20 min.   Total Time: 5 hr., 30 min.

This thick, sweet spread is the result of cooking apples with sugar, spices, and cider. Southerners slather apple butter on pancakes and hot biscuits. How long to cook it is important. When done, the brown mixture should cling to the spoon.

8   Gala apples, peeled and diced

8   Granny Smith apples, peeled and diced

2   cups apple cider

2   cups sugar

2   tsp. ground cinnamon

½   tsp. ground cloves

¼   tsp. ground nutmeg

1. Preheat oven to 275°. Cook diced apples and cider in a large Dutch oven over medium heat 40 minutes or until apples are very tender, stirring occasionally. Stir until apples are mashed.

2. Stir in sugar and remaining ingredients. Pour apple mixture into a lightly greased 13- x 9-inch baking dish. Bake at 275°, stirring every hour, for 4½ hours or until spreading consistency. Cover and chill. Makes about 5 cups.

ROAD FOOD FEAST

by Les Thomas

I once drove 400 miles for a pecan praline. My name is Les. I'm a road food junkie.

You can't find the kind of treats I crave at golden arches or packed in handy buckets. I love the home-grown treasures of the South—wrapped in orange peels; boiled in salty peanut hulls; and sandwiched in warm, fluffy biscuits baked by little old ladies at 3 in the morning. You'll find them at rickety little wooden roadside stands, behind hand-lettered signs, and sometimes on simple tables with no proprietor in sight—just a metal box that lets you pay on the honor system. Not even Colonel Sanders could franchise that.

Honk if you pass me on the highway this holiday season. I'll be the one in the loaded-down SUV, aka the "cornucopia," on my way home to Texas from Alabama. Santa travels light compared to me. Those are my Florida pomelos in the back seat, right next to the Georgia pecans, the Tennessee biscuits, and the Virginia hams. There's that shrinking bag of pecan pralines that I drove half-way across Louisiana to get from Tee-Eva's stand on Magazine Street, a roadside treat in the heart of New Orleans. I bought

them for stocking stuffers. Now I doubt they'll even make it to Baton Rouge.

Maybe they're just roads to you, but to me the highways of the South stretch out like endless aisles in the market of my dreams. Christmas gives me a better excuse to shop, but to tell the truth, I browse the South's foodways all year long. Visiting Georgia? Don't miss the magnificent pecan brittle at Ellis Bros. Pecans. Traveling Texas? Be sure to stop for fresh homemade kolaches at the Czech Stop in West.

Too bad they don't make scratch-and-sniff highway maps. On a warm winter's day, when I roll down the windows, a drive on U.S. 27 through the middle of Florida feels as welcome and refreshing as a bite of a sweet orange plucked fresh from a citrus grove. Trees along the roadside grow their own Christmas ornaments and brighten every jour-ney along the citrus trail. Roadside stands and canneries dot the high-way. At a pick-it-yourself orchard, I can bag enough fruit—including some basketball-size pomelos—to last through the winter.

Not long ago—and a little farther north—I pulled into Henpeck Market in Franklin, Tennessee. The old-

fashioned market is a road food junkie's dream. Counters bulge with homemade cookies, sandwiches, and delicious cakes. I left there that snowy morning with a stack of biscuits with country ham that Lizzie Mai Jackson got up to make before sunrise.

Out on the highway, I had to smile. I had a full tank of gas and enough biscuits to get me to Mississippi.

Homemade Ketchup

HOMEMADE KETCHUP

Hands-on Time: 1 hr., 15 min.   Total Time: 5 hr., 5 min.

Ketchup traces its origins to China, but it was New Englanders who added tomatoes and gave us what we now consider one of America's favorite condiments.

46 medium tomatoes (about 12 lb.), quartered
2 medium onions, coarsely chopped
2 (3-inch) cinnamon sticks
1½ tsp. whole cloves

2 garlic cloves, chopped
Cheesecloth
Kitchen string
1½ cups white vinegar (5% acidity)
¾ cups sugar

1½ tsp. salt
1½ tsp. paprika
⅛ tsp. ground red pepper

1. Combine tomatoes and onions in 1 very large Dutch oven or 2 medium Dutch ovens. Bring vegetables to a boil over medium-high heat; reduce heat to low, and simmer, uncovered, stirring often, 45 minutes. Remove from heat; let cool slightly. Process tomato mixture in a blender until smooth.
2. Place cinnamon sticks, cloves, and garlic on a 3-inch square of cheesecloth, and tie with kitchen string; place spice bag and vinegar in a saucepan. Bring to a boil over medium-high heat; reduce heat to medium-low, and simmer, uncovered, 30 minutes. Remove and discard spice bag; reserve vinegar.
3. Cook tomato mixture, uncovered, in a large Dutch oven over medium-high heat, stirring often, 2½ hours or until reduced by half. Add reserved vinegar, sugar, and remaining ingredients. Cook, uncovered, 30 to 40 minutes or until thickened.
4. Quickly pour hot mixture into hot jars or bottles, filling to ½ inch from top. Remove air bubbles; wipe jar rims. Cover at once with metal lids, and screw on bands. Process in boiling-water bath 20 minutes, or if using bottles, cover and keep refrigerated. Makes 6 (1-pt.) jars.

TARRAGON VINEGAR

Hands-on Time: 10 min.   Total Time: 10 min., plus 3 weeks for standing

This herb-laced vinegar is a tasty gift to give. Tie fresh tarragon sprigs to a decorative bottle with ribbon as a hint of the sweet scent of the vinegar.

1½ (1-oz.) packages fresh tarragon (about 25 sprigs)

4 (12.7-oz.) bottles Champagne wine vinegar (7 cups)

Fresh tarragon sprigs (optional)

1. Twist tarragon gently, bruising leaves with fingertips to release flavor, and place in a large glass container.
2. Bring vinegar to a boil in a large saucepan, and pour over tarragon. Cover and store in a cool, dark place at room temperature 3 weeks.
3. Pour vinegar mixture through a wire-mesh strainer into hot, sterilized bottles, discarding solids. Add additional fresh tarragon sprigs, if desired. Seal bottles, and cool to room temperature. Store in refrigerator up to 3 months. Makes 5 (½-pt.) bottles.

mama's way or your way

One marmalade is a rich summer classic. The other equally delectable version adds a modern twist.

<u>MAMA'S WAY:</u>
- Makes a big batch for sharing
- Only 3 ingredients
- Uses traditional canning method

<u>YOUR WAY:</u>
- Uses a combo of oranges, grapefruit, and lemon
- Updated flavor with a hint of vanilla
- No need for canning method

mama's way

SUNNY ORANGE MARMALADE

Hands-on Time: 30 min.   Total Time: 2 hr., 40 min., plus 8 hr. for chilling

This recipe is a little time-consuming, but it's well worth the effort.

12 oranges (about 6 lb.)   9 cups sugar
2 lemons

1. PEEL oranges, and cut rind into thin strips. Chop pulp, discarding seeds. Cut lemons into thin slices, discarding seeds.
2. COMBINE orange rind, chopped pulp, lemon slices, and 4 cups water in a large Dutch oven; bring to a boil over medium-high heat. Reduce heat to low, and simmer 15 minutes. Remove from heat; cover and chill 8 hours or overnight.
3. COMBINE chilled fruit mixture and sugar in Dutch oven; bring to a boil over medium-high heat. Reduce heat to low, and simmer, stirring occasionally, 1½ hours or until a candy thermometer registers 215°.
4. PACK hot marmalade into hot, sterilized jars, filling to ¼ inch from top. Remove air bubbles; wipe jar rims. Cover at once with metal lids, and screw on bands. Process in boiling-water bath 5 minutes; cool. Makes 5 (1-pt.) jars.

CITRUS-VANILLA BEAN MARMALADE

Hands-on Time: 20 min. **Total Time:** 2 hr., 15 min., plus 1 day for chilling

Traditional marmalade with a whisper of bitterness is transformed into a sweet citrus jam with a hint of spicy vanilla.

1 vanilla bean
2 large Valencia or navel oranges
2 medium-size red grapefruit
1 lemon
2 cups sugar
⅛ tsp. kosher salt

1. Split vanilla bean lengthwise, and scrape out seeds.

2. Grate zest from oranges to equal 1 Tbsp. Repeat with grapefruit. Grate zest from lemon to equal 1 tsp.

3. Peel and section oranges, grapefruit, and lemon, holding fruit over a bowl to collect juices.

4. Stir together zest, fruit segments, sugar, kosher salt, ⅓ cup fruit juices, vanilla bean and seeds, and 1¾ cups water in a large saucepan. Bring mixture to a boil over medium-high heat; reduce heat to low, and simmer, stirring occasionally, 50 minutes or until a candy thermometer registers 225° and mixture is slightly thickened. Cool completely (about 1 hour; mixture will thicken as it cools). Remove and discard vanilla bean. Pour into 2 (½-pt.) jars or airtight containers, and chill 24 hours. Store marmalade in refrigerator up to 3 weeks. Makes 2 (½-pt.) jars.

METRIC EQUIVALENTS

The recipes that appear in this cookbook use the standard U.S. method
for measuring liquid and dry or solid ingredients (teaspoons, tablespoons, and cups). The
information in the following charts is provided to help cooks outside the United States
successfully use these recipes. All equivalents are approximate.

Metric Equivalents for Different Types of Ingredients

A standard cup measure of a dry or solid ingredient will vary in weight depending on the type of ingredient. A standard cup of liquid is the same volume for any type of liquid. Use the following chart when converting standard cup measures to grams (weight) or milliliters (volume).

Standard Cup	Fine Powder (ex. flour)	Grain (ex. rice)	Granular (ex. sugar)	Liquid Solids (ex. butter)	Liquid (ex. milk)
1	140 g	150 g	190 g	200 g	240 ml
¾	105 g	113 g	143 g	150 g	180 ml
⅔	93 g	100 g	125 g	133 g	160 ml
½	70 g	75 g	95 g	100 g	120 ml
⅓	47 g	50 g	63 g	67 g	80 ml
¼	35 g	38 g	48 g	50 g	60 ml
⅛	18 g	19 g	24 g	25 g	30 ml

Useful Equivalents for Dry Ingredients by Weight

(To convert ounces to grams, multiply the number of ounces by 30.)

1 oz	=	1/16 lb	=	30 g
4 oz	=	¼ lb	=	120 g
8 oz	=	½ lb	=	240 g
12 oz	=	¾ lb	=	360 g
16 oz	=	1 lb	=	480 g

Useful Equivalents for Length

(To convert inches to centimeters, multiply the number of inches by 2.5.)

1 in			=		2.5 cm	
6 in	=	½ ft	=		15 cm	
12 in	=	1 ft	=		30 cm	
36 in	=	3 ft	=	1 yd	90 cm	
40 in			=		100 cm	= 1 m

Useful Equivalents for Liquid Ingredients by Volume

¼ tsp					=	1 ml	
½ tsp					=	2 ml	
1 tsp					=	5 ml	
3 tsp	=	1 Tbsp		=	½ fl oz =	15 ml	
		2 Tbsp	=	⅛ cup =	1 fl oz =	30 ml	
		4 Tbsp	=	¼ cup =	2 fl oz =	60 ml	
		5⅓ Tbsp	=	⅓ cup =	3 fl oz =	80 ml	
		8 Tbsp	=	½ cup =	4 fl oz =	120 ml	
		10⅔ Tbsp	=	⅔ cup =	5 fl oz =	160 ml	
		12 Tbsp	=	¾ cup =	6 fl oz =	180 ml	
		16 Tbsp	=	1 cup =	8 fl oz =	240 ml	
		1 pt	=	2 cups =	16 fl oz =	480 ml	
		1 qt	=	4 cups =	32 fl oz =	960 ml	
					33 fl oz =	1000 ml	= 1 l

Useful Equivalents for Cooking/Oven Temperatures

	Fahrenheit	Celsius
Freeze water	32° F	0° C
Room temperature	68° F	20° C
Boil water	212° F	100° C
Bake	325° F	160° C
	350° F	180° C
	375° F	190° C
	400° F	200° C
	425° F	220° C
	450° F	230° C
Broil		

SUBJECT INDEX